中外英语教师课堂元话语比较研究
Metadiscourse in the Classroom: A Comparative Analysis of Native and Non-Native EAP Teachers

仵欣欣　著

本书获山东省社会科学规划研究项目"基于自建语料库的中外英语教师课堂元话语比较研究"（20CYYJ01）的资助

苏州大学出版社

图书在版编目(CIP)数据

中外英语教师课堂元话语比较研究：英文／仵欣欣著. —苏州：苏州大学出版社，2022.12
ISBN 978-7-5672-4128-2

Ⅰ.①中… Ⅱ.①仵… Ⅲ.①英语-教师-话语语言学-对比研究-中国、国外 Ⅳ.①H0

中国版本图书馆 CIP 数据核字(2022)第 234203 号

书　　名：	中外英语教师课堂元话语比较研究
	Metadiscourse in the Classroom: A Comparative Analysis of Native and Non-Native EAP Teachers
著　　者：	仵欣欣
责任编辑：	汤定军
策划编辑：	汤定军
装帧设计：	刘　俊
出版发行：	苏州大学出版社(Soochow University Press)
社　　址：	苏州市十梓街1号　邮编：215006
印　　装：	广东虎彩云印刷有限公司
网　　址：	www.sudapress.com
E - mail：	tangdingjun@suda.edu.cn
邮购热线：	0512-67480030
销售热线：	0512-67481020
开　　本：	700 mm×1 000 mm　1/16　印张：19.5　字数：310千
版　　次：	2022年12月第1版
印　　次：	2022年12月第1次印刷
书　　号：	ISBN 978-7-5672-4128-2
定　　价：	78.00元

凡购本社图书发现印装错误，请与本社联系调换。服务热线：0512-67481020

Acknowledgements

This book would not have been possible without the support of a wide range of organisations and individuals, and I wish to warmly acknowledge their support here. I would first of all like to extend my heartfelt appreciation to Dingjun Tang, the editor for this book, whose constructive and professional suggestions pushed me to turn this book into a more elegant version of its current form.

This book derives from the research of my PhD at the University of Aberdeen in the UK. I would like to thank the University of Aberdeen and the Chinese Scholarship Council for their academic scholarships covering my tuition fees and living stipends, which made possible my dream of pursuing a PhD.

My sincerest and greatest thanks go to my supervisors, Professor Robert Millar and Dr Agni Connor, for their endless patience, extensive knowledge and continued support. Their invaluable comments and constant encouragement in either regular tutorial sessions or written feedback have been increasingly sharpening my thoughts on the current research. I could not have wished for better supervisors than Robert and Agni, and my success in the current research and beyond is a product of their guidance.

I am indebted to the supportive research environments at the University of Aberdeen. The PGR forum of the school gave me the opportunities to present my research and receive comments from academic staff and PhD colleagues. Other academic staff such as Dr Tania Fahey Palma gave me some insightful advice at the early stage of this research. Dr Shona Potts provided me with many helpful suggestions during our encounters in the office kitchen. A special thank to all the doctoral students I have met at the University of Aberdeen and other universities. The friendship and exchange of ideas with them made my PhD process much more interesting and manageable than it otherwise would have been.

During my writing process, I am very grateful to the administrative staff in the school office who provided me with every possible support. Special thanks go to Dr Jon Cameron and Mr Kyle Anderson for their assistance in providing an office for me to concentrate on my writing. I would also like to thank the university library and IT services for always helping me solve any kind of technical issues in time. In particular, Mr Ewan Grant patiently helped me with some Ref Works issues. Mrs Kim Richmond taught me many useful office skills, which has considerably facilitated my data analysis and file editing. These technical skills will definitely also contribute to my future academic career. Moreover, the rich variety of workshops and seminars provided by the university has broadened my horizon in a range of fields.

This book would not have been possible without the involvement of all the participants who generously allowed me to get access to their lessons. I cannot make them known in the interests of privacy. I extend my thanks to them here. I must also thank Ms Julie Bray and Ms Alison McBoyle who offered me great assistance in recruiting possible participants.

I would also like to extend my heartfelt appreciation to the support of my friends, in particular Ms Elizabeth Gyurgyak, for her careful proofreading of my book and many other writings. I would also like to thank Hui Ni and Chang Yan for their encouragement and help in proofreading my final book. I would also like to express my gratitude to my colleagues at Dezhou University in China, who gave me a lot of support during my PhD process.

Finally, I give my heartfelt thanks to my dear parents and parents-in-law for their unceasing love and support. I would also like to say to my husband, Chuantong, that no amount of thanks would suffice for his love, support and encouragement. His positive, constructive attitude to my PhD research and other aspects of life has been my major source of motivation. My special thanks also go to my son, Fanjin, to whom I dedicate this book.

Contents

List of tables / vi
List of figures / viii
List of abbreviations / ix

Chapter 1 Introduction

1.1 Introduction / 001
1.2 Background of the current research / 001
1.3 Assumptions and research questions / 004
1.4 Theoretical framework / 005
1.5 Significance of the current research / 006
1.6 Organisation of the book / 007

Chapter 2 An overview of research in metadiscourse

2.1 Introduction / 009
2.2 Origin and development of the term *metadiscourse* / 017
    2.2.1 SFG-inspired broad approach / 019
    2.2.2 Jakobson's function-based narrow approach / 020
2.3 Definitions of metadiscourse / 022
    2.3.1 Definitions in the broad approach tradition / 024
    2.3.2 Definitions in the narrow approach tradition / 029
    2.3.3 Definition adopted in this research / 030
2.4 Classifications of metadiscourse / 031
    2.4.1 Classifications in the broad approach tradition / 031
    2.4.2 Classifications in the narrow approach tradition / 042

2.4.3　Classification adopted in this research　/ 047
2.5　Other terms pertinent to metadiscourse　/ 048
　　2.5.1　Metalanguage　/ 048
　　2.5.2　Metacommunication　/ 052
　　2.5.3　Discourse markers　/ 055
2.6　Overview of metadiscourse research in academic genres　/ 058
　　2.6.1　Cross-disciplinary research on metadiscourse in academic genres　/ 060
　　2.6.2　Cross-linguistic research on metadiscourse in academic genres　/ 064
　　2.6.3　Cross-cultural research on metadiscourse in academic genres　/ 067
2.7　Summary　/ 071

Chapter 3　An overview of research in classroom discourse

3.1　Introduction　/ 073
3.2　A brief history of research in classroom discourse　/ 073
3.3　Major approaches to the study of classroom discourse　/ 076
　　3.3.1　The interaction analysis approach　/ 077
　　3.3.2　The discourse analysis approach　/ 081
　　3.3.3　The conversation analysis approach　/ 084
3.4　Overview of metadiscoursive research in classroom discourse　/ 089
　　3.4.1　Metadiscourse research across classroom discourse and written discourse　/ 089
　　3.4.2　Metadiscourse research in one-way classroom discourse　/ 091
　　3.4.3　Metadiscourse research across monologic and dialogic modes of classroom discourse　/ 094
3.5　Rationales for the current research　/ 096
3.6　Summary　/ 100

Chapter 4 An analytical framework for teachers' classroom metadiscourse

4.1 Introduction / *101*

4.2 Interpersonal model of metadiscourse analysis / *102*

    4.2.1 Interactional metadiscourse / *103*

    4.2.2 Interactive metadiscourse / *105*

    4.2.3 The list of metadiscourse items / *108*

4.3 Integration of corpus linguistics with metadiscourse analysis / *109*

    4.3.1 Overview of basic concepts in corpus linguistics / *110*

    4.3.2 Three categories of corpus linguistic research / *112*

    4.3.3 Integrating corpus-based analytical method into metadiscourse research / *116*

4.4 Summary / *119*

Chapter 5 Methodology

5.1 Introduction / *121*

5.2 Research questions / *122*

5.3 Overall research design / *123*

5.4 Data preparation / *127*

    5.4.1 Rationales for data collection methods / *127*

    5.4.2 Recruitment of participants / *131*

    5.4.3 Data recording / *134*

5.5 Data treatment / *135*

    5.5.1 Transcription / *135*

    5.5.2 Identification of potential metadiscourse markers / *137*

    5.5.3 Elimination of irrelevant metadiscourse items / *140*

    5.5.4 Compilation of corpus / *142*

    5.5.5 Coding of corpus / *144*

5.6 Data analysis / *145*

5.7 Research ethics / *146*

5.8 Summary / 149

Chapter 6　A corpus linguistic analysis of metadiscourse use across native and non-native EAP teachers

6.1　Introduction / 150

6.2　Overall result of metadiscourse markers in both ET and CT sub-corpora / 151

6.3　Interactional metadiscourse markers in both ET and CT sub-corpora / 154

 6.3.1　Hedges / 155

 6.3.2　Boosters / 173

 6.3.3　Attitude markers / 188

 6.3.4　Engagement markers / 198

 6.3.5　Self-mentions / 212

6.4　Interactive metadiscourse markers in both ET and CT sub-corpora / 215

 6.4.1　Transitions / 215

 6.4.2　Frame markers / 221

 6.4.3　Endophoric markers / 228

 6.4.4　Code glosses / 232

6.5　Summary / 236

Chapter 7　Conclusion

7.1　Introduction / 237

7.2　Summary of the book / 237

 7.2.1　Uniformity of metadiscourse use / 238

 7.2.2　Variations of rhetorical preferences / 240

 7.2.3　Diversifications of lexical types of metadiscourse / 242

7.3　Implications of the current research / 243

 7.3.1　Theoretical implications for the study of metadiscourse markers / 243

    7.3.2   Pedagogical implications for language teachers and teacher education　/ 245

  7.4 Limitations and suggestions for further research　/ 249

References　/ 252

Appendix 1　**List of metadiscourse items**　/ 277

Appendix 2　**Participant information sheet**　/ 285

Appendix 3　**Consent form for teachers**　/ 289

Appendix 4　**Consent form for students**　/ 291

Appendix 5　**Transcription conventions**　/ 293

List of tables

Table 2.1   Speech acts and their corresponding functions   / 021
Table 2.2   Vande Kopple's classification of metadiscourse   / 035
Table 2.3   Crismore's classification of metadiscourse   / 036
Table 2.4   Crismore, Markkanen and Steffensen's revised classification of metadiscourse   / 038
Table 2.5   Hyland's (1998a) classification of metadiscourse   / 039
Table 2.6   Hyland's (1998b) classification of metadiscourse   / 040
Table 2.7   Hyland's (2005) classification of metadiscourse   / 041
Table 2.8   Mauranen's classification of metadiscourse   / 042
Table 2.9   Ädel's (2006) classification of metadiscourse   / 044
Table 4.1   Interpersonal model of metadiscourse for the current research   / 102
Table 5.1   Overall amount and distribution of data in each sub-corpus   / 144
Table 6.1   Overall frequency and distribution of metadiscourse markers in both sub-corpora   / 152
Table 6.2   Linguistic realisations of hedges   / 156
Table 6.3   Summary of individual hedging adverbs in both sub-corpora   / 161
Table 6.4   Summary of individual hedging auxiliaries in both sub-corpora   / 164
Table 6.5   Summary of individual hedging verbs in both sub-corpora   / 168
Table 6.6   Summary of individual hedging adjectives in both sub-corpora   / 170
Table 6.7   Summary of individual hedging multi-word expressions in both sub-corpora   / 172
Table 6.8   Linguistic realisations of boosters   / 174
Table 6.9   Summary of individual boosting adverbs in both sub-corpora   / 179
Table 6.10 Summary of individual boosting modal auxiliaries in both sub-corpora   / 182
Table 6.11 Summary of individual boosting verbs in both sub-corpora   / 183

Table 6.12	Summary of individual boosting adjectives in both sub-corpora	/ 185
Table 6.13	Summary of individual boosting multiword expressions in both sub-corpora	/ 187
Table 6.14	Linguistic realisations of attitude markers	/ 189
Table 6.15	Summary of individual attitude verbs in both sub-corpora	/ 193
Table 6.16	Summary of individual attitude adjectives in both sub-corpora	/ 194
Table 6.17	Summary of individual attitude adverbs in both sub-corpora	/ 197
Table 6.18	Linguistic realisations of engagement markers	/ 199
Table 6.19	Top 20 frequent lexical items for directives in both sub-corpora	/ 203
Table 6.20	Summary of addressee-oriented pronouns in both sub-corpora	/ 206
Table 6.21	Summary of questions for engagement markers in both sub-corpora	/ 209
Table 6.22	Linguistic realisations of self-mentions	/ 212
Table 6.23	Summary of self-mentions in both sub-corpora	/ 213
Table 6.24	Linguistic realisations of transition markers	/ 216
Table 6.25	Comparison of the lexical categories of transitions in both sub-corpora	/ 220
Table 6.26	Linguistic realisations of frame markers	/ 222
Table 6.27	Comparison of the lexical categories of frame markers in both sub-corpora	/ 227
Table 6.28	Linguistic realisations of endophoric markers	/ 228
Table 6.29	Summary of endophoric markers in both sub-corpora	/ 230
Table 6.30	Linguistic realisations of code glosses	/ 233
Table 6.31	Summary of code glosses in both sub-corpora	/ 234

List of figures

Figure 2.1   Ädel's (2010) classification of metadiscourse   / 045

Figure 4.1   An example of the concordance tool in AntConc   / 117

Figure 4.2   An example of the concordance plot tool in AntConc   / 118

Figure 4.3   An example of the collocates tool in AntConc   / 119

Figure 5.1   The overall raw number of occurrences by the search word *about*   / 138

Figure 5.2   The raw occurrences of the search word *about* in each sub-corpus   / 139

Figure 5.3   Proportions of metadiscourse categories used by teachers in the ET sub-corpus   / 146

Figure 6.1   Proportions of metadiscourse categories used by teachers in the ET sub-corpus   / 153

Figure 6.2   Proportions of metadiscourse categories used by teachers in the CT sub-corpus   / 154

Figure 6.3   Distribution of normalised frequencies of hedges in both sub-corpora   / 157

Figure 6.4   Overall frequency distribution of hedges in both sub-corpora   / 158

Figure 6.5   Normalised frequencies of hedging lexical categories in both sub-corpora   / 159

Figure 6.6   Normalised frequencies of booster lexical categories in both sub-corpora   / 175

Figure 6.7   Overall frequency distribution of boosters in both sub-corpora   / 176

Figure 6.8   Normalised frequencies of hedging lexical categories in both sub-corpora   / 177

Figure 6.9   Normalised frequencies of attitude markers in both sub-corpora   / 190

Figure 6.10   Overall frequency distribution of attitude markers in both sub-corpora   / 191

Figure 6.11   Normalised frequencies of lexical categories of attitude marker in

Figure 6. 12   both sub-corpora   / *192*

Figure 6. 12   Normalised frequencies of engagement markers in both sub-corpora   / *200*

Figure 6. 13   Overall frequency distribution of engagement markers in both sub-corpora   / *201*

Figure 6. 14   Normalised frequencies of lexical categories of engagement markers in both sub-corpora   / *202*

Figure 6. 15   Distribution of normalised frequencies of transitions in both sub-corpora   / *217*

Figure 6. 16   Overall frequency distribution of transitions in both sub-corpora   / *218*

Figure 6. 17   Normalised frequencies of lexical categories of transitions in both sub-corpora   / *219*

Figure 6. 18   Distribution of normalised frequencies of frame markers in both sub-corpora   / *224*

Figure 6. 19   Overall frequency distribution of frame markers in both sub-corpora   / *225*

Figure 6. 20   Normalised frequencies of pragmatic categories of frame markers in both sub-corpora   / *226*

List of abbreviations

AFL   Academic Formulas List

ALWL   Academic Lecture Word List

AWL   Academic Word List

BAAL   British Association of Applied Linguistics

BASE   British Academic Spoken English

BNC   British National Corpus

CPD   Continuous professional development

CT(s)   Non-native English-speaking teacher(s) from China

EAP   English for academic purposes
EFL   English as a foreign language
EF/SL   English as a foreign/second language
ELF   English as a lingua franca
ET(s)   Native English-speaking teacher(s) from the UK
IRF   Initiation-response-feedback
L1   First language
L2   Second language
L2CD   Second language classroom discourse corpus
LT & L   Language teaching and learning
MA   Master of Arts
MD   Metadiscourse
MICASE   Michigan Corpus of Academic Spoken English
MOOCs   Massive Open Online Courses
NESTs   Native English-speaking teachers
NmlFrq.   Normalised frequency
NNESTs   Non-native English-speaking teachers
PGR   Postgraduate
ptw   Per thousand words
RawFrq.   Raw frequency
RSA   Royal Society of Arts
SIG   Special interest group
SL/FL   Second language/foreign language
T2K-SWAL TOEFL 2000 Spoken and Written Academic Language
TOEFL   Test of English as a Foreign Language

CHAPTER 1

Introduction

1.1 Introduction

This chapter introduces the overall landscape of the current research. It begins with a brief introduction of the chapter. This is followed by a description of the background of the present study, mainly involving the theoretical and practical considerations of focusing on a comparative analysis of cross-cultural metadiscourse (MD) use in spoken academic genres. The next section presents the assumptions, based on which the research questions of the current research are proposed. This leads to an account of the theoretical framework. Then, the significance of the current research, including theoretical and pedagogical significance, is briefly illustrated. The subsequent section outlines the organisation of the whole book, followed by a summary of this chapter.

1.2 Background of the current research

The current research explores classroom metadiscourse used by native English-speaking English for academic purposes (EAP) teachers in the UK and non-native English-speaking EAP teachers in China. The primary reasons for focusing on the current research involve both practical and theoretical facets. In relation to the practical facet, the current research grew from my personal experience as an English as a foreign language (EFL) lecturer at a university in China. During my teaching practice, I used to encounter the question of how, in varied ways, to guide students through the lessons and keep them actively engaged in classroom activities, and also how to best accomplish pedagogical tasks in the classroom setting which usually lasts for one or two hours. As a non-native English-speaking EFL teacher, I also pondered the authentic way of teachers' classroom discourse, which forms both the means of organising teaching and the important source of students' input.

Metadiscourse, as a rhetorical strategy for organising discourse and engaging audiences, could offer us insights into those aspects. In other words, for a particular subject like EFL teaching, it is supposed that native English teachers' metadiscoursive strategies in delivering a lesson may provide some insights for non-native EFL teachers. This insight could be better provided by a thorough comparative analysis of the native and non-native teachers' metadiscourse use in comparable classroom teachings. Nevertheless, very rare comparative analyses have been found in this area. Therefore, the current research is designed to fill this gap by focusing on teachers' classroom metadiscourse use across the native and non-native English-speaking contexts in the UK and China. It also narrows down the lessons into one type of lesson, that is, EAP writing courses in both cultural settings, with a view to minimising the effect of genre factors such as lesson types to the comparative results. The detailed reasons for choosing EAP writing courses will be further elaborated later in Section 3.4.

In terms of the theoretical facet, the current research is motivated by the significance of metadiscourse use in English language teaching, along with the gaps in existing metadiscourse research into spoken academic genres in general and classroom discourse in particular. Metadiscourse has become a widely acknowledged term in discourse analysis and language education. Although there is no consensus in its definition, it is generally agreed that metadiscourse refers to the self-reflective linguistic expressions used to negotiate interactional meanings in a discourse, assisting the addressers to express a viewpoint and engage with addressees as members of a particular community (Hyland, 2005). Previous research in both spoken and written academic discourse has demonstrated its significance in facilitating comprehension and addresser-addressee interaction (e.g. Chaudron & Richards, 1986; Crismore et al., 1993; Mauranen, 1993a). Nevertheless, a plethora of previous research has been focusing on written academic discourse, and there is still a lack of research into spoken academic genres, such as teachers' classroom discourse.

In addition, in an EFL educational context, teachers' classroom discourse is vital for effective classroom teaching and learning. It is both the means of lesson organisation and one important resource of input for students. Moreover, teachers' classroom discourse may also provide second language (L2) learners with "linguistic models of how to interact meaningfully and appropriately in communicative situations, although students at this point in their development may only notice a few at a time" (Friginal et al., 2017, p.89). Despite such a crucial role of teachers' classroom discourse, most current research into it focuses on teacher-students interaction, such as corrective feedback, teachers' questioning strategies, power relationship and identity construction (Lindwall et al., 2015). Whereas how teachers' use of metadiscourse strategies may contribute to the organisation of and interaction in classroom teaching is still underexplored, in particular the cross-cultural analysis of teachers' metadiscourse use from a comparative perspective. These two general gaps regarding metadiscourse research in spoken academic genres and teachers' classroom discourse serve as two important theoretical rationales for the current research.

1.3 Assumptions and research questions

The current research is based on two hypotheses. First, despite a relative uniformity of teachers' metadiscourse use in EAP classroom teaching imposed by the requirements of the genre, there is significant intercultural variation in the rhetorical preferences of teachers (e.g. Mauranen, 1993a, 1993b). Second, the use of metadiscourse in the Chinese non-native English-speaking teachers' classroom discourse may be not as diversified as those in the British native English-speaking teachers' classroom discourse (e.g. Friginal et al., 2017; Mauranen, 1993b). As noted above, teachers' classroom discourse can serve as a means of classroom organisation, main source of students' input and linguistic model. Therefore, the current research aims to analyse those varied preferences and diversifications in order to inform teachers' language awareness and language teacher training and education, to contribute to an improved understanding of the nature of teacher talk in English as a foreign/second language (EF/SL) classrooms and to enhance existing research of metadiscourse in spoken academic genres. In order to test these two hypotheses and accomplish the above aims, the current research formulated the following three research questions:

(1) What are the frequencies and distributions of teachers' metadiscourse use in classrooms by native English-speaking EAP teachers in the UK and non-native English-speaking EAP teachers in China?

(2) What are the similarities and differences between the classroom metadiscourse use of native English-speaking EAP teachers in the UK and that of non-native English-speaking EAP teachers in China?

(3) What are the possible reasons for these similarities and differences?

1.4 Theoretical framework

The current research employs a self-compiled corpus, which consists of two sub-corpora. These two sub-corpora are created based on the transcriptions of the video-recordings of eight separate teachers. One sub-corpus (named ET sub-corpus) consists of four native English-speaking EAP teachers' classroom discourse, and the other (named CT sub-corpus) incorporates four non-native English-speaking EAP teachers' classroom discourse. Each teacher was recorded for two sessions of their classroom teachings, ranging from 90 to 120 minutes. In order to compare teachers' metadiscourse use between these two sub-corpora, the current research adopts a discourse analysis approach to provide a relatively comprehensive understanding of the cross-cultural similarities and differences of metadiscourse use (Dörnyei, 2007). It presents an analysis of the frequencies and distributions of metadiscourse markers in light of their individual metadiscourse functions and their comprehensive functions together with their most likely co-occurrences with other metadiscourse markers.

In the first place, the current research proposes a two-layered analytical framework that integrates corpus linguistics with Hyland's (2005) interpersonal model of metadiscourse. However, as Hyland's model is based on written academic discourse, it warrants close examination in involving new instances of metadiscourse markers specific to the current spoken academic genre. Consequently, the current research also makes reference to reported instances from other metadiscourse research into spoken academic discourse, for example, Yan's (2010) research into Chinese EFL teachers' classroom discourse and Lee and Subtirelu's (2015) research into metadiscourse use by EAP teachers and lecturers. Accordingly, altogether two broader categories, including nine subcategories of metadiscourse are identified, as will be further illustrated later in this book. However, Hyland's (2005) interpersonal model of metadiscourse determines the definition and taxonomy of metadiscourse markers and serves as the basis for subsequent metadiscourse analysis.

In addition, the use of corpus tools such as concordance and concordance plot can greatly facilitate our analysis and consequently build up our understanding of metadiscourse phenomena. First, the concordance plot is run to generate the total occurrences or raw frequencies of metadiscourse markers. Second, the concordance tool is used to assist the identification of metadiscourse markers by referring to their immediate contexts as is shown in their respective concordance lines, thus facilitating the quantitative analysis of the frequencies, lexical types and ranges of metadiscourse markers.

1.5 Significance of the current research

The current research has important theoretical and practical significance. In terms of theoretical significance, the current research aims to fill the gap in metadiscourse research which is devoid of a focus on spoken academic discourse by carrying out a comparative analysis of metadiscourse use between English language teachers from the British and Chinese cultural contexts. In addition, it also extends existing cross-cultural research of metadiscourse which mainly centres on written academic discourse by presenting the comparison of native English-speaking EAP teachers in the UK and their non-native counterparts in China. This may provide an analytical model for the comparative analysis of metadiscourse between native speakers with non-native speakers from other cultural contexts.

Besides, the practical significance mainly refers to the pedagogical significance. First, the current research may help to raise teachers' awareness (in particular ES/FL teachers) in classroom instructional contexts. Second, based on the assumption that native English-speaking EAP teachers have a broader repertoire of metadiscourse strategies, the current research is intended to help non-native English-speaking teachers in China to make more diversified and flexible use of metadiscourse makers and rhetoric strategies. Third, the current research also attempts to provide insights for native EAP teachers, who are having an increasing number of students from multi-lingual and multi-cultural backgrounds. It may inform them about the instructional backgrounds of their Chinese students, who normally account for a large proportion of their students' cohort. Such familiarity with students' educational backgrounds may help teachers to predict students' prior knowledge and cater their classroom discourse to students' comprehensibility. Fourth, the current research may serve as the first step towards raising teachers' classroom language awareness and it may lead to better language proficiency training in teacher education programmes. Finally, the analytical procedure of the current research may provide an example for teachers' reflective practice, and allow them to see the impact of their discourse practices on student learning.

1.6 Organisation of the book

This book encompasses seven chapters. This introductory chapter provides a brief overview of the background, assumptions, research questions, theoretical frameworks, significance and organisation of the current research. Chapters 2 and 3 present respectively literature related to the research in metadiscourse and its application to classroom discourse analysis. Through such a review of literature, the gaps and rationales for the current research are outlined, based on which the research questions are proposed. Chapter 4 illustrates the analytical framework for the metadiscourse use in the current research. Chapter 5 describes the research design, the data preparation, treatment and analysis method employed in the current research. Chapter 6 works on the functional analysis of metadiscourse markers across native and non-native EAP teachers. Chapter 7 concludes the current research with a recap of the major findings, highlights its achievements and acknowledges the limitations, and then points out some possible venues for further research.

CHAPTER 2

An overview of research in metadiscourse

❋ 2.1 Introduction

Prior to dealing with the major issues of metadiscourse, it is essential to know something about the two levels of discourse: main discourse and secondary discourse. This is because this conception has been the basis for the defining of *metadiscouse*, coined by Zellig Harris (Harris, 1959, 1970) in his article "Linguistic Transformations for Information Retrieval". In order to summarise scientific discourses into a sequence of kernel sentences with roughly the same information as the original discourse, Harris introduces the term *kernel*, the set of elementary sentences and combiners, such that all sentences of the language are obtained from one or more kernel sentences with combiners, by means of one or more transformations. He then identifies in this article the main kernels and metadiscourse kernels in a discourse. He defines metadiscourse kernels as the linguistic elements of a discourse which entails information of a secondary importance. For example, *we have found that* ... He goes on to state that this metadiscoursal kernel is the talk about the main kernel and can be omitted in the summarising process. This expression of the two kernels embodies and is roughly equivalent to the idea of the two levels of discourse. However, it has not attracted much attention of researchers in the field of linguistics and discourse analysis, which may be due to the obscure metaphorical use of the expression "kernel".

Nevertheless, the conception of two levels or layers of discourse has been advocated by many researchers (e. g. Crismore & Farnsworth, 1990; Vande Kopple, 1985; Williams, 1981) and gained a more prominent position especially after Lautamatti (1978) and Sinclair (1981). Lautamatti (1978) distinguishes two levels of material in written discourse, namely, the topical material which refers to the discourse topic, and the non-topical material which is equivalent to what is called metadiscourse. These two levels of materials altogether constitute the overall meaning of discourse. Similarly, Sinclair (1981) explicitly proposes the notion of the two "planes of discourse", the primary plane and the secondary plane of discourse, also called primary discourse or secondary discourse. In his view, the primary plane of discourse refers to the propositional content or subject matter of the discourse, and provides information for the listener/reader. This is also what, in Hyland's (2005) words, is "the communicative content of discourse". The secondary plane of discourse, also called metadiscourse, represents the non-propositional part of the discourse, which guides the listeners/readers through the discourse and builds a bond between the speaker/writer and the listeners/readers. In other words, metadiscourse can be employed to act on listeners/readers and to direct them rather than inform them. For example, metadiscourse is used to show the steps of the discourse procedure (*first*, *second*, *finally*, etc.), or to show the degree of certainty (*it seems*, *probably*, etc.).

The preliminary foundation of the concept of metadiscourse is based on an assumption that creating a discourse is a "social engagement" (Hyland, 2005). It is a widely used term in discourse analysis and language education to refer to the self-reflexive expressions used to negotiate interactional meanings in a text, assisting the writers or speakers to express their viewpoint and engage with readers or listeners. This suggests that in producing a discourse, writers or speakers attempt to achieve two major functions for the interlocutors. One is the textual function, in which they employ the best possible ways to guide readers or listeners to understand what they intend to convey by anticipating readers or listeners' attitudes, using logically coherent expressions, or sometimes signposting their views. The other is interpersonal metadiscouse, in which this discourse is also used to convey their own attitude towards the readers or listeners, for example, to build a rapport with them. Hyland (2005) states that "a text has to talk to readers or hearers in ways that they find familiar and acceptable, which means the process of comprehension and participation is not just a matter of informational clarity, but of the individual writer's or speaker's projection of a shared context" (Hyland, 2005). Moreover, he also proposes metadiscourse as a robust analytic framework for exploring these aspects of language. Based on this, Mauranen (2010) claims that metadiscourse is a "crucial aspect of human communication, which deserves to be studied in its own right" (p. 37).

One important function of metadiscourse is to reveal the interactions between interlocutors, whether in spoken or written form. Bearing this in mind, however, Hyland (2005) also argues that interaction in written discourse is less obvious compared with that in spoken discourse. Despite this being rather less obvious, an array of research has been conducted on metadiscourse use in different written genres, in particular in written academic discourse, for example research articles (Hyland, 2005), theses and dissertations (Hyland, 2004a). Research has also been carried out on the cross-cultural uses of written metadiscourse (Ädel, 2006; Mauranen, 1993b). These studies have built up our understanding of how metadiscourse is used in written academic contexts.

In contrast to the popular study of metadiscourse in written discourse, the metadiscourse use in spoken context is far less researched despite the fact that few research articles (e.g. Lee & Subtirelu, 2015; Zare & Tavakoli, 2017) on spoken discourse have appeared. Existing research in spoken language mainly focused on certain metadiscoursive aspects of university lectures. Some have focused on classroom discourse markers such as *so* or *OK* (Chaudron & Richards, 1986; Flowerdew, John & Tauroza, 1995; Jung, 2006; Thompson, 2003). Others have investigated certain interpersonal characteristics, such as the use of asides (Strodt-Lopez, 1991), personal pronouns (Fortanet, 2004; Lee, 2009; Morell, 2004), and rhetorical, display, and referential questions in university lectures (Crawford Camiciottoli, 2005; Morell, 2007). More recent research has been conducted to compare metadiscourse use in university seminars and lectures (Lee & Subtirelu, 2015) and study metadiscourse in science classes (Tang, 2017). Although the findings are mixed, most of these studies suggest the metadiscursive use of language in facilitating learners' understanding and involvement in the authentic classroom teaching activities. Such important functions of metadiscourse use, together with its relatively rare studies in spoken academic genres, forms one of the important rationales of this research. In the following section, an overview of metadiscourse research will be presented in detail.

Meanwhile, since the emergence of metadiscourse in the field of applied linguistics in the 1980s (Vande Kopple, 1985; Williams, 1981), there have emerged a body of research from various perspectives, which can largely be incorporated into two traditions (Ädel & Mauranen, 2010). These two traditions have formed different definitions and consequently varied approaches to metadiscourse. One is the broad approach and centres on both textual organisation and writer/speaker and reader/listener interaction. The other is the narrow approach and centres on textual organisation or reflexivity. These two approaches have also been labelled by other terms respectively, such as the "integrative" model versus

Chapter 2   An overview of research in metadiscourse

"non-integrative" model (Mauranen, 1993b), "interactive" model versus "reflexive" model, and "thin" approach versus "thick" approach (Ädel & Mauranen, 2010).

These two approaches can be deemed to be at opposite ends of a continuum. The broad approach is located at the quantitative end and usually begins with retrieving relevant instances of metadiscourse based on pre-determined lists of specific subcategories. These pre-defined lists are typically composed of words or lemmas, which are considered inherently metadiscursive. Then, the frequency and distribution of these instances or occurrences are examined. This approach has its merits in that it is generally a corpus-based research and the occurrences can be retrieved automatically. Thus, it allows for dealing with a large set of data which could be impossible by previous manual analysis, and makes it possible for quick comparison of metadiscourse use across different genres and contexts.

Nevertheless, this retrieval of pre-determined instances, ranging from "connectives" such as *therefore* to "self-mentions" such as *we*, runs the risking of missing some metadiscourse instances which may not be listed beforehand, as metadiscourse is generally agreed on as an open category which is ready to include new instances (Ädel & Mauranen, 2010). Moreover, because what counts as metadiscourse in one context may be primary discourse in another context, this leads to the fact that some retrieved metadiscourse may also include instances which are not metadiscourse in its specific context. This can be illustrated by the following two extracts from Ädel's work (2006, pp. 30 –31).

Extract 2.1

One does not need to read the papers to notice how the antagonism towards immigrants has increased. Lately *I have discussed* the increasing hostility towards immigrants with my friends, relatives and fellow workers. Almost everyone I spoke to wants tougher immigration rules.

Extract 2.2

I will briefly discuss the Prime Minister's role and then elaborate on the President's functions. Then *I will analyse* each presidency showing how the president's role has evolved.

In Example 2.1 above, the self-mention marker *I* does not refer to the current text according to Ädel's (2006) delimitation of metadiscourse, but instead refers to *I* in the real world. Therefore, it cannot be regarded as metadiscourse. However, in Example 2.2 above, the "I"s refer to the writer in the current text, so both of them are metadiscourse. This evidences the importance of context in determining whether one category is metadiscourse or not. Therefore, the decontextualised broad approach above may weaken its analytical power and result in superficial observation.

At the other end of the continuum, the *narrow* approach is more qualitative-oriented. It often begins with retrieving the possible candidates of metadiscourse first, followed by the exclusion of the irrelevant instances. Then subsequent analysis is centred on the extended units of metadiscursive meanings, generally involving the examination of lexico-grammatical occurrence patterns (e.g. Bondi, 2010) and/or immediate discourse functions. This approach is characterised by its examination of metadiscourse occurrences in their certain contexts, thus allowing for a dynamic and in-depth understanding of metadiscourse use, although usually based on a smaller data of corpus compared to that of the broad approach.

Despite their respectively quantitative and qualitative nature, these two approaches are not totally exclusive to each other. Historically, the broad approach emerges earlier than the narrow approach, they are now, however, increasingly used in a complementally manner to each other. The broad approach sometime entails some qualitative methods and analyses the linguistic functions based on manual coding of metadiscourse items (e.g. Hyland, 1998a), while the narrow approach also makes use of the corpus to analyse the frequency and distribution of metadiscourse items (e.g.

Ädel, 2006).

Although being categorised under these two general research approaches, there is an inherent ambiguity in delimiting what is and what is not metadiscourse in both traditions. This may probably be due to at least two reasons as recognised by Schiffrin (1980). The first concerns the wide range of phenomena that can be considered metalinguistic. As Schiffrin (1980, pp. 199 – 201) claims, we have conversations that not only focus predominantly on talk, such as those in a linguistic class or a psychotherapy session, but also allow talk to emerge as a subtopic within ongoing talk about something else such as *I'll put it this way.* or *What do you mean by that?* The second reason is the multifunctionality of language. Metalinguistic acts may perform other non-metalinguistic functions simultaneously. Schiffrin quoted an example from Lyons (1977, p. 55) that a metalinguistic act such as requesting an interlocutor to define a word may be also related to phatic function of preventing a breakdown in communication, and conative function of making an appeal to the interlocutor.

Hyland (2017, pp. 17 – 19) makes a more detailed illustration of fuzziness in metadiscourse study. He identifies the following four aspects. First, there is ambiguity in what a metadiscourse is. As it has been generally described as the "discourse about discourse", this is open to a variety of interpretations, thus hard to underpin what is and what is not metadiscourse. Hyland uses the distinction between propositional and non-propositional content to indicate the metadiscourse units and those which are not metadiscourse. But this interpretation has been challenged by Ädel (2006, p. 182), who argues that "we should not equate it [metadiscourse] with non-propositional or non-ideational material, but instead conceptualise it as a discourse phenomenon, which, to some extent, can stand in juxtaposition to the text's content or subject matter".

The second aspect of ambiguity emerges from the different ways of formal realisation of metadiscourse, which can be realised by varied linguistic units, ranging from words and phrases to clauses, sentences, or even paragraphs. This complicates the coding and the comparative analysis of metadiscourse occurrence. It also leads to the fact that researchers differ in their views of the analytical units of metadiscourse. For example, the noun phrase "our conclusion" may be considered to be one metadiscourse unit of a frame marker or code-oriented metadiscourse signposting the subsequent discourse, or two metadiscourse units consisting of the self-mention or personal metadiscourse "our" and the frame marker or code-oriented metadiscourse "conclusion".

The third reason for fuzziness resonates with Schiffrin (1980) and concerns the multifunctionality of metadiscourse. Hyland points out that not only the same metadiscourse form may perform more than one function simultaneously, but also that a particular linguistic function may be performed by several metadiscourse units. For example, the metadiscourse form "quite" may function as a booster in the phrase "quite extraordinary", or as a hedge in "quite good". Likewise, metadiscourse functions, such as concessive connections between statements, could be expressed by *although*, *even if*, *admittedly*, *of course*, etc. Therefore, Hyland argues that metadiscourse underlines the problem of "poly-pragmatic meanings" (Hyland, 2017, p.18).

Finally, the ambiguity of this concept also results from the lack of consensus in relation to what metadiscourse actually does in a text. It is normally conceived as the writer or speaker's rhetorical manifestation used to "bracket the discourse organisation and the expressive implications of what is being said" (Schiffrin, 1980, p.231; Cf. Hyland, 2017). This seemingly simple interpretation has been interpreted in different ways. This may partly interpret the reasons for the emergence of different approaches to metadiscourse research.

As with the widely recognised ambiguity of metadiscourse (see also Ädel, 2017), the study of its definition and taxonomy themselves deserves considerable attention and explication. Therefore, in this part of an overview of metadiscourse, we will first devote much space to reviewing the origins and available definitions of metadiscourse in terms of its two major approaches, and based on this produce a working definition used for this research. In order to get a clearer understanding of this concept, terms related to metadiscourse will be illustrated following the review of its definitions. Then, the classifications of metadiscourse will be reviewed to further clarify its characteristics. Finally, the empirical and theoretical studies of metadiscourse will be presented based on extensive literature review survey.

2.2　Origin and development of the term *metadiscourse*

Etymologically, the prefix "meta-" has evolved in meaning over history. In ancient Greek, it means "beyond", "with", "among", "next to" or "after" (Ädel, 2006, p. 229); while in modern English, it has a sense of self-reference, roughly meaning "something is 'about' itself or its own kind of thing" (Craig, 2016, p. 1). This prefix has been used in various scientific fields, such as in computer science (*metadata* means the data used to process data) and in linguistics (*metacognition* means people's awareness of their mental processes). It is probably based on the etymological meaning that the term *metadiscourse* was generally defined as "discourse about discourse" in the early days of its development although this interpretation has been criticised by many researchers as being too broad and obscure.

With regard to the origin of the term, it is generally agreed that the term was coined by Zellig S. Harris (1959), whose preliminary attempt then was to develop an information retrieval system in order to construct abstracts for scientific articles. However, this term did not attract much attention of researchers in linguistics for a considerable period. About two decades later, Joseph M. Williams (1981) explicitly defined and explicated the term in his book *Style: Ten Lessons in Clarity and Grace*, on the explication of writing styles. Based on the assumption that language has two levels of meaning. One is the content level, which represents the ideas the discourse intends to convey. The other is the metadiscourse level, in which language is used to describe how these ideas are represented at the content level. Williams (1981) describes metadiscourse as the language that refers not to the substance of the writer's ideas, but to the writer's thinking and act of writing (e.g. *we/I will argue, claim, suggest*, etc.), the readers' actions (e.g. *as you recall, look at the next example*, etc.), and the logic and form of what the writer has written (e.g. *first, second; therefore, however*, etc.). This distinguishes metadiscourse from the content level of discourse. Since then, metadiscourse has witnessed a robust development and the term was frequently used and further studied by many researchers such as Vande Kopple (1985) and Crismore (1989) in various written and spoken discourses.

The boom in metadiscourse study can also be evidenced from studies on other parallel terms. From roughly the same period, some researchers in the field of linguistics also used other terms to describe the same or similar area of language use. For example, "meta-communication" (Rossiter, 1974), "signalling words" (Meyer et al., 1980; Meyer, 1975), "non-topical material" (Lautamatti, 1978), "meta-text" and "the modalities of texts" (Enkvist, 1978), "meta-talk" (Schiffrin, 1980), "gambits" (Keller, 1979), discourse marker (Schiffrin, 1987) and reflexivity (Mauranen, 1993b). The reasons for categorising these terms as metadiscourse lie in at least two aspects (Crismore, 1989). The first is that they belong to the secondary level, or the non-content aspect of discourse. The second is that their main function is to guide the readers/listeners as to how to understand the author/speaker and message. It is the term "metadiscourse" that is most widely used throughout the scholarly literature. For this reason, the term "metadiscourse" will be used throughout this study.

As noted above, metadiscourse research is a *fuzzy* field to study. One aspect of its fuzziness can be attributed to the various parallel terms used alternatively by different scholars as mentioned above. More prominently, these scholars then developed varied methods to address this linguistic phenomenon. Based on Ädel & Mauranen (2010), these can be roughly divided into two approaches to the study of metadiscourse, namely, the *broad* approach and the *narrow* approach. Corresponding to these two prevailing approaches to the study of metadiscourse, their respective theoretical origins can be identified, both of which are concerned with the functions of language. The so-called broad approach of metadiscourse study can be traced back to Halliday's (1985) systemic functional grammar, while the narrow approach originates from Jakobson's (1998) functional view of linguistics. In order to have a better knowledge of the fluidity of its development process, these two theoretical foundations will be discussed briefly in the following sections.

2.2.1 SFG-inspired broad approach

The broad approach model is sometimes referred to as the SFG-inspired model. SFG is short for systemic functional grammar, which was later reconceptualised to be called systemic functional linguistics (SFL) (Halliday, 1973, 1985). Based on Halliday's SFG, human language has three macro-functions: ideational, interpersonal and textual. Each discourse is an integrated expression of these three functions, and each function can be conveyed or realised by certain lexical and grammatical items. Ideational function, also called representational or informational function, refers to the content of assertions or text, and is the "means of the expression of our experience, both of the external world and of the inner world of our own consciousness" (Halliday, 1973, p. 58). For example, those lexical and grammatical elements in clauses that express transitivity, being labelled as "agent", "process" and "goal".

Interpersonal function addresses positioning between speaker/author and listener/reader and serves as mediator. It includes the linguistic elements which express "our personalities and personal feelings on the one hand, and forms of interaction and social interplay with other participants in the communication situation on the other hand" (Halliday, 1973, p.58). For example, the linguistic elements which indicate the choice of mood and the model verbs. Textual function manages the coherence of discourse into a text and positions the author/speaker in relation to it. It mainly includes the linguistic elements of the cohesive devices, "themes (what is being written/[spoken] about) as related to rhemes (what is written/[spoken] about the themes), and given information (mentioned in or derivable from preceding text) as related to new information (not mentioned in or derivable from preceding text)" (Vande Kopple, 1985, p.86).

Vande Kopple (1985) was the first scholar to introduce M. A. K. Halliday's three metafunctions to the field of metadiscourse. He recommended to assign Halliday's ideational metafunction to propositional content or primary discourse, while the interpersonal and textual metafunction to metadiscourse. He goes on to claim that metadiscourse does not expand the propositional information of the text, but has the potential to affect the reader's or listener's interaction with the text. This way of characterising metadiscourse was advocated and employed by many scholars (Crismore & Farnsworth, 1990; Schiffrin, 1987; Crismore & Farnsworth, 1989; Crismore, 1989; Crismore et al., 1993; Hyland, 1998a) contemporary of or later than Vande Kopple. However, with the further study of the two ways of interpreting language, scholars' views diverge in the relationship between metadiscourse and Halliday's three metafunctions (Hyland, 2005).

2.2.2 Jakobson's function-based narrow approach

One of the influential representatives of the narrow approach to metadiscourse, the reflexive model proposed by Ädel (2006), has Roman Jakobson's functional model of language as a starting point. According to Jakobson (1998, pp. 69 –79), each speech act contains six factors: 1) the *addresser* who sends a 2) *message*; 3) the *addressee* to whom the addresser sends the message; 4) the *context* graspable by the addressee, either verbal or capable of being verbalized; 5) a *code* common to the addresser and the addressee; and finally 6) a *contact*, a physical channel and psychological connection between the addresser and the addressee, enabling both of them stay in communication. He notes that each of these six factors determines a different function of language, which can be expressive, directive, poetic, referential, metalinguistic and phatic respectively. These speech acts and their corresponding functions can be shown in Table 2.1 below:

Table 2.1 Speech acts and their corresponding functions

Speech acts	Functions
Addresser	Expressive
Addressee	Directive
Message	Poetic
Context	Referential
Code	Metalinguistic
Contact	Phatic

Based on Jakobson's functional model of language, Ädel (2006, pp. 163 –165) claims that metadiscourse expressions include three of the six functions, namely, the expressive, directive and metalinguistic, with their corresponding components of the speech event, the code, addresser and addressee. She goes on to claim that these three functions can be realised by various linguistic expressions. The expressive function aims at reflecting some emotion in the addresser or expressing the addresser's attitude towards what she is talking about. It can be realised by metadiscourse items which explicitly refer to the writer or speaker, typically with the first person pronouns such as *I*, *we*, *our*, or *ours*. The directive function aims to create a certain response in the addressee or influence the addressee's interpretation of what is conveyed in the discourse. It can be realised by metadiscourse items such as vocatives (e.g. *dear reader/listener*), imperatives (e.g. *note that*), or second personal pronouns (e.g. *you, your, yours*).

The third, the metalinguistic function, is concerned with making the code more accessible to the addressee. According to Jakobson (1980, pp. 91-92), typical examples of realising this include requesting clarifications by the addressee (e.g. *I don't follow you—what do you mean?*), anticipating questions by the addresser (e.g. *Do you know what I mean?*), or explaining the meaning of a word (e.g. *An X is a Y*). Then Ädel (2006, p. 165) extends these realisation items to "illocution markers", which explicitly comment on which speech act is being performed (e.g. *to conclude*), units that show the organisation of the text to the reader (e.g. *what we will discuss in the following is …*), and any linguistic material that comments on the style or form of the message (e.g. *stated briefly, generally speaking*).

2.3 Definitions of metadiscourse

The definition of metadiscourse has undergone a number of changes from its emergence. Traditionally, metadiscourse has been defined as "discoursing about discourse" (Crismore, 1984, p. 280), "discourse about discourse" (Vande Kopple, 1985, p. 83), "writing about writing" (Williams, 1985, p. 226), or "communication about communication" (Mao, 1993, p. 266), all of which seems to "demonstrate a theoretical fine-tuning as time develops" (Amiryousefi & Rasekh, 2010). However, it seems that they are to some extent too broad and fuzzy, and those general definitions contribute little to pinning down what is and what is not metadiscourse in a clear sense. As is claimed by Nash (1992, p. 100):

Chapter 2 An overview of research in metadiscourse

The word "metadiscourse" may have a reassuringly objective, "scientific" ring, but its usage suggests boundaries of definition no more firmly drawn than those of, say, "rhetoric" or "style". One reader may perceive a clear stylistic intention in something which another reader dismisses as a commonplace, "automatized" use of language.

More recently, researchers also propose a variety of definitions for metadiscourse (Ädel, 2006, 2010; Hyland & Tse, 2004). Among the researchers, Hyland is probably one of the most frequently quoted one in the field of metadiscourse study. He defines metadiscourse as "the linguistic resources used to organize a discourse or the writer's stance toward either its content or the reader" (Hyland, 2000, p.109). According to him, writers may choose from a variety of cohesive and interpersonal features to relate their texts to their contexts by assisting their readers to connect, organize, and interpret their texts in a way preferred by both the writers themselves and the particular discourse community sharing common beliefs and values. This means all metadiscourse features act as textual metadiscourse or interpersonal metadiscourse.

This textual and interpersonal distinction, however, is conceived unhelpful and misleading as it fails to notice that meanings can overlap and contribute to academic arguments in a variety of ways. As Hyland & Tse (2004) argue, the explicit signalling feature of textuality is a general feature for the realization of discourse. It is pertinent to the writers' awareness of self and of the reader when writing. As Hyland & Tse (2004, p.164) states:

> By making reference to the text, the audience, or the message, the writer indicates his or her sensitivity to the context of the discourse and makes predictions about what the audience is likely to know and how they are likely to respond. What is commonly referred to as textual metadiscourse is therefore actually the result of decisions by the writer to highlight certain relationships and aspects of organization to accommodate readers' understandings, guide

their reading, and make them aware of the writer's preferred interpretations. It contributes to the interpersonal features of a text.

Therefore, in this sense, it can be arguably stated that the previous textual and interpersonal taxonomy of metadiscourse can be both incorporated into a holistic interpersonal model of metadiscourse. This is a development of the previous categorization of metadiscourse. In this new interpersonal model, Hyland and Tse (2004) employed the two terms interactive and interactional dimensions first proposed by Thompson (2001) to replace the textual and interpersonal distinction. *Interactive*, in Thompson's terms, refers to the writer's management of the information flow to guide readers through the text, and *interactional* refers to his or her explicate interventions to comment on and evaluate material.

Overall, the definition of metadiscourse has been shifting away from a primary-secondary distinction to an interpersonal resource, which is interpreted as a resource for the writer to intrude into the discourse and to interact with the reader (Crismore & Farnsworth, 1990). Hyland (2005) emphasized the interactional feature of metadiscourse because he developed the idea that writer/speaker and reader/listener are constantly interacting with each other while a text is being produced and consumed. In what follows, a working definition based on a systematic overview of the available definitions in two traditions of metadiscourse study will be tentatively proposed. Before reviewing the existing definitions in the two traditional approaches, the origin of the term *metadiscourse* itself, and the theoretical origins of these two research traditions will be illustrated.

2.3.1 Definitions in the broad approach tradition

2.3.1.1 Joseph Williams's definition

Joseph Williams is one of the earliest researchers to elaborate clearly on metadiscourse in a broad sense, although he exclusively focuses on written discourse. In his eminent work *Style: Ten Lessons in Clarity and Grace*, Williams (1981) states that metadiscourse does not refer to what we are primarily saying about out subject matter, but to the language we use when we write about our own act and context or writing about it. It is prevalent in many aspects of our writing. Metadiscourse verbs announce the things to do in what follows—*to explain*, *suggest*, *expand*, *argue*, *summarise*, etc. Metadiscourse is used to list the procedures and parts of presenting things—*firstly*, *secondly*, *thirdly*, *finally*, etc.; to show logical connections—*therefore*, *nevertheless*, *in conclusion*, etc.; to indicate the extent of out certainty—*perhaps*, *probably*, *it seems that*, etc. It is used in any discourse in which "we filter our ideas through a concern with how our reader will take them" (Williams, 1981, p.125).

He also noted the characteristics of metadiscourse use in different genres. For example, metadiscourse features are investigated more in genres such as personal narratives, arguments and memoirs, but relatively less in other kinds of writing such as technical manuals, operating instructions, laws, etc. Moreover, he also points out we should be cautious when we use metadiscourse because too much metadiscourse may bury the ideas we intend to convey. He uses one example to illustrate this interesting point. For example, in the following sentence:

The last point I would like to make here is that in regard to men-women relationships, it is important to keep in mind that the greatest changes have probably occurred in the way men and women seem to be working next to one another.

He said that only part of the sentence addresses relationships between men and women:

... greatest changes have ... occurred in the way men and women ... working next to one another.

And the rest tells readers how to understand what they are reading:

The last point I would like to make here is that in regard to ... it is important to keep in mind that ... probably ... seem to ...

If we delete this writing about reading, the sentence would become more direct:

The greatest changes in men-women relationships have occurred in the way men and women work next to one another.

And now we can make it more direct by reshaping it into a more coherent sentence:

Men and women have changed their relationships most in the way they work together.

However, he goes on to suggest that there is no rigid regulation or broad generalisation on how much metadiscourse shall be included in a discourse. Probably the reasonable way is to read widely in our field and meanwhile keep an eye on how metadiscourse is used by relatively successful writers, and then follow suit.

2.3.1.2 Vande Kopple's definition

Vande Kopple (1980; Cf. Crismore, 1983) defines metadiscourse as writing that signals the presence of the author and that calls attention to the speech act itself. Then, based on Williams (1981), Vande Kopple (1985) further illustrates the two levels of discourse in writing a discourse. "On one level, we supply information about the subject of our text. On this level we expand propositional content. On the other level, the level of metadiscourse, we do not add propositional material but help our readers organise, classify, interpret, evaluate, and react to such material" (Vande Kopple, 1985, p. 83). But his definition remains to be too general, defining metadiscourse as the discourse about discourse or communication about communication.

2.3.1.3 Avon Crismore's definition

Another influential researcher in the early stages of metadiscourse research is Avon Crismore (1983). She seems to have overcome some of the vagueness surrounding Vande Kopple's (1980) characterisation, and defines metadiscourse as author's explicit or implicit intrusion into the discourse to direct, rather than inform how the listeners'/readers' interpretation of the discourse. The problem in this definition is, as pointed out by Beauvais (1989), that Crismore (1983) does not draw a clear distinction between "direct" and "inform". Later in 1993, probably influenced by Vande Kopple's (1985) two levels of discourse, Crismore, Markkanen & Steffensen (1993, p. 40) redefines metadiscourse as the "linguistic material in texts, either spoken or written, which does not add the propositional content, but helps listeners/readers to organise, interpret and evaluate the information given". The term "proposition" used in this definition is also a vague category, but it is generally referred to as the information about the outside world, which "concerns thoughts, actors or states of affairs in the world outside the text" (2005).

In an article written by Markkanen, Steffensen and Crismore (1993), the claim is made that language used in both spoken and written communication serves what Halliday (1973) calls three macro-functions—ideational, interpersonal and textual. The latter two functions play an important role in writing instruction. Based on this, they define metadiscourse as "linguistic items that explicitly serve the interpersonal and textual functions, i.e. the linguistic material which does not add propositional information but which signals the presence of the author" (Markkanen et al., 1993, p.138). They stress the function of metadiscourse in helping readers organise, interpret and evaluate the information in a text. They also claim that the use of metadiscourse may vary from one language or culture to another. This makes the comparison of metadiscourse use across language or culture essential in order to have a better knowledge of metadiscourse use.

2.3.1.4 Ken Hyland's definition

Ken Hyland is among the most frequently quoted and most influential researchers in the study of metadiscourse. He has been devoted to the study of metadiscourse from a broad approach, in particular in the field of academic written discourse, for over twenty years. During these more than two decades of research, he has developed an increasingly fine-tuned definition of metadiscourse. As early as 1998, in his article "Persuasion and Context: The Pragmatics of Academic Metadiscourse", he defines metadiscourse as "those aspects of the text which explicitly refer to the organisation of the discourse or the writer's stance towards either its content or the reader" (Hyland, 1998a, p.438). He embraces the view of Crismore and Farnsworth (1990) that metadiscourse is used to refer to the non-propositional aspects of discourse which help to organise a coherent text and convey a writer's personality, credibility, reader sensitivity and relationship to the message. He then reshapes the definition of metadiscourse as "the linguistic resources used to organise a discourse or the writer's stance towards either its content or the reader" (Hyland, 2000, p.109). Later in his instrumental book *Metadiscourse: Exploring Interaction in Writing*, Hyland (2005) provides a revised definition:

> Metadiscourse is the cover term for the self-reflective expressions used to negotiate interactional meanings in a text, assisting the writer or speaker to express a viewpoint and engage with readers/listeners as members of a particular community.

This suggests a transformation of Hyland's viewing metadiscourse as being composed of a binary relationship of textual and interpersonal functions to an integrated interpersonal model. Because the textual function of metadiscourse is also for the purpose of facilitating the readers'/listeners' understanding and interpretation of the discourse, it can also, in this sense, have the interpersonal function inherent in it. Therefore, it seems more sensible to incorporate them into an integral interpersonal model of metadiscourse. This is the most widely quoted model of metadiscourse both in written and spoken metadiscourse research. Overall, the broad approach stresses the interpersonal function of metadiscourse, and includes both what Halliday claims are the textual and the interpersonal elements of metadiscourse. It differs from the following narrow approach in that the latter normally includes only the textual aspect but excludes the interpersonal one.

2.3.2 Definitions in the narrow approach tradition

As discussed above, compared to the broach approach, the narrow approach to metadiscourse limits its scope to the aspect of textual organisation, excluding the interpersonal aspect of discourse. In addition, the narrow approach usually adopts a different term, "metatext", as an alternative to metadiscourse in its broad sense. The most prominent representatives who adopt a narrow approach to metadiscourse are Mauranen (1993b) and Ädel (2006). Their definitions of metadiscourse will be reviewed briefly in subsequent section.

2.3.2.1 Anna Mauranen's definition

Anna Mauranen (1993b) is the first researcher who explicitly used the term *metatext* to refer to the narrow approach to metadiscoursive linguistic phenomenon. She defines metatext as essentially text about the text itself and states that it comprises the linguistic elements which fall into the non-propositional content. For example, in the sentence "*The paper concludes by explaining why* the results of empirical work done by Chang do not correspond to the expected results", the italicised part serves the function of metatext, organising the propositional content following it in this sentence and to comment on it as a conclusion and explanation.

2.3.2.2 Annelie Ädel's definition

Built on the work of Mauranen (1993b) to a great extent, Ädel (2006) proposed a reflexive model to the study of metadiscourse. Although Ädel is generally considered belonging to the narrow approach camp (Ädel & Mauranen, 2010), she distinguishes her reflexive model to Mauranen's narrow approach, by claiming that Mauranen's metatext "consider ... only the text itself and not the writer persona and the imagined reader of the current text, restrict the concept of metadiscourse too severely" (Ädel, 2006, p. 180). Thus, she expands the narrow approach by incorporating the linguistic elements that refer to the writer and the reader of the ongoing text. Through this, what Ädel strives to achieve is a middle ground between the broad approach and the narrow approach.

Instead of employing the term "metatext", Ädel uses the term *metadiscourse* in her research. In her extensively quoted book *Metadiscourse in L1 and L2*, she defines it as the "text about the evolving text, or the writer's explicit commentary on her own ongoing discourse" (Ädel, 2006, p. 20). This shows the writer's awareness of the current text and its language use *per se* and also the current writer and reader in their roles as writer and reader. What is worth noting is that Ädel concentrates on written text in this book, but she claims that metadiscursive phenomena commonly occur in spoken language as well. Later Ädel (2010, p. 75) redefines metadiscourse as "reflexive linguistic expressions referring to the evolving discourse itself or its linguistic form, including references to the writer-speaker qua writer-speaker and the (imagined or actual) audience qua audience of the current discourse". Based on this extended definition, a classification model of metadiscourse aimed to be applicable to both spoken and written academic context is proposed, which will be discussed in the classification section below.

2.3.3 Definition adopted in this research

On the whole, the above section has provided a detailed description of major issues related to the concept of metadiscourse. First, the origin and development of metadiscourse is introduced. Second, the theoretical origins

Chapter 2 An overview of research in metadiscourse

of the two traditions, that is, the broad approach and the narrow approach to metadiscourse research are outlined. Following this, the definitions proposed by pioneering scholars within each of those two traditions are presented and compared to illustrate the development of this notion. Finally, three pertinent terms that are similar to or have some overlaps with metadiscourse are also discussed to further clarify the nature of metadiscourse. Based on the above illustration, and in light of the objectives of the current research, that is to explore teachers' use of metadiscourse devices to guide students through the lesson and involve students, the current research adopts the broad approach to metadisourse and follows Hyland's (2005) definition of metadiscourse. Based on the specific spoken academic contexts of the current research, the working definition for the current research is reformulated as below:

> Metadiscourse in this book refers to the cover term for the self-reflective expressions used by teachers to negotiate interactional meanings in classroom teaching discourse, assisting teachers to organise the lesson and engage with students to participate actively in the classroom interactional activities.

2.4 Classifications of metadiscourse

This section seeks to describe the classifications of metadiscourse in literature in relation to the broad and narrow approaches discussed above. By spelling out variable categories in each tradition, and then based on metadiscursive features in the classroom in this research, the taxonomy of metadiscourse adopted in the current research will be presented accordingly.

2.4.1 Classifications in the broad approach tradition

2.4.1.1 Joseph Williams's classification

Williams (1981) put forward an early classification of metadiscourse which later served the basis for other classifications. He identifies the following three basic types of metadiscourse. The first type includes Hedges and Emphatics. These are used to show how certain we are. Hedges give us room to backpedal and make exceptions, such as *sometimes, perhaps, in certain ways, might, for the most part*, etc., whereas an appropriate emphatic allows us to underscore what we really believe, or would like our reader to think we believe. For example, *it is generally agreed that, it is obvious that, undoubtedly*, etc. However, it would make us sound arrogant or sometime defensive if used too much. The second type involve Sequences and Topicalizers. These are linguistic expressions such as words, phrases or sentences that signal the textual organisation and lead the reader through the text. Examples of sequences are *first, second, finally, therefore*, etc., and examples of topicalizers are *with regard to, tuning now to*, etc. The second type is Attributors and Narrators. They tell the source or origin of the ideas, facts or opinions or the text. Attributors refer to those linguistic expressions which reflect the third person as a source, such as *it has been observed, according to, has maintained that*, etc., while narrators refer to those linguistic expressions with the author as a source, such as *I think, I have concluded, I was concerned with*, etc.

William's classification of metadiscourse represents a preliminary version in the overall categorising process. He does not adopt the two broad terminologies of textual and interpersonal metadiscourse, but some of their subcategories are overlapped to some extent. Compared to some later categorisations, some categories such as evaluatives, code glosses, and illocutionary markers are not mentioned here. Nevertheless, this classification does match some of the elements of discoursing and signals the writer-reader relationships and interaction as discussed above in Williams's definition of metadiscourse.

2.4.1.2 Vande Kopple's classification

Vande Kopple's major contribution is his classification of metadiscourse, which is the basis for many influential classifications after him. Borrowing a range of names and examples from Williams (1981) and Lautamatti (1978), he claimed that there are at least seven categories of metadiscourse and made a relatively detailed explanation of them. These seven categories of metadiscourse include text connectives, code glosses, illocution markers, validity markers, narrators, attitude markers, and commentary. Influenced by the three ideational, textual and interpersonal macro-functions proposed by Halliday (1973), these seven categories are integrated into two broad textual and interpersonal categories.

The first type of metadiscourse relates to text connectives, which can facilitate readers' understanding of the textual organisation and internal links of different parts of the text. It compromises the following four subcategories.

1) Sequencers. For example, *first, next, in the third place.*
2) Logical or temporal connectors. For example, *nevertheless, however, at the same time, as a sequence.*
3) Reminders about material presented earlier and announcement of material appearing later in texts. For example, *as I noted above, as we shall see in the next section.*
4) Topicalizers of reintroducing information already being treated in texts or explicitly connect new information to old information. For example, *with regard to, there are, as for, for example.* Here the term *topicalizers* is borrowed from Williams (1981).

The second type of metadiscourse is code glosses, which can assist readers to grasp the specific meanings of certain parts in texts, such as the words being used to define the new terms in a text. These words do not expand the propositional content but help readers understand and interpret the text. The third type of metadiscourse is represented by illocution markers, which can help readers understand what speech or discourse act is being performed at certain points in our texts. For example, *I hypothesize that, we claim that, I promise to, to sum up and for example.* The fourth type of metadiscourse is related to narrators, which are primarily used to inform readers of who said or wrote something. For example, *according to ...*, *... announced that*, and *... reported that*.

The fifth type of metadiscourse relates to validity markers, which can be used to indicate how we assess the probability or truth of the propositional content we express and to show how committed we are to that assessment. It contains three subcategories.

1) Hedges—which allow us to show some uncertainty or "sound small notes of civilised diffidence" (Williams, 1981, p. 45). For example, *to a certain degree*, *may*, *perhaps*, *seem*.

2) Emphatics—which allow us to "underscore what we really believe ... or would like our readers to think we believe" (ibid). For example, *clearly*, *undoubtedly*, *it's obvious that*.

3) Attributors—linguistic expressions being used to guide readers to judge or respect the truth value of the propositional contents as we wish them to. For example, *according to Einstein*.

The sixth type of metadiscourse is attitude markers. These help to show our attitudes to the propositional content. For example, *surprisingly*, *I find it interesting that*, and *it is alarming to note that*. The seventh type of metadiscourse is commentaries, which is generally used to address readers directly and engage them in an implicit dialogue with the writer(s). For example, linguistic expressions used to comment on the probable moods, views or reactions or the propositional material such as *most of you will oppose the idea that*; to recommend a mode of procedure such as *you might wish to read the last chapter first*; to guide the readers' expectation such as *you will probably find the following material difficult at first*; or to comment on readers' actual or hoped-for relationship to the writer, such as *my friend*. In order for easier comparison with other classification models, we summarise the overall classification in Table 2.2 as follows:

Table 2.2 Vande Kopple's classification of metadiscourse

Categories	Subcategories
Text connectives	• Sequencers • Logical or temporal connectors • Reminders about material presented earlier and announcement of material appearing later in texts. • Topicalizers
Code glosses	
Illocution markers	
Narrators	
Validity markers	• Hedges • Emphatics • Attributors
Attitude markers	
Commentaries	

Vande Kopple's above classification of metadiscourse is based on Halliday's (1973) three macro-functions of language and helps the reader understand, evaluate and react to the text. Moreover, it signals the author's presence and attitude towards the content and the reader. Nevertheless, some overlaps among these categories can also be observed, for example, attributors and narrators can be grouped as sources, reminders and illocutionary markers, which can be labelled as self-mentions by Hyland and Tse (2004). Later, these seven categories were grouped by Crismore and Farnsworth (1990) and Crismore et al. (1993) into two major categories, namely textual metadiscourse and interpersonal metadiscourse.

2.4.1.3 Crismore's classification

Avon Crismore (1990) examined the impact of metadiscourse on sixth-grade students' learning and attitudes and the relationship of certain learner variables such as ability and anxiety to the text variables such as metadiscourse and voice. The inclusion of either of these two forms of metadiscourse or the use of interpersonal voice (the first and second person pronouns) or impersonal voice (the third person pronouns) differentially affect retention of information from social studies passages and attitudes toward the passages and the subject matter, as shown in Table 2.3 below.

Table 2.3 Crismore's classification of metadiscourse

Categories	Subcategories	Functions	Examples
Informational metadiscourse	Announcement of main ideas, rationales, purposes, and strategies	Inferential, informational—when it indicates how to understand the primary message in terms of its content and structure and of the author's purposes or goals. Referring—global or local scale	*my main idea is that*, *the reason for X is that*, *my purpose for you is*, *in this section I will trace the history of X*
Attitudinal metadiscourse	Hedges	Expressive, attitudinal—when it indicates how to understand the author's perspective and attitudes toward the primary discourse and toward the reader.	*probably*, *it is possible that*
	Emphatics		*surely*, *it is certain that*
	Evaluatives		*fortunately*, *most important*

In light of Halliday's (1973) textual and interpersonal macro-function of language and Vande Kopple's (1985) seven categories of metadiscourse, Crismore and Farnsworth (1990) selected four major types from Vande Kopple, and applied them into the analysis of popular and science discourse. These four types are integrated into the two broad textual and interpersonal functions. Among them, code glosses fall into the textual function, modality markers and attitude markers the interpersonal function, while the commentaries are considered to perform both textual and interpersonal functions, which can be shown as follows:

1) Code glosses (textual): *I will call them x, in short*

2) Modality markers (interpersonal)

Hedges: *probably, suggest that*

Emphatics: *obviously, undoubtedly*

3) Attitude/evaluative markers: *it is regrettable that, we are struck by*

4) Commentaries (interpersonal and textual): The distribution of each ally may now be considered in turn, we will present these data in two

Chapter 2 An overview of research in metadiscourse

ways, see discussion below:

—**General commentary**:

Informative: except for colour, varying from island to island

Previews: we will discuss distribution in the next section

Reviews: as suggested above

Action markers: I now report that

—**Scientific commentary**:

Quantitative: measure 19

Source: Gould, Woodruff 1974

Graphics: Table 5

Latin terminology: c. bandalli

Captions: converted from original data in micrometer units

It can also be seen from this classification that the original modality markers by Vande Kopple (1985) has been reduced from three subcategories to only two: emphatics and hedges. One typical feature is that the commentary has been expanded to incorporate the general commentary and scientific commentary to make it more applicable to this specific research of metadiscourse in popular and professional science discourse. The classification here, especially of the scientific commentary, are only applicable to scientific discourse, rather than some other genres. This limits its generalisation. However, this may also reflect the fact that there is no consensus on one universally applicable classification of metadiscourse.

Crismore, Markkanen & Steffensen (1993) further developed the classification of metadiscourse in their comparative study of the phenomenon in persuasive writing by American and Finnish university students. This classification is also based on Vande Kopple (1985), but they made some modifications. They still follow the two broad textual and interpersonal categories of metadiscourse. But some of the subcategories within these two broad categories are either eliminated or renamed. These revised classification models for metadiscourse categories are shown in Table 2.4 as follows:

Table 2.4 Crismore, Markkanen and Steffensen's revised classification of metadiscourse

Broad categories	Categories	Subcategories
Textual metadiscourse (used for logical and ethical appeals)	Textual markers	• Logical connectives • Sequencers • Reminders • Topicalizers
	Interpretive markers	• Code glosses • Illocution markers • Announcements
Interpersonal metadiscourse (used for emotional and ethical appeals)	Hedges Certainty markers Attributors Attitude markers Commentary	

From this classification, it can be found that several changes exist in comparison with the Vande Kopple's (1985) classification. In the broad category of textual metadiscourse, the narrator category and the temporal sequence subcategory are dropped. The original four categories are reshaped into two categories. The first category, textual markers, replaced the text connectives. The original illocution markers, code glosses and the subcategory of announcement in the text connective category are reshaped into the second category and given a new name, interpretive markers. In the broad category of interpersonal metadiscourse, the name of original category of validity markers are dropped. Its subcategories of hedges and attributors in the validity markers category are posited to be individual categories, and emphatics are renamed certainty markers.

It is noteworthy that the above classifications by Crismore, et al and that by Vande Kopple are based on the analysis of written texts in English, which may not be automatically applicable to texts written in other languages or spoken discourse. They also admit the multi-functionality of metadiscourse which could complicate its delimitation or classification. However, one important features of this categorisation is that it is a functional classification. This use of similarity in functions of linguistic items in metadiscourse as a criterion is likely to provide more reasonable basis for cross-cultural comparative analysis.

2.4.1.4 Ken Hyland's classification

Hyland's study on metadiscourse is one of the most influential in the field of academic text, especially in academic writing to date. His classification of metadiscourse has been heavily influenced by that of Crismore et al. (1993), which distinguishes textual and interpersonal types of metadiscourse. The following section will review the development process of his metadiscourse classifications. His earliest research on metadiscourse is on its application in the business discourse, specifically the metadiscourse in the CEO's letters. In this article, Hyland (1998a, p. 228) adopted and modified Crismore et al.'s (1993) classification model, and identified the following categories as shown in Table 2.5 below, with their correspondent functions and examples.

Table 2.5　Hyland's (1998a) classification of metadiscourse

Categories	Subcategories	Function	Examples
Textual metadiscourse	Logical connectives	Express semantic relation between main clauses	*in addition*, *but*, *therefore*
	Sequencers	Denote sequence of text material	*first*, *next*, *finally*, *then*
	Frame markers	Explicitly refer to discourse acts or text stages	*finally*, *to repeat*, *my goal is*
	Endophoric markers	Refer to information in other parts of the text	*noted above*, *see below*
	Code glosses	Help readers grasp meanings of ideational material	*namely*, *e.g.*, *in other words*
Interpersonal metadiscourse	Hedges	Withhold writer's full commitment to statements	*might*, *perhaps*, *it is possible*
	Emphatics	Emphasize force or writer's certainty in message	*in fact*, *definitely*, *it is clear*

Categories	Subcategories	Function	Examples
	Attributors	Indicate the source of quoted information	according to, X says
	Attitude markers	Express writer's attitude to propositional content	surprisingly, hopefully
	Relational markers	Explicitly refer to or build relationship with reader	between us, you can see, I, we

In the same year, Hyland proposed a similar classification model in another article on metadiscourse in academic texts, as shown in Table 2.6 below.

Table 2.6 Hyland's (1998b) classification of metadiscourse

Categories	Subcategories	Function	Examples
Textual metadiscourse	Logical connectives	Express semantic relation between main clauses	in addition, but, therefore, thus, and
	Frame markers	Explicitly refer to discourse acts or text stages	finally, to repeat, our aim here, we try
	Endophoric markers	Refer to information in other parts of the text	noted above, see Fig 1 below
	Evidentials	Refer to source of information from other texts	according to X, Z states
	Code glosses	Help readers grasp meanings of ideational material	namely, e.g., in other words, such as
Interpersonal metadiscourse	Hedges	Withhold writer's full commitment to statements	might, perhaps, it is possible, about
	Emphatics	Emphasize force or writer's certainty in message	in fact, definitely, it is clear, obvious
	Attitude markers	Express writer's attitude to propositional content	surprisingly, I agree, X claims
	Relational markers	Explicitly refer to or build relationship with readers	frankly, you can see, note that
	Person markers	Explicit reference to author(s)	I, we, my, mine, our

Comparing the above two classification models, we can find that there are slight differences between them. The classification model for the business discourse has the sequencers included in the textual metadiscourse broad category, but it was dropped and incorporated into the fame marker category in the classification model of academic discourse. The attributor category was classified in the interpersonal metadiscourse in the business discourse classification model, but in that of the academic discourse, it was classified into the textual category and renamed *evidentials*. In addition, a new category of person markers was added into the interpersonal metadiscourse in the classification model for academic discourse. On the one hand, this shows the refinement of metadiscourse categories according to the specific research contexts, with the eliminating and renaming of certain categories. On the other hand, it also evidences that metadiscourse is an open category to which new items can be added to meet the specific needs of certain contexts. Then, in studies since 1998, Hyland's classification model of metadiscourse in the academic context, which he called the interpersonal model of metadiscourse, has been established (Hyland, 2005; Hyland & Tse, 2004, 2010), as shown in the following Table 2.7.

Table 2.7 Hyland's (2005) classification of metadiscourse

Categories	Subcategories	Function	Examples
Textual metadiscourse	Logical connectives	Express semantic relation between main clauses	*in addition*, *but*, *therefore*, *thus*, *and*
	Frame markers	Explicitly refer to discourse acts, sequences, or text stages	*finally*, *to repeat*, *our aim here*, *we try*
	Endophoric markers	Refer to information in other parts of the text	*noted above*, *see Fig. 1 below*
	Evidentials	Refer to source of information from other texts	*according to X*, *Z states*
	Code glosses	Help readers grasp meanings of ideational material	*namely*, *e. g.* *in other words*, *such as*
Interpersonal metadiscourse	Hedges	Withhold writer's full commitment to statements	*might*, *perhaps*, *it is possible*, *about*
	Boosters	Emphasize force or writer's certainty in message	*in fact*, *definitely*, *it is clear*, *obvious*
	Attitude markers	Express writer's attitude to propositional content	*surprisingly*, *I agree*, *X claims*

continued

Categories	Subcategories	Function	Examples
Interpersonal metadiscourse	Relational markers	Explicitly refer to or build relationship with readers	*frankly*, *you can see*, *note that*
	Self-mentions	Explicit reference to author(s)	*I*, *we*, *my*, *mine*, *our*

As is shown above, the overall classification has retained its original form, with only the previous two categories of emphatics and personal markers have been renamed to boosters and self-mentions respectively. Although Hyland (2005) claims it is applicable to both spoken and written context, his application research of this interpersonal model is mainly in the area of written academic context. Recently, this classification model has been applied by many researchers in spoken academic contexts as well (e. g. Lee & Subtirelu, 2015; Zare & Tavakoli, 2017).

2.4.2 Classifications in the narrow approach tradition

2.4.2.1 Anna Mauranen's classification

Although based on the classification of metadiscourse by Vande Kopple (1985), Mauranen (1993b) follows a narrower interpretation of metadiscourse and identifies four types of metatext, namely connectors, reviews, previews, and action markers. The linguistic realisation of these metatext items could range from single words to sequences of sentences, which can be illustrated by Table 2.8 below:

Table 2.8 Mauranen's classification of metadiscourse

Types of metatext	Linguistic realisation	Examples
Connectors	conjunctions, adverbial and prepositional phrases to indicate relationships between propositions in text	*however*, *for example*, *as a result*
Reviews	clauses (sometimes abbreviated), including an explicit indicator that an earlier stage of the text is being repeated or summarized	*So far we have assumed that the corporate tax is a proportional tax on economic income.*

Types of metatext	Linguistic realisation	Examples
Previews	clauses, sometimes abbreviated, including an explicit indicator that a later stage of the text is being anticipated	*We show below that each of the initial owners will find this policy to be utility maximizing.*
Action markers	clauses indicators of discourse acts performed in the text	*The explanation is, to express this argument in notation, to illustrate the size of this distortion.*

2.4.2.2 Annelie Ädel's classification

Ädel (2006) expands Mauranen (1993b) to incorporate both "metatext" and "writer-reader interaction" in to metadiscourse. On the one hand, the discourse functions of "metatext" aspects are to guide the reader through the text and to comment on the use of language in the text. The major focus is on the structure, discourse actions and wording of the text. For example, *to summarise, to conclude, will be discussed in the following*, etc. On the other hand, the discourse functions of "writer-reader interaction" are to help the writer to interact with the potential reader in ways that may create maintain a relationship with the reader and that allow the writer to influence the reader by involving the reader directly in different ways. For example, *Correct me if I'm wrong, but …*; *You will probably think that …*, etc.

After identifying these basic types of metadiscourse, Ädel (2006) reshapes the categorisation of metadiscourse into "personal" and "impersonal" types. Personal types of metadiscourse are the metadiscursive expressions which explicitly refer to the current writer and/or potential reader, while impersonal types of metadiscourse are those which implicitly refer to the current writer and/or possible reader. Therefore, from a personal and impersonal perspective, metadiscourse are further classified into four categories: (1) "text-oriented metadiscourse", which is used to refer to the current text itself and its language use; (2) "writer-oriented metadiscourse", which refers to the writer persona of the current text. Persona means the "created personality put forth in the act of communicating" (Campbell, 1975, p. 394). It is used here to distinguish the "actual writer [from] the character projected as the writer of the text" (Ädel, 2006, p. 222). These four categories can be shown in Table 2.9.

Table 2.9 Ädel's (2006) classification of metadiscourse

Types of metadiscourse	Object of reference	Examples
Text-oriented metadiscourse	Current text itself and its language use	*in this essay; in the following*
Writer-oriented metadiscourse	Writer persona of the current text	*as I stated above; by this I principally mean ...*
Reader-oriented metadiscourse	Imagined reader of the current text	*So you see, there were many reasons for ...; you may be thinking ...*
Participant-oriented metadiscourse	Writer and reader of the current text	*As we have seen, ...; Therefore, I will give you ... for your reference*

It is noteworthy that both Mauranen's and Ädel's classification models above are based on written texts. In order to extend the study of metadiscourse to the spoken discourse, Ädel (2010) proposed a revised and extended model, which she calls the reflexive model of metadiscourse and endeavours to make applicable to both written and spoken academic context. Under the two broad functions of metatext and audience interaction, the revised functional model consists of four major categories and 23 concrete discourse functions, as shown in Figure 2.1 below.

In this classification model, the first category of metatext, metalinguistic comments, includes five functional subcategories. Among them, repairing involves self- or other-initiated correction or cancelation to preceding contribution. Reformulating refers to the language which offers an alternative expression and an added value of expansion to the preceding contribution. Commenting on linguistic form/meaning is the metalinguistic reference to the linguistic form, word choice and meaning. Clarifying is used to spell out the addressor's intentions in order to avoid misinterpretation. Managing terminology normally gives definition, provide terms or labels for the phenomena being talked about.

The second category of metatext, discourse organisation, includes discourse functions of managing the topic and those of managing the *phoric* [*phoric* here refers to the various locations and portions in the current discourse (Ädel, 2006, p.101)]. In those functions of managing the topic, introducing the topic is used to opening a topic. Delimiting topic explicitly states how the topic is constrained. Adding to topic is used to explicitly comment on the addition of a topic or subtopic. Concluding topic is used to close the topic. And the last one marking asides is used to open or close a "topic sidetrack" or digression.

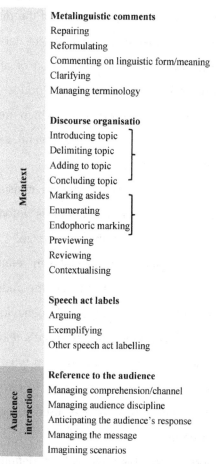

Figure 2.1　Ädel's (2010) classification of metadiscourse

In those functions of managing the phorics, enumerating is used to indicate how different parts of the discourse are ordered. Endophoric marking points to a certain location in the discourse, whether before or after the current point (unlike previewing and reviewing), for example, when the audience is instructed to look at a table, or turn to a specific part in a handout. Hyland (1998b) uses a similar term, "endophoric marker", but he uses it to refer to reviewing and previewing, which is different from its usage here. The following two categories' previewing and reviewing points forward and backward respectively to the discourse, to announce what is to come and remind the audience what has already taken place in the discourse. Contextualising is used to comment on the situation of writing or speaking and contains traces of the production of the discourse.

The third category of metatext, speech act labels, includes three subcategories. Arguing is used to stress the action or arguing for or against an issue. Exemplifying is used to explicitly introduce an example. Other speech act labelling refers to those speech acts which are used not frequently enough to have their own label. She listed several examples of giving a hint, suggesting, mentioning and emphasising.

The category of reference to the audience consists of five discourse functions. Managing comprehension/channel is intended to ensure the addresser and addressee(s) are "on the same page", to check or at least refer to participants' understanding and uptake in relation to the channel. Managing audience discipline is used to instruct the audience in what to do, or to reprimand or compliment the audience's behaviour. Anticipating the audience response is used to predict the audience's reaction. Managing the message typically emphasises the core message in what is being conveyed, or state what the addresser wishes the audience to remember based on the discourse. Imagining scenarios is a strategy used to guide the audience to see something from a particular perspective.

In short, this model resonates well with its definitions in that the two broad categories of metatext and audience interaction are figured out in detail in relation to how to be reflexive to the evolving discourse or its linguistic form. It is a pioneering classification of metadiscourse specifically designed to be used in both spoken and written academic discourse. Thus, it sheds light on the theoretical and empirical development of metadiscourse study in the comparative study of spoken and written academic discourse, in particular the less researched fields of spoken academic discourse.

2.4.3 Classification adopted in this research

Hyland's (2005) interpersonal model of metadiscourse is adopted as the primary theoretical foundation for the current research. This is due to the following several reasons. First, as the current research is aimed at exploring the teachers' reference to and interaction with the students, the broad approach to metadiscourse could better suit this purpose as opposed to the narrow approach (e. g. Ädel, 2010; Mauranen, 1993a) which merely focusing on discourse reflexivity. Second, this broad approach to metadiscourse is mainly derived from and used for research into academic genres, and has been improved based on a variety of previous taxonomies of metadiscourse studies (e. g. Crismore, 1990; Vande Kopple, 1985, 2002). Third, although Hyland's (2005) interpersonal modal of metadiscourse is mainly designed to investigate written academic discourse, this model has demonstrated its robustness and effectiveness in exploring the discourse organisation and audience involvement mechanisms in spoken academic discourse, in particular teachers' classroom instructional discourse after slight modification of certain metadiscourse markers (e. g. Lee & Subtirelu, 2015; Yan, 2010; Zhang, 2017).

Moreover, this interpersonal modal of metadiscourse has a clear-cut categorisation and list of metadiscourse items, thus can facilitate the examination of the frequency and distribution of metadiscourse markers. Such frequency and distribution of teachers' metadiscourse use in guiding students through the lesson and interacting with students are assumed to be variables that can distinguish the distinctive features of the native and non-native English-speaking EAP teachers in both the UK and China. Although it has had to be modified according to the specific characteristics of spoken academic discourse, this interpersonal modal of metadiscourse provides a rather flexible framework to integrate all the above related considerations. Therefore, it would be more appropriate to follow a broad approach to metadiscourse and adopt Hyland's interpersonal modal of metadiscourse functions in the current research.

2.5 Other terms pertinent to metadiscourse

In order to get a better understanding of this widely recognised fuzziness of metadiscourse, this section will present the terms that have a bearing on metadiscourse, and distinguish those terms which have some overlap with metadiscourse.

2.5.1 Metalanguage

Metalanguage as a term has a longer history than metadiscourse. It has been noted that the term *metadiscourse* was coined by Zellig Harris in 1959. Contrastively, based on Ädel (2006), metalanguage, as a calque from Polish, originates in modern logic. According to this argument, it was coined in the 1930s by the mathematician and logician Alfred Tarski and was first introduced into the field of linguistics by Roman Jakobson in the 1950s. It was only in recent decades, however, that metalinguistic phenomena have been discussed and regarded as an important part of text production and reception in the field of discourse studies. In its process of development, metalanguage has been defined in various ways by different standards, with the most prevalent definition as "language about language". Nevertheless, most of these definitions show that the term *metalanguage* is

Chapter 2 An overview of research in metadiscourse

generally bound up with the notion of object language. Based on Craig (2016, p.6), in formal semantics, metalanguage is "a language that refers to another language, which is called an object language *and in turn refers to non-linguistic entities*". This definition embodies the idea that metalanguage and object language are conceived to be two closely related but contrastive terms. The former is stated as a language in which we speak of the verbal code itself, whereas the latter refers to the language in which we speak about the things that are external to language itself.

More concretely, Ädel (2006, p.161) summarised the meanings of metalanguage into four broad categories from its technical and non-technical usages. Ranking from less technical to more technical usages, the meanings of this term may include the following four categories. The first category concerns the "mention" of any term and not the referent in the object world. This is the reflexive level of language use, which means many aspects of language can be talked about with language itself. From this perspective, language is used specifically to refer to the code itself, rather than any substance in the outside world. For example, in the sentence "Mary is a noun", "Mary" does not refers to any girl with this name in the real world, but the word or code itself in this particular sentence. In this view, words which are deemed as metalanguage on one occasion can also be the object language on some other occasions. Metalanguage or object language can be transformed from one to another depending on its local context. Second, linguistic terminologies, ranging from less-technical terminology such as *word*, *phrase* or *sentence*, to highly specialised and abstract ones, such as *relative clause*, *basilect*, or *definiendum*. Third, dictionary definitions or the "defining of metalanguage" (Preston, 2004, p.306). This aspect of metalanguage refers to the headwords which are listed paradigmatically in a dictionary. They are presented not to refer to the substance in the outside world, but to be specially defined, explained and commented upon. Finally, highly formalised linguistic codes. For example, specific codes such as *p*, *q*, or *r* used in the scientific analysis of language as logic. Also in the field of information technology, some abstract codes may be used to describe other codes, such as SGML, which defines rules for how the structure of a document can be described, with words being marked with <w> <w/>, sentences with <s> <s/>, and paragraphs with <p> <p/>.

From the above four aspects of metalanguage, it can be seen that the less-technical usages incorporate a broader amount of metalanguages than the following more technical ones. In effect, these technical and non-technical taxonomies in metalanguage have drawn the continuous attention of a body of researchers in the study of metalanguage as well as metadiscourse. Dennis Preston (2004), in his book chapter "Folk Metalanguage", elaborates on various types of lay metalanguage and distinguishes between folk and expert (linguists') metalanguages. He defined folk metalanguage as "overt knowledge of and comment about language by non-linguists", compared to the expert metalanguage which is the "talk about language by professional linguists and students in the world of linguistics" (Preston, 2004, p.75). Here, the term "lay metalanguage" and "fold metalanguage" are roughly the same as the less-technical usage of metalanguage as summarised in the second point by Ädel (2006) above. "Expert metalanguage" is to some extent equal to the more technical usages of metalanguage mentioned in the first point above.

In another article of the same collection of book, Theo van Leeuwen (2004) puts forward, in a more systematic way, the two broad approaches to the idea of metalanguage. According to him, the first approach is oriented towards representation, in which metalanguage does not represent the world directly but represents representations of the world. This kind of metalanguage is a specialised scientific register and is similar to the above "expert metalanguage". The second approach is oriented towards communication and regarded as an indispensable part of everyday communication, hence as one important component of the "object language". This also resonated with the first meaning proposed by Ädel (2006) as indicated above.

In a similar vein, in the field of metadiscourse study, Hyland (2017) argues that the growing interest in metadiscourse is driven mainly by two attempts, one to "understand relationship between language and its context of use" and the other to "employ this knowledge in the service of language and literacy education". It is rather likely that these two impetuses will lead to the further taxonomy of practical and academic metadiscourses. Likewise, Craig (1999) also draws a distinction between metadiscourse which constitutes the practical talk of everyday life and also the "research and theory about talk", in other words, everyday metadiscourse and theorized concepts.

Metalanguage and metadiscourse share similarities; discrepancies exist as well, however. They overlap roughly in terms of two aspects. The first aspect is in their overarching definitions, with the former being the study of language about language and the latter discourse about discourse. Secondly, the starting point of their research are both based on the "familiar observation that language is a unique communicative system in that it can be used to describe and represent itself" (Jaworski & Coupland, 2004, p. 3; Willoughby et al., 2015).

However, metalanguage and metadiscourse differ from each other in subtle ways as well. Metalanguage not only predates metadiscourse conceptually, as mentioned at the beginning of this section, but also covers a relatively narrower scope compared to that of metadiscourse. This is because metadiscourse goes beyond the study of language about language, and embraced a much broader range of phenomena (Mauranen, 2010), covering "secondary" discourse (Crismore, 1989; Crismore & Farnsworth, 1990), "non-topical" text matter (Lautamatti, 1978, 1987), "non-propositional" content (Mauranen, 1993b), or interpersonal and textual meta-functions of language (Vande Kopple, 1985, 2002). In addition, metadiscourse develops further than metalanguage in that metadiscourse incorporates the pragmatic aspects of language, as is stated by Craig (2016, p.6), " ... distinct from the older concept of metalanguage, metadiscourse is primarily concerned with the pragmatics of communication". This, from a distinctive perspective, evidences the powerful developing potential of the research in metadiscourse.

2.5.2 Metacommunication

The term "metacommunication" was first advanced by Ruesch and Bateson (1951/1968) in their book *Communication: The Social Matrix of Psychiatry*, to mean the "communication about communication". According to Ruesch and Bateson (ibid), metacommunication, arising with the evolution of mammals, is a "new order" of communication and explains "some distinctively complex, creative and deeply paradoxical qualities of social interaction" (Craig, 2016, p.1). Later on, Bateson (1972, 1999) developed the theory of metacommunication and claimed that human verbal communication operates simultaneously at three levels of abstraction, i.e., denotative level, metalinguistic level and metacommunicative level. The first level refers to the literal content of what is said, while the latter two levels are more abstract levels. Metalinguistic level is the messages about the language being used, and metacommunicative level concerns the relationship between the communicators. These metalinguistic and metacommunicative levels can be either implicit or explicit. They are explicit in such occasions when someone explicitly say "Let's be friends" or by expressing the knowledge that the word *media* is a plural noun, but more commonly these explicit expressions are rendered as implicit, by *acting* in a friendly way or by *using* the word "media" as a plural noun.

Enlightened by observing monkeys at play, Bateson notes that one of the most important types of metacommunication is the implicit metacommunicative message on how to interpret explicit signals which communicate meanings such as friendliness or hostility. He goes on to argue that this is what metacommunication should mainly focus on, as much of our communication has the potential to generate paradox insofar as every message includes an implicit metacommunication about the relationship between the communicators. In other words, any message can only be produced in some particular context and manner, which implies a certain relationship between the interlocutors.

Thus, he emphasized the necessity of taking context in to account in the studying of metacommunication to deal with the issue of paradox between the implicit message and the explicit message. He employs the example of the simple message "please pass the salt" said at dinner, which could imply varied relationship between the speaker and the hearer, depending on the situational context and the use of metacommunicative signals such as facial expression and tone of voice. To be concrete, it could be deemed as a bid to start a conversation, or it could be a conversational move intended to end a conversation. Moreover, at a metalinguistic level, words can mean different things in variable situations. "The salt" in the above example can mean "the salt shaker on the table in front of you" in one situation or "the bag of rock salt by the wall behind you" in another. Meaning always has to be interpreted in context, but the context is framed by metalinguistic and metacommunicative aspects of the message. Hence the relation between meaning and context is closely interdependent.

The concept of metacommunication has been applied in a range of academic and professional fields based on variable understandings of the concept itself. It is sometimes used in certain therapy groups in which participants may be trained to speak directly about their here-and-now experience of ongoing interaction, based on the conception of metacommunication as the explicit discussion of the communication process. More commonly, metacommunication is conceived as nonverbal signals that modify the meaning of verbal expressions, and used, for example, to convey sincerity or sarcasm, or to manage conversational turn-taking. Although oversimplified, these common definitions are roughly consistent with Bateson's concept of metacommunication. For example, they often highlight the potential for metacommunicative signals to contradict verbal utterances in order to produce confusing "mixed messages", or the potential for misunderstanding between members of different cultural groups, by whom the same nonverbal framing cues may be interpreted differently (Craig, 2016).

Based on Bateson's metacommunication, Erving Goffman (1974), in his work *Frame Analysis*, developed an elaborate microsociological scheme for analysing "the organisation of experience" in social interaction. Although Goffman does not discuss metacommunication explicitly, he distinguishes several forms of communication that function metacommunicatively, such as directional signals and ways of breaking frame. The concept of metacommunication has also been applied and extended to the field of interpersonal communication to develop a system for coding and analysing interpersonal interaction at the relational level (see, e.g. Rogers & Escudero, 2014). Drawing on metacommunication theory, a general theory of communication named coordinated management of meaning (CMM) was developed to provide heuristic models to guide professional analysis, intervention and the facilitation of communication processes ranging from intimate relationships to public participation forums. In addition to interpersonal relationships, metacommunication has been proved to be equally applicable to other kinds of interactional relationships, such as international relations (Rich & Craig, 2012), political debate and other sites of public confrontation (Simons, 1994).

Scholars of language and social interaction have studied metacommunication through the closely related concept of metadiscourse or reflexive language use, a concept that includes both the metalinguistic and the metacommunicative levels of communication (as defined by Bateson) while highlighting the role of language pragmatics. The concept of metadiscourse invites detailed studies of the specific means by which communicators accomplish metacommunicative functions such as framing (e. g. Tannen, 1993), or (mis)understanding across languages, cultures or social situations. Other studies (Taylor, 1997; Cameron, 2000) have revealed the fundamental importance of metadiscourse in the aggregate for language, culture and the theory and practice of communication.

Overall, metadiscourse has an important role in shaping social practices and normative beliefs about language and communication. It follows that discourses of communication theory and philosophy also function pragmatically as forms of metadiscourse, insofar as they diffuse beyond the narrow confines of an academic discipline and are taken up by social actors and used by them to interpret, justify, or criticize communicative conduct. In this light, it can be argued that communication scholars, who possess relevant expert knowledge, have an obligation to participate in public discourse on communication problems and practices as interpreters and critics of the commonplace assumptions about communication embedded in ordinary metadiscourse, and as creative innovators of new and better ways of talking about how we communicate (Craig, 2005).

2.5.3 Discourse markers

Following Fraser (1999), the term *discourse markers* was first put forward by Labov & Fanshel (1977), and later exposited by Levinson (1983). Since the late 1980s, discourse markers have aroused the attention of many scholars (Schiffrin, 1987; Fraser, 1990; Halliday, 1994) and has been defined in different ways. Generally speaking, discourse markers refers to the "linguistic devices used by speakers to make the relations between the previous and the ongoing texts salient in order to build the coherence of discourse units" (Yeh & Huang, 2016). In her ground-breaking monograph

Discourse Markers, Schiffrin (1987, p. 40) defines it as the "linguistic, paralinguistic or non-verbal elements that signal relations between units of talk by virtue of their syntactic and semantic properties and by virtue of their sequential relations as initial or terminal brackets demarcating discourse units". Another pioneering researcher, Fraser (1990), specified discourse markers as linguistic units that "impose a relationship between some aspect of the discourse segment they are part of ... and some aspect of a prior discourse segment ..." (p. 938).

Meanwhile, like that of metadiscourse, this concept of discourse markers has been expressed by a variety of parallel terms. For example, discourse operators (Redeker, 1990, 1991), connectives (Stukker & Sanders, 2012), sentence connectives (Halliday & Hasan, 1976), pragmatic connectives (Fraser, 1988), pragmatic markers (Fraser, 1988, 1990; Schiffrin, 1987), discourse particles (Schourup, 1985; Bayer et al., 2016), and discourse markers (Tanghe, 2016; Marmorstein, 2016). According to Bidaoui (2016), some researchers use certain expressions of this notion based on whether the focus of their research is based on formal or functional aspects of discourse markers. The term *discourse particles* is used when they focus on the formal perspective, whereas discourse markers is usually used when they focus on the functional perspective. Other researchers choose the term to use depending on the number of words involved in the concept. For example, Fischer (2006) uses the term *discourse particles* when one word is involved, and uses the term *discourse markers* when two or more words is incorporated. Nevertheless, discourse marker is preferred over a plethora of competing terms (Fraser, 1999), not only because it aptly conveys how the linguistic item signals discourse relations, but also because it "probably has the widest currency in the field" (Buysse, 2012, p. 1764).

Research in discourse markers has broadened its scope in the past over three decades. Although some theoretical issues such as the delimitation work of its basic definitions and categorisations still exist, a solidified theoretical framework has currently been established. The research has been extended to include not only the discourse markers of non-native English speakers (e. g. Fuller, 2003; Aijmer, 2004; Fung & Carter, 2007, 2011; Mukherjee, 2009; Polat, 2011; Aijmer, 2004; Fung & Carter, 2007, 2011; Mukherjee, 2009; Polat, 2011), but also those of other languages, such as French (Hansen, 1998), Indonesian (Wouk, 1999) and Spanish (Cuenca & Marín, 2009). In addition, other language varieties such as learner language has also come into prominence in recent years (Granger, 2009), although spoken learner corpora, an important resource for studying discourse markers in learner language, develops later than the written form due to the time-consuming collection and transcription process.

Discourse markers share a range of similar characteristics with that of metadiscourse. First and foremost, there seems no clear boundary between the terms of metadiscourse markers and discourse markers, because metadiscourse markers are sometimes also called discourse markers, and they are used interchangeably in some research (Shi, 2015). Second, similar to the view on metadiscourse, discourse markers have also traditionally been viewed as secondary or inferior to propositional content, as they are seen as the linguistic components which do not contribute to the ideational meaning of a discourse (Bidaoui, 2016). Moreover, since the late 1980s, the delimitation in the field of discourse markers, such as its definitions and taxonomies (e. g. Blakemore, 1988; Redeker, 1991; Fraser, 1999; Schourup, 1999; Fischer, 2006), has been a very important aspects of research focus. This issue has been and still is one of the major issues in the study of metadiscourse, although the scope of discourse markers seems to be less vague than that of metadiscourse.

Despite the above shared features of discourse markers and metadiscourse, they also distinguish from each other in several aspects. As is noted by Shi (2015) in a comprehensive analysis, first of all, metadiscourse can be realised by a series of linguistic units ranging from words, phrases, clauses, sentences, to sequences of sentences or passages. However, discourse markers are typically very short and concise linguistic units. Second, metadiscourse can be some loose linguistic items, while discourse markers are usually well-knit linguistic units. Third, discourse markers are used more frequently compared with that of metadiscourse. Discourse markers are themselves the result of frequent use in metadiscourse. Therefore, the number of discourse markers are generally less than that of metadiscourse. Metadiscourse is a system open to the emergence of new metadiscourse items.

2.6 Overview of metadiscourse research in academic genres

This section reviews metadiscourse research in academic genres. As metadiscourse research in written academic genres accounts for the predominant majority, it will be reviewed prior to the exploration of metadiscourse study in spoken academic genres. Overall, a review of the literature has revealed that metadiscourse research is usually conducted from a comparative perspective. The current research identified three major categories from the existing literature, that is, cross-disciplinary, cross-linguistic and cross-cultural perspectives. Such studies in written context have enhanced our understanding of metadiscourse phenomena. They may also shed new light on research into spoken academic metadiscourse. In addition, there have been sporadic metadiscourse studies in spoken academic contexts, and the majority of them are mainly in the classroom teaching contexts. Therefore, metadiscourse research in spoken academic contexts will be introduced separately in Section 3.3 below on the overview of metadiscourse research in classroom teaching contexts.

As discussed above, it was from the early 1980s that the study of metadiscourse began to witness a robust development. However,

Chapter 2 An overview of research in metadiscourse

metadiscourse research prior to the 2000s was mainly limited to a few pioneering researchers (e. g. Williams, 1981; Vande Kopple, 1985; Crismore, 1983, 1989, 1990) who primarily centred on clarifying the term, including its definitions, characteristics and classifications, with relatively few empirical studies on metadiscourse. It is during the past two decades or so that metadiscourse has begun to draw a wider attention from researchers, being studied in a variety of genres, such as in news article genres (Fu & Hyland, 2014; Kuhi & Mojood, 2014; Makkonen-Craig, 2011; Peterlin & Moe, 2016), business and commercial genres (Fu, 2012; Fuertes-Olivera et al., 2001; Gilmore, 2015; González, 2005; Hyland, 1998a; Leibbrand, 2015; López-Ferrero & Bach, 2016; Vásquez, 2015). Moreover, metadiscourse has been found to be an effective way of engaging listeners or readers in preaching or religious texts (Malmström, 2014). It is also said to contribute to the argumentative and interactional effect of editorials (Khabbazi-Oskouei, 2013, 2016; Shokouhi et al., 2015).

The above-mentioned studies can be classified under the general rubric of non-academic genres. However, they account for a relatively small proportion of the overall research into metadiscourse, when compared with academic genres. Metadiscourse research in academic genres, in particular written academic genres, is the most prevalent area being investigated. A survey of existing literature reveals that most metadiscourse research in written academic genres is conducted in a comparative manner, such as between texts written by writers with different language proficiency levels (Aull & Lancaster, 2014; Dobbs, 2014; Intaraprawat & Steffensen, 1995; Lee & Deakin, 2016; Noble, 2010). In view of the significance and comparatively large proportion of metadiscourse study in academic genres and the focus of this book, this overview will examine three broad categories of metadiscourse research in written academic genres: cross-disciplinary, cross-linguistic and cross-cultural studies.

Notably, the classification of these different categories is not intended to be exhaustive, but rather to make prominent the contrastive characteristics of metadiscourse research, as it is often the case that many studies involve more than one comparative factors simultaneously in one piece of research. For example, some research may focus on mixed factors of cross-cultural/disciplinary (Li & Wharton, 2012), cross-linguistic/disciplinary (Dahl, 2004), or cross-cultural/linguistic (Çandarli, Bayyurt & Marti, 2015; Pérez-Llantada, 2010; Yang, 2013). There is also comparison of metadiscourse use in research articles in terms of mixed factors of cross-disciplinary/paradigmatic (Hong & Cao, 2014; Hu & Cao, 2015). Therefore, the following classification is based on the primary comparative factors used in their respective studies.

2.6.1 Cross-disciplinary research on metadiscourse in academic genres

As one of the most influential researchers in metadiscourse research, Ken Hyland has conducted a series of metadiscourse research studies based on cross-disciplinary comparison since the 1990s. In his first piece of cross-disciplinary research, based on an analysis of 28 research articles, with seven from each of four separate academic disciplines (i.e. microbiology, marketing, astrophysics and applied linguistics), Hyland (1998b) examined how the appropriate use of metadiscourse is affected by its rhetorical context. Based on previous taxonomy of metadiscourse (Vande Kopple, 1985; Crismore, 1990), he developed a slightly revised model of metadiscourse and claimed that it helps to guide readers to better construct appropriate contexts and interpret shared disciplinary assumptions. This early research adds to a significant dimension of rhetorical differences among variable disciplinary communities and provides new insights into the concept of metadiscourse. In an attempt to examine whether academic research writing is a self-effacing task with little or no writer presence, Hyland (2001) explored the use of self-mention, one of the metadiscourse categories, in a corpus of 240 research articles in eight disciplines. Through this research, he showed how self-mention, in particular its subcategories of self-citation and exclusive first person pronouns can be used as a powerful rhetorical strategy for emphasising a writer's contribution.

Drawing on a corpus of 240 dissertations totalling four million words, which consists of 20 masters' and 20 doctoral dissertations from each of six academic disciplines—electronic engineering, computer science, business studies, biology, applied linguistics, and public administration, Hyland (2004a, 2010) conducted two similar studies employing both quantitative and qualitative approaches. These two studies comprise frequency counts of metadiscourse items, text analysis, and interviews with postgraduate students. Both studies reveal how L2 writers deploy metadiscourse resources to offer a credible representation of themselves and work in different fields, and thus how metadiscourse can be used to uncover the rhetorical and social distinctiveness of disciplinary communities.

In a more recent study, Hyland and Jiang (2016) carried out a longitudinal study into the use of stance, an important concept under the umbrella term of metadiscourse, with a view to determining whether authorial projection has changed over the past 50 years. Based on a corpus of 2.2 million words abstracted from the top five journals in each of four disciplines—applied linguistics, sociology, electrical engineering and biology—at three distinct time periods of 1965, 1985 and 2015, they found "a somewhat surprising picture" (Hyland & Jiang, 2016, p. 269) that stance frequencies have been increasing in hard sciences and declining in social sciences. They pointed out that research articles in hard science, in particular those in electrical engineering, display an increased use of stance markers, most notably self-mention. This shows at least a slow change of traditional knowledge construction practice toward rhetorical convergence as hard and soft science fields adjust their stance to changing circumstances.

Based on a corpus of 160 research articles across eight disciplines and a corpus of 120 research articles across six disciplines respectively, Jiang and Hyland (2015, 2016) conducted two studies on a relatively overlooked means of expressing a stance, that is, through a Noun Complement structure in which a stance head noun takes a nominal complement clause, for example, in the sentence "The fact that science has a history is not an argument against the possibility of scientific truth". By developing a new rhetorically based classification of stance nouns, they show that the "metadiscursive noun + post-nominal clause" pattern is another key element of metadiscourse, providing writers with a means of organising discourse into a cohesive flow of information and constructing stance towards it. This structure can not only be widely used to express author comment and evaluation, but also exhibit considerable variation in the way that it is used to build knowledge across different disciplines.

Hyland's (2005) interpersonal model of metadiscourse, or sometimes the similar Hyland and Tse's (2004) model, provides the analytical framework for many subsequent studies on interpersonal or interactive metadiscourse phenomena. Based on Hyland's (2005) interpersonal model of metadiscourse, Estaji and Vafaeimehr (2015) examined the variations in the patterns of use, type and frequency of interactional metadiscourse markers in the introduction and conclusion of research papers. Through the analysis of a corpus with 21 articles in each of mechanical and electrical engineering disciplines, it was found that there are minor differences in the frequency and type of metadiscourse markers used in the introduction and conclusion of these two disciplines. Moreover, the Chi-square test result demonstrates that there is no significantly difference between the two disciplines. This could probably be due to the reason that these two disciplines both fall into the category of natural science. Drawing on the same interpersonal metadiscourse model by Hyland (2005), Khedri, Heng and Ebrahimi (2013) explored the use of interactive metadiscourse markers in research article abstracts in two disciplines within the social sciences.

With their research based on an analysis of 60 research article abstracts in applied linguistics and economics, they found that there were marked differences across the two disciplines in the use of interactive metadiscourse markers.

Adopting Hyland & Tse's (2004) model, Kan (2016) investigated the use of interactional metadiscourse in all parts of 20 articles from Turkish language education and literature. The result reveals that interactional metadiscoure markers are used more frequently in the domain of Turkish language education than in the domain of literature. Specifically, it was found that there is no statistically significant difference in the uses of attitude markers, engagement marker and self-mentions in studies on Turkish language education and literature, but it demonstrates significant difference in their use of hedges and boosters.

Other researchers employ some other models in their cross-disciplinary metadiscourse studies. For example, Abdi (2002) adopted an early model of metadiscourse developed by Vande Kopple (1985) to examine the ways writers use interpersonal metadiscourse to partly reveal their identity and their selected mode of interaction in two disciplines: social sciences and natural sciences. The analysis indicates that social sciences writers make more frequent use of interpersonal metadiscourse than natural sciences writers do. Further comparison shows that they differ significantly in the use of attitude markers and hedges but there was little variation in the use of emphatics. The result reveals that the choice of validity markers is closely dependent on the type of article being studied.

By adopting a narrow approach (Ädel, 2006) different from the above studies reviewed so far, Salas (2015) compared the use of reflexive metadiscourse in research articles from three disciplines (medicine, economics and linguistics) written in Spanish. The analysis shows that significantly fewer metadiscourse markers are used in economics and medicine than in linguistics. Certain subcategories, such as self-mentions, relational markers, directives, discourse verbs and code glosses show significant differences across the three disciplines. This narrow approach resonates with the above broad approach in that both suggest authors from different academic disciplines vary in their use of metadiscourse to guide and interact with the audience.

The above review shows that cross-disciplinary research into metadiscourse mainly centres on the comparison between social sciences and natural sciences, or within social or natural sciences. Through these comparisons of metadiscourse use in texts or different sections of written texts, for example, the abstract, introduction or conclusion, researchers attempt to map out, from a more comprehensive perspective, the distinctive features of written texts in each disciplinary genre. This might shed light on how writers construct their texts, signal their presence and guide their readers by employing appropriate metadiscourse resources. Furthermore, it can be seen that these comparisons are also generally conducted within the written academic genres, with very few such studies being carried out in their spoken equivalents. This in turn forms part of the rationale for the current research, which will be further illustrated in Section 3.4.

2.6.2 Cross-linguistic research on metadiscourse in academic genres

Compared with cross-disciplinary and cross-cultural research, cross-linguistic research of metadiscourse in academic genres accounts for a lesser proportion in the contrastive studies of metadiscourse. In view of the importance of English in cross-cultural communication, studies of this kind primarily centre on the comparison between English and other various languages, such as Chinese, Turkish, Spanish, or Catalan. As noted by Mauranen (2010) from a text reflexivity perspective, metadiscourse is a "discourse universal" in that it is "such a major element of communication that languages generally possess means for expressing it" (p.21).

Drawing on Hyland's (2005) interpersonal model of metadiscourse,

Mu, Zhang, Ehrich and Hong (2015) compared the usage of metadiscourse in English and Chinese research articles published in applied linguistics journals and investigated how metadiscourse may contribute to knowledge construction in research articles. The results show that both types of articles use statistically significantly more interactive metadiscourse which serves to organise discourse than interactional metadiscourse which indicates writers' attitude and evaluation of themselves, text and readers. However, English articles employ more varied metadiscourse devices than that of Chinese articles, that is, the total frequency of English metadiscourse is 647.8 per 10,000 words, while it is 240.3 per 10,000 characters in Chinese.

In another comparative study of English and Chinese research articles, Kim and Lim (2013) focused on the introduction section in articles in educational psychology. In light of Hyland and Tse's (2004) model of metadiscourse, they drew a similar conclusion to that of Mu et al. (2015) in that English articles have a higher density of metadiscourse than their Chinese counterparts do. However, the two types of articles also share similarities in metadiscourse use. For example, both English and Chinese research article introductions use far more interactive than interactional forms, and evidentials and transitions (58.6% and 18.5% of all interactive uses respectively) are the most frequent metadiscourse used in both types of articles. The authors then interpreted this from a socio-cultural perspective. They claimed that under the influence of English as a lingua franca (ELF), Chinese academic writing has been becoming more reader-responsible, which means the writer controls the level of personality in a text to establish a more distant relationship between the author, text and readers, and gives the readers some room to interpret the text according to their personal knowledge and perception. They pointed out the implication for ESL Chinese students to be aware of this change as what was stated in previous literature was that "Chinese writing favours simplicity and its cohesiveness is interpreted from the context" (Lee, 2004, p. 296).

Apart from comparisons of metadiscourse use between English and Chinese, there is also comparative analysis of English with other languages. Drawing on Hyland's (2005) model of metadiscourse, Lee and Casal (2014) compared the result and discussion sections of engineering masters' theses written in English and Spanish. They found that compared with Spanish theses, English theses employ not only considerably more metadiscourse, but also greater transitions, endophorics and evidentials to assist readers in navigating through the line of argumentation. In a comparison of English with Turkish academic book review genres, Bal-Gezegin (2016), employing Hyland's (2000) taxonomy of metadiscourse, noted that English book reviews have a higher frequency of metadiscourse use than that of Turkish, in particular in the use of hedging devices.

In addition to the comparison between two different languages, Martín-Laguna & Alcón (2015) moved further to compare the opinion essays written by secondary school students in three different languages: English, Spanish and Catalan. By employing Hyland's (2000) classification of metadiscourse, they showed that although there is more variety of metadiscourse use in Catalan and Spanish, no significant variation was observed among these three languages. This leads the authors to conclude that language input affects students' metadiscourse use in writings, which may provide insights for teachers' writing instruction as will be conducted in the current research.

Moreover, it can also be found that all the studies above adopted Hyland's interpersonal model of metadiscourse as their analytical framework. It is also worth mentioning a neatly cross-lingual study is based on the comparison of research articles with their corresponding translations (English and Slovene) represented by Peterlin either employing Hyland's (2005) model or that of Mauranen (1993b). Her research mainly focuses on the comparison of textual organising devices of metadiscourse (Peterlin, 2005, 2008), or on specific hedging devices (Peterlin, 2010), or engagement markers in research articles (Peterlin & Moe, 2016).

2.6.3 Cross-cultural research on metadiscourse in academic genres

Another important aspect of metadiscourse study is cross-cultural research. This can be divided into three types. First, texts written by native English speakers, such as British and American, and non-native English speakers in other cultural contexts, such as Turkish, Iranian, Spanish and Finnish. Second, texts written by both different native cultural groups and native with non-native groups, such as between American, British and Norwegian or Swedish. Third, texts written by writers from different non-native cultural settings, such as Chinese, Spanish and Polish. This will be presented in detail in what follows.

The first aspect involves cross-cultural research of metadiscourse use in texts written by native and non-native writers. In an early study, Crismore, Markkanen and Steffensen (1993) compared the writings of two groups of students from American and Finnish universities, with a view to investigating the cultural influence on metadiscourse use. They also took into account the role of gender variables in this research. The results show that there are some cultural and gender variations in the types and amounts of metadiscourse use, although both cultural groups of students use all categories and subcategories. Compared with American students and female students, more metadiscourse items are used by Finnish students and male students. Students from both countries employ more interpersonal than textual metadiscourse, with Finnish male students using the most and American male students the least. This pioneering cross-cultural research on metadiscourse evidences the universality of the metadiscourse phenomenon. More importantly, it calls for more cross-cultural research into its use and more attention to metadiscourse in writing instruction. This extends the scope of research in metadiscourse and sheds new light on later comparative studies of this type.

More recently, Ozdemir and Longo (2014), based on Hyland's (2005), analysed the cultural differences in the use of metadiscourse between American and Turkish postgraduate students' abstract sections in their Master of Arts (MA) theses, which were written in English. They found that Turkish students use more metadiscourse transitions, frame markers and hedges in their master thesis abstracts than American students do, but they employ fewer occurrences of evidential, endophorics, code glosses, boosters, attitude markers, and self-mentions. In order to find the differences between the metadiscourse use by American native authors and Iranian non-native authors, Gholami & Ilghamit (2016) compared their frequency of interactive and interactional metadiscourse markers in biological research articles written in English. They observed that Iranian authors use slightly more interactive and interactional metadiscourse markers than their American counterparts. In addition, they also showed that there is a strong positive correlation between the frequency of metadiscourse markers and impact factor of the journals. This may provisionally confirm the important role of metadiscourse markers in improving the coherence and organisation of research articles for potential publishing in high-impact journals.

Apart from the above comparison between American authors and authors from non-native settings, there is also a comparison between British writers and non-native groups. Based on Hyland's (2005) interpersonal model of metadiscourse and conceiving that metadiscourse is context dependent, Golmohammadi, Suluki, Daneshmand & Salahshoor (2014) analysed the use of metadiscourse in the discussion sections of 40 research articles written in English by Iranian and English scholars. They found that the two groups differ in their use of self-mentions and engagement markers. In addition, this research also drew on the socio-cognitive approach of van Dijk (2008) to interpret the analysis, and suggested that social constructions and cognition of participants may also have a great influence on the use of interactional metadiscourse strategies.

In addition, there is also a comparison between Anglo-Americans and non-native writers. For example, Abdollahzadeh (2011) studied the interpersonal metadiscourse in the conclusion sections of applied linguistics articles written in English by Anglo-American and Iranian academic writers. They drew a similar conclusion to Golmohammadi, Suluki, Daneshmand & Salahshoor (2014) in that both groups use a considerable amount of hedges, but Anglo-American writers employ more emphatics and attitude markers. Likewise, Mauranen (1993b) conducted a contrastive rhetorical study between texts written by Finnish and Anglo-American academics. The analysis demonstrates that Anglo-American academics use more metadiscourse (termed *metatext* by Mauranen) than Finnish academics. She thus concluded that Anglo-American writers are more reader-oriented compared with their Finnish counterparts. This resonates with Crismore's (1989) view that metadiscourse is a reader-friendly linguistic phenomenon. Later, Mauranen's (1993b) assumption was further explored by Valero-Garces (1996) and Moreno (1997). It was perhaps surprising that they come to opposite conclusions. Valero-Garces' (1996) research resonates with Mauranen's assumption by showing that Anglo-American writers are more reader-oriented than Spanish speaking academics. Nevertheless, Moreno (1997) claimed that it is the writing convention of the research article genre, rather than the peculiarity of Spanish and English language writing cultures that affect writers' rhetorical strategies in using metatext. This may be ascribed to the reasons that Moreno's research is based on the comparison of two languages and only confined to the analysis of the causal relations of metadiscourse.

The second type of cross-cultural research into metadiscourse use is the comparison among three groups, between sub-settings of native and non-native groups. For example, Ädel (2006, 2008) examined essays written in English by three cultural groups of university students—two corpora of British and American native speakers, and one corpus of first language (L1)

Swedish. She observed considerable differences not only between learners and native speakers, but also between British and American writers. Thus, she identified four possible reasons for this variation: cultural conventions, genre comparability, register awareness and general learner strategies. In a similar vein, adopting Ädel's (2010) reflexive model of metadiscourse, Hasselgård (2016) compared the texts in two disciplines (linguistics vs. business) written in English by three novice groups of Norwegian learners, British and American native students. Based on a comparison in three dimensions, namely disciplines, English L1 vs. L2, and British vs. American writes, it was found that Norwegian learners use a higher frequency of metadiscourse than L1 novice writers do in both disciplines, although not all types of metadiscourse are equally different. Results from cross-disciplinary comparison shows that overall more metadiscourse is used in linguistics than business. She went one step further to compare writings by all three novice groups with published research articles within the same disciplines and noticed that more metadiscourse is used by learners and L1 novices than research articles written by the professional academics.

The third type of cross-cultural research into metadiscourse use is among different non-native English speakers from different cultural backgrounds. For example, Hong & Cao (2014) investigated the use of interactional metadiscourse in descriptive and argumentative English essays written by three groups of English as a foreign language (EFL) learners with Chinese, Spanish and Polish as their mother tongue respectively. Through a mixed quantitative and qualitative research method, they found that these three groups of EFL leaners differ significantly in their use of boosters, attitude markers, self-mentions and engagement markers. Descriptive and argumentative essays also differ in their use of hedges and self-mentions. This suggests that the use of metadiscourse is affected by cross-cultural homogeneity and heterogeneity factors and essay types as well, which has pedagogical implications for teaching interactional metadiscoursive resources to young EFL learners from different cultural backgrounds.

From the above review, it can be found that metadiscourse studies in spoken academic genres mainly focus on exploring teachers' metadiscourse use and its relationship with student comprehension and learning, monologic or dialogic type of metadiscourse and their comparison, and the comparison of overall spoken academic metadiscourse to written ones. This shows that there is a gap in the comparison of teachers' metadiscourse use across cultural contexts. In order to fill this gap, the present research will devote to exploring the cross-cultural comparison between teachers across the UK and the Chinese educational contexts. Specifically, this research will focus on comparing English language teachers' use of metadiscourse in EAP writing classrooms in UK and Chinese universities.

2.7 Summary

To sum up, this chapter has outlined the origion and development of the term *metadiscourse*, its definitions and classifications, and proposed the working definition and taxonomy of the current book. Additionally, this chapter has also introduced other related terms similar to metadiscourse, and presented a systematic review of relevant research in metadiscourse. It can be seen that the majority of metadiscourse studies are comparative in one way or another. Studies conducted so far have "increased our understanding of how writers of various genres with different institutional statuses use metadiscoursal resources within and across disciplinary and cultural domains" (Lee & Subtirelu, 2015, p.53). Based on various specific research contexts, and through the comparison of English texts written by native and non-native writers, or texts written in English and other languages, such investigations achieve similar or sometimes contrastive results. Their variable findings, in turn, also evidence the context dependent nature of metadiscourse use. As also noted by Mauranen

(2010), "there is space for more work on contextual parameters which have a bearing on metadiscourse" (p. 38). This makes it all the more interesting and worthwhile to explore the intricate nature of metadiscourse in various contexts.

Furthermore, as indicated above, previous studies of metadiscourse mainly centre on written discourse, especially those in academic settings, while spoken academic discourse is scarcely researched. "Speaking has entered the scene much more recently, as in other approaches to academic discourse" (Ädel & Mauranen, 2010, p. 1). In particular, the contrastive study of metadiscourse use between native and non-native English teachers in the same or similar academic setting is still an area that has not received much attention. Although researchers have conducted an array of research into the comparative use of metadiscourse between native and non-native speakers of English, these studies largely focus on the written discourse as described above (e.g. Ädel, 2006; Jiang & Hyland, 2015; Khedri et al., 2013), or comparison between written and spoken (Ädel, 2010). The sporadic cases of comparison on spoken discourse in classroom contexts are mainly between different types of classes, such as monologic lectures and dialogic seminars (Lee & Subtirelu, 2015; Zare & Tavakoli, 2017). With a view to filling this gap, the present research seeks to investigate the cross-cultural comparison of teachers' classroom metadiscourse use between native English-speaking teachers in the UK and non-native English-speaking teachers in China. Specifically, this research will focus on comparing English language teachers' use of metadiscourse in EAP writing courses in both cultural contexts.

CHAPTER 3

An overview of research in classroom discourse

3.1 Introduction

This chapter presents a landscape for pertinent research into classroom discourse. In the first place, it briefly outlines the evolution of classroom discourse research. This is followed by a review of four widely employed approaches to the study of classroom discourse. In the fourth section, it moves further to provide an overview of metadiscourse research in classroom discourse. Based on such systematic review of relevant research in this line of inquiry, the fifth section clarifies the rationales for the particular focus of the current research in detail. The last section recaps the major content of this chapter.

3.2 A brief history of research in classroom discourse

Classroom discourse can be defined in both the narrow and broad senses. In the narrow sense, it is defined as the oral interaction that takes place in a classroom context between teachers and their students and between students themselves (Thoms, 2012). That is to say, classroom discourse refers only to verbal or linguistic elements in its narrow sense. Broadly speaking, classroom discourse can be referred to as all forms of discourse that take place in the classroom, including verbal discourse and non-verbal discourse. Verbal discourse refers to the linguistic elements of classroom discourse produced by "the teachers and the learners, teacher-learner and learner-learner interactions" (Tsui, 2008, p. 261), while non-verbal discourse refers to the non-linguistic or paralinguistic elements of discourse, for example, gestures, prosody, and silence. According to Tsui (2008, 2017), these linguistic and non-linguistic elements constitute the observable dimension of classroom discourse, which is the focus of a large body of earlier studies. In addition to this dimension, research in classroom discourse has also increasingly attended to the sociocultural factors, such as the physical environment, the socioeconomic and cultural backgrounds of participants, as well as their psychological states, such as teachers' and learners' perceptions, emotions, beliefs and orientations. These sociocultural factors fall into the unobservable dimension of classroom discourse.

Research into classroom discourse has a long tradition. It is claimed that the earliest research pertinent to classroom interaction and classroom events can be traced back to the 1930s (Flanders, 1960, p. 729; Skukauskaite et al., 2015, p. 44). Until the 1950s, research in this early stage was mainly carried out for the purpose of teacher training, with a view to assessing student teachers' performance and identifying the effective teaching strategies (Flanders, 1960; Cf. Tsui, 2008). Since the 1960s, however, research on English as a second language/foreign language (SL/FL) classroom discourse has expanded exponentially, especially since the publication of the seminal work, *Interaction Analysis in the Classroom: A Manual for Observers* by Flanders (1960). Based on this work, researchers set out to develop observation instruments for measuring how teachers' variable behaviours affect the learning opportunities of students (Green & Joo, 2017).

Research into classroom discourse has witnessed an evolving from a

Chapter 3 An overview of research in classroom discourse

quantitative paradigm to a qualitative paradigm. The significant characteristic of classroom discourse research during the 1960s and 1970s, even beyond the 1970s, was that it mainly used the quantitative and observational research methods, without involving the recording and transcribing of classroom discourse (Galton et al., 1999). However, since the 1970s, there has been a shift towards qualitative analysis. The importance of variable contextual factors is recognised for its effect on students' learning achievement. Such work continued through the 1990s, especially from the perspective of linguistic ethnography (e. g. Gee & Green, 1998; Creese, 2008). The view of classroom teaching and learning "as a journey through time for those involved" (Mercer & Dawes, 2014, p. 436) has stimulated a new research method named *event history analysis* to study the impact of teachers' and students' questions as *moves* in the process of classroom interaction.

Over the past decades, classroom discourse has attracted considerable attention from researchers in the areas of linguistics and education from a range of perspectives. For instance, research from an ethnographic perspective has investigated the influence of culture on language use and literacy practices (e. g. Gee, 1996; Bloome et al., 2004). Studies from a discourse analysis perspective have examined the widely accepted tripartite initiation-response-feedback (IRF) exchange pattern in classroom interaction (e. g. Sinclair & Coulthard, 1975; Mehan, 1979). Following a conversation analytical perspective, researchers have explored the contingent talk-in-interactions in classroom teaching, such as turn taking, adjacency pairs, or repairs (e. g. Hellermann & Vergun, 2007; Seedhouse, 2012; Seedhouse, 2015). Researchers from a L2 acquisition perspective have probed into the effect of comprehensible input and modified interaction on students' L2 learning.

Teachers' classroom discourse plays an important part in the classroom teaching and learning process. It is not only the means of organising instructions, but also an important input for students, especially in English as an SL/FL context. Moreover, teachers' classroom discourse may also provide L2 learners with "linguistic models of how to interact meaningfully and appropriately in communicative situations, although students at this point in their development may only notice a few at a time" (Friginal et al., 2017, p. 89). However, the most extensively investigated aspects of classroom discourse are in teacher-students interaction, such as corrective feedback, teachers' questioning strategies, power relationship and identity construction (Lindwall et al., 2015). Whereas the extent to which teachers' metadiscourse use may contribute to the organisation of and interaction in classroom teaching is still underexplored, particularly in the instructional context where teachers' monologue is dominant. The current research is designed to fill this gap by focusing on the functions of metadiscourse use in classroom organisation and teacher-students interaction in classroom teaching.

3.3 Major approaches to the study of classroom discourse

Since research on classroom discourse became an important topic in general education in the 1950s, there have emerged a series of research traditions and methodologies. Different scholars have adopted variable perspectives on the study of classroom discourse. Based on exiting literature, a body of researchers have produced an array of comparative or summative overview of the approaches or methodologies adopted in classroom discourse research (Rex et al., 2006; Rex & Green, 2008; Tsui, 2008, 2015; Mercer, 2004; 2010, 2014; Walsh, 2006a, 2011, 2013). In the following part, three principal approaches—Interaction analysis, discourse analysis and conversation analysis—used in the L2 classroom discourse will be presented.

3.3.1 The interaction analysis approach

The first approach relates to interaction analysis (IA), originating in behavioural psychology. It involves the use of coding systems to investigate classroom discourse. "Coding systems" is the core term in interaction analysis. It is also mentioned by different scholars as "observational schemes" (Kumaravadivelu, 1999), "coding schemes" (McKay, 2006) or "observation instruments" (Walsh, 2006a, 2011, 2013). These coding systems are generally composed of a series of predefined categories designed for describing the verbal behaviours of teachers and students in their classroom interaction. The categories adopted in a research reflect the researcher's assumptions on what should be incorporated in the classroom discourse research. Based on these predetermined categories in the coding systems, the researcher records the classroom and establishes the classroom profiles through the recordings and subsequent statistical analysis. It is argued by some researchers (e.g. Cohen et al., 2013) that this provides an objective and scientific analysis of the classroom discourse.

Interaction analysis was the most widely used approach of analysing classroom interaction in the 1960s and 1970s (Walsh, 2011). Since then, the number of coding systems has increased dramatically. There are more than 200 coding systems available (Bellack et al., 1966) in the field of general education, and about 26 systems used for analysing interaction in L2 classrooms (Chaudron, 1988). These systems, however, differ in their scope of classroom activities they attempt to examine. Some systems are rather comprehensive with a view to account for the overall feature of classroom interaction, while others are more specialised with the purpose of interpreting the moves of a particular type of communication pattern happened in a classroom context. The former is usually named the generic coding schemes, while the latter is called the limited coding schemes (McKay, 2006). They are also sometimes mentioned as the system-based approach and "ad hoc" approach respectively (Wallace, 1998; Walsh, 2006a, 2011, 2013). In order to have a clearer understanding of the coding systems used for interaction analysis, the two coding systems will be reviewed briefly in the following part.

Generic coding schemes

According to Chaudron (1988), generic coding schemes may differ from each other mainly in two dimensions, namely, recording procedure and multiple coding. In terms of the former, some researchers may record and then code one particular classroom activity every time it occurs in some generic coding schemes, whereas other researchers may record and then code merely what they conceive is happening at one specified period of time. In terms of the latter dimension, researchers may assign more than one code to a certain classroom activity. For instance, they may code one classroom activity by its pedagogical function such as scaffolding, or by its modality such as linguistic or non-linguistic features.

A brief overview will be presented of the representative examples of generic coding schemes. One of the earliest coding schemes was put forward by Bellack, Kliebard, Hyman & Smith (1966) in their work *The Language of the Classroom*, in which they identified the frequently occurring pedagogical moves of *structure, solicit, respond* and *react* in common teaching cycles. These *solicit, respond and react* moves are similar to the later influential *initiation, response and feedback* (IRF) exchange patterns proposed by Sinclair and Coulthard (1975). As such, it helps to uncover the mechanisms of classroom interaction process and represents a great contribution to the study on classroom discourse.

A prominent development is made by Flanders (1960), who proposed a finely tuned coding scheme known as Flanders Interaction Analysis Categories (FIAC), which includes three broad categories of teacher and students talk. The first category is teacher talk, which includes those subcategories of accepting students' feelings, praising or encouraging,

Chapter 3   An overview of research in classroom discourse

accepting or using ideas of students, asking questions, lecturing, giving direction, criticising or using authority. The second category relates to pupil talk, including response to teacher talk and initiation of talk. The last category involves a period of silence or confusion. This scheme has inspired a considerable range of coding schemes in second language and foreign language education. It is questionable, however, in that it is unlikely to adequately account for the complexity of contemporary classrooms where classroom interaction is more of a dynamic process than a linear one and teacher and learner roles are more equal and student-students interaction is commonplace.

Another important development in classroom interaction analysis is the emergence of Communicative Orientation of Language Teaching (COLT) coding scheme put forward by Allen, Fröhlich and Spada (1984), and later a revised version was developed by Spada and Fröhlich (1995). The main aim is empowering the researcher to link the instructional input with potential learning outcomes. Because of the widespread advocate for communicative language teaching (CLT) at that time, this scheme also entails categories that dealing with the communicative features of classrooms. Thus, it is devised to include two parts. Part A describes activities of the classroom, focusing mainly on classroom organisation, tasks, materials and levels of learner involvement; and Part B describes the communicative features of classroom discourse, focusing on the evidence of an information gap, the existence of sustained speech, the quantity of display and referential questions (Walsh, 2011).

This scheme is much more complex than previous observation instruments. It comprises altogether seventy-three categories and makes use of a series of both quantitative and qualitative approaches to analysis. This makes it possible to account for the extent to which one class exhibits communicative features. However, COLT shares some of the limitations characterised other generic coding schemes, its reliance on predetermined categories restricts its capability to capture the holistic landscape of classroom discourse. As is also noted by Spada & Fröhlich (1995, p. 10), "if one is interested in undertaking a detailed discourse analysis of the conversational interactions between teachers & students, another method of coding and analysing classroom data would be more appropriate".

Moreover, as is criticised by Brown & Rodgers (2002), most of these instruments require considerable training to use because of their sophistication. Although these coding schemes were popular in classroom discourse research in the 1960s and 1970s, they declined later as a result of their cumbersome design as well as the time-consuming process of transcribing and analysing the observational data. In view of these drawbacks of generic coding schemes, an alternative is to develop a relatively limited coding schemes which are tailored to a specific classroom discourse type such as peer interaction or to deal with one particular aspect of classroom interaction such as teachers' questioning strategies. This limited coding scheme will be reviewed in the following section.

Limited coding schemes

In contrast to generic coding schemes, limited coding schemes may be fine-tuned by focusing on one specific classroom discourse type or certain aspect of classroom interaction through a process of what Wallace calls "guided discovery" (1991, p. 78; Cf. Walsh, 2006a). The coding system is to be based on an analysis of the interaction. In other words, the limited coding schemes should be developed inductively from the data, as opposed to the deductive approach of the pre-specified categories in the above mentioned generic coding schemes. Through being designed in relation to a particular problem of questions within one specific context, this scheme allows researchers to concentrate on the microcosms of classroom interaction. This is what might be missed by the generic coding schemes in which the observing patterns "have to be matched to *a priori* categories that the schemes have delineated" (Lee, 2011, p. 12). Furthermore, the limited coding scheme process is much more from the inside looking out and less from the outside looking in. It may enable the participants to have a sense of ownership of the research design process and give them more insights into the classroom discourse in question. More importantly, by focusing on the specific detail of certain classroom interaction, such schemes may allow practitioners to access and understand the complex phenomena that may otherwise take years of class experience to acquire (Walsh, 2006a, 2011). Therefore, this limited coding scheme is more likely to promote understanding and generate explanation than the highly structured generic coding schemes.

Overall, the coding schemes adopted in interaction analysis of classroom discourse share an array of characteristics (Walsh, 2011). First of all, they use some system of ticking boxes to make marks and record what the researcher sees and are considered an objective and scientific approach to the analysis of classroom discourse. Second, it should be made clear that they are primarily designed for teaching education, in particular for developing competencies and raising awareness. Finally, they assume that classroom discourse progresses in a sequential way (e.g. teacher talk—student talk—teacher talk). This is simply not the case, because there are many interruptions, overlaps, repetitions, hesitations and so on in the naturally occurring language classrooms. The above review shows that this interaction approach can only present a fragmented picture of classroom reality. Its inherent shortcomings inevitably led to the emergence of alternative analytical approaches such as classroom discourse analysis (Kumaravadivelu, 1999), which will be reviewed briefly in the next section.

3.3.2 The discourse analysis approach

Discourse refers to written or spoken texts which have been produced in a particular context or for a specific purpose (Walsh, 2013). Discourse analysis is the umbrella term for analysing words and utterances above the level of sentences, with the primary aim of looking at the ways in which words and phrases function in a context. It has been variously defined by a number of researchers across different times, but these definitions share the same concentration on the discourse context of interactions. For example, McCarthy (1991, p. 5) defines discourse analysis as "the study of the relationship between language and the contexts in which it is used". Celce-Murcia & Olshtain (2000) refers it to the "study of language in use that extends beyond sentence boundaries" (p. 4); it is also referred to as the "study of spoken and written texts as a means of understanding their internal and external structure or logic" (Walsh, 2013, p. 23).

Discourse analysis can be traced back to a variety of fields as early as the 1960s and 1970s. Generally speaking, it was usually related to two parallel interests. One is text linguistics, which deals with written texts from a range of fields and genres. The other is discourse analysis, which represents "a more cognitive and social perspective on language use and communication exchanges and which included spoken as well as written discourse" (Celce-Murcia & Olshtain, 2000, p. 4). As an analytical approach, discourse analysis has been implicitly or explicitly adopted by the majority of previous studies in L2 classroom interaction.

Perhaps one of the earliest and most prominent piece of research into classroom discourse adopting the discourse analysis approach is by Sinclair and Coulthard (1975). They proposed that most classroom teaching and learning activities follow a structure of initiation, response and feedback (IRF), in which a teacher initiates a talk, followed by a student response, then the teacher provides a feedback to the student's response. For example, a teacher initiates an interaction by asking "what's the past tense of go?", a student then responses by answering "went", and finally the teacher provides a feedback by saying "went, excellent". This triadic exchange pattern has exerted great influence on classroom discourse study

Chapter 3 An overview of research in classroom discourse

and has been widely adopted by researchers ever since to analyse its effect on the first and second/foreign language classroom contexts (e.g. Mehan, 1979; Wells, 1993; Nystrand, 1997; Nassaji & Wells, 2000; Cazden, 2001).

Nevertheless, this exchange pattern has its limitations due to a variety of reasons. First and foremost, the IRF pattern on classroom discourse was put forward in the 1970s, and the data used in this research was collected in the primary school classrooms in the 1960s. At that time, the classroom teaching was conducted in a more formal and ritualized way, with a clear status and power relations between the teacher and students. The IRF pattern, with two moves of teacher talk and one move of student talk, seems to show that teachers generally speak more than students in most classrooms. However, during the past over half a century, great changes have taken place in the classroom teaching patterns. Classroom teaching nowadays, however, are normally characterised by less reliance on teacher-fronted and lockstep models of teaching, instead with more equal turn-taking and partnership between the teacher and students, and even more learner-initiated communication. This transformation has, to some extent, rendered the traditionally powerful IRF model obsolete in interpreting the complex classroom interaction and events (Walsh, 2006a, 2011). Second, it might be problematic that this discourse analysis pattern assigns one specific function rigidly to one structural move. As is the case with most functional analysis, a certain utterance could probably perform more than one functions due to crucial contextual factors such as who said it, to whom how and why they said it and so on. This is also true for the multi-party setting of a classroom (Stubbs, 1983; Levinson, 1983), in which there are so many things going on at the same time.

To sum up, like the conversation analysis approach, which will be reviewed in the following section, discourse analysis also deals with the naturally occurring conversation. But unlike conversation analysis, discourse analysis approach represents a more rigid way of analysing classroom discourse. With structural-functional linguistics as its starting point, it underscores the necessity of building an "order" for the utterances by fixing them into pre-confined pedagogical or linguistic categories based on their structural patterns and functions. For example, a teacher's utterance of the sentence "the window's open" might function as a request (please close it), but it could also be an explanation (that's why it's so cold), a definition (as a way of showing the meaning of open), or even a drill (everyone repeats). In this sense, any attempt to analyse classroom discourse adopting a discourse analysis approach may "involve some simplification and reduction" (Walsh, 2011, p. 83). In short, discourse analysis of classroom discourse fails to account for the dynamic nature of classroom interaction and the relationship between its pedagogic purpose and language use in the specific contexts.

3.3.3 The conversation analysis approach

Conversation analysis (CA), sometimes called conversational analysis (see Cazden, 1986; Ten Have, 2007; Heritage, 1985; Levinson, 1983, for a detailed introduction), is the systematic study of talk-in-interaction and mainly involves the examination of naturally occurring talk in order to have a better understanding of what is accomplished by involved speakers. Its primary aim is to "discover the natural living order of social activities as they are endogenously organised in ordinary life, without the exogenous intervention of researchers imposing topics and tasks or displacing the context of action" (Mondada, 2013, p.34). Thus, it can be seen that conversation analysis is descriptive, featured by its emic and bottom-up approach.

The term *conversation analysis* can be used in a broad or narrow sense. Broadly speaking, it points to any study of people talking together, "oral communication", or "language", no matter whatever analytical approach being adopted. In a narrow sense, it involves one particular tradition of analytic work that was initiated by Harvey Sacks, Emanuel A. Schegloff, and Gail Jefferson (1974). Specially, it refers to an interdisciplinary approach to the study of human communication, from ordinary conversation to institutional talk, in terms of the turn-taking, adjacency pairs and preference organisation, sequences, repair, opening and closing of conversation. As with most current discourse studies, it is in its narrow sense that conversation analysis is referred to and reviewed in this section.

The study of conversation analysis can be traced back to an ethnomethodological tradition of sociology in the 1960s led by Harold Garfinkel (e. g. Mori & Zuengler, 2008; Huth, 2011; Liddicoat, 2011; Seedhouse, 2004, 2012). Ethnomethodology refers to "the study of common-sense reasoning and practical theorising in everyday activities" (Ten Have, 2007, p.6). It attempts to explore the ways in which how the social interaction is achieved through everyday communication, be it verbal or non-verbal, and the means by which people "account for" their social experiences. In the early 1970s, Sacks, Schegloff, and Jefferson (1974) set out to investigate the basic organisational turn-taking for conversation in their seminal article "A Simplest Systematics for the Organisation of Turn-Taking in Conversation". In this article, a range of procedures and expectations underlying ordinary social activities, such as sequential organisation, topical organisation, preference organisation, etc., have been described and explicated. It is claimed to be the landmark of conversation analysis to take form as "an independent area of study" (Cancino, 2015, p.116).

In order to have a better understanding of conversation analysis, it is necessary to review briefly ethnomethodology and its relationship with conversation analysis. There are subtle differences between ethnomethodology and conversation analysis. Ethnomethodology focuses on the principles in which people base their social actions, while conversation analysis studies merely the principles through which people interact with each other by the use of language (Seedhouse, 2004). Therefore, it can be argued that the fundamental relationship of ethnomethodology and conversation analysis is that the former subsumes the latter. The idea that conversation analysis is derived from ethnomethodology lies in two factors. First, similar to ethnomethodology, conversation analysis also seeks to explore how social order is achieved in and through social interaction. Second, it is an empirically-based methodology that endeavours to make detailed analysis of the on-going discourse, or talk-in-interaction (Liddicoat, 2011; Cf. Cancino, 2015, p.116).

Conversation analysis approach is considered to be a process-oriented qualitative analysis to spoken interaction (Walsh, 2006a). This process orientation takes functions of language as a means of social interaction (Sacks et al., 1974) and conceives social contexts as dynamic, that is, being constantly negotiated by and through participants through their language use and the ways in which they manage the sequential organisations of their utterances (Walsh, 2011, p.84). Since its emergence, conversation analysis was first used in the study of everyday conversation, typically those recordings of telephone calls. Later, it expanded its scope to the naturally occurring conversations in institutional settings, such as new interviews, medical consultation, and classroom interaction. Conversation analysis has been applied to the field of applied linguistics and education, in particular in classroom context. Its systematic examination of the moment-by-moment, turn-by-turn unfolding of social interaction, by means of repeated listening or viewing the audio or video recordings, has greatly contributed to research into classroom teaching and learning.

The application of conversation analysis approach to classroom discourse presupposes that they are related to each other. They are perceived to be relevant in the sense that interaction is viewed as a dynamic process which is context-shaped and context-renewing. That is to say, the meaning of one contribution is based on the previous sequence of interaction and meanwhile serves as the context for the subsequent contribution. This microscopic view of context underlines the close relationship of one person's utterance to another and the central role of sequential organisation in shaping the social order of spoken discourse. Based on this view, conversation analysis examines the practice at work that enables participants to make sense of the existing moment-by-moment interaction and make contributions of their own. Likewise, in a classroom interactional context mainly constituted by teacher(s) and students, in order to achieve the pedagogical goals of classroom teaching and learning, teacher(s) and students need to make sense of the on-going interaction and to unsure its continuous progression.

This dynamic view of interaction encourages us to view the classroom as a multi-context construct, which can be assessed by analysing the language use arising from the data in light of the specific pedagogical goals. That is to say, the types of instructional organisation in classroom interaction are derived from the participants' interaction, as is shown from the data, without matching them to predetermined notions. This analysis from the emerging data rather than confined by a pre-conceived category avoids the failure of involving some possible features which may be neglected when using predetermined theoretical frameworks. It is seen as one of the most distinctive features of conversation analysis compared with those of interactional or discourse analysis approach (Walsh, 2011).

In addition, because a priori in conversation analysis approach has not been established, this analytical scheme is open to include newly emerging aspects of communication. The development of any different points of view, joint understanding or misunderstanding can be further probed through the continuous data of recorded and transcribed talk. Like those of other qualitative approaches, extracted examples can be used to show specific analytical features in conversation analysis. In this sense, researchers do not need to prove the validity of abstracted categorisations (Mercer, 2010,

p. 8).

Nevertheless, despite these strengths, there are also some inherent shortcomings to this analytical approach. First, as the conversation analysis approach is typically involved with the recording and detailed transcription of data, it is rather time-consuming. Thus, it is difficult and therefore rarely used to deal with large scale of data. Second, as classroom interaction is an extremely complex activity, affected by a number of factors such as the progress of the lesson itself, local contexts of the class, and prior knowledge and experiences of teachers and learners, etc. Conversation analysis, however, typically concentrates on a localised small-scale analysis of interaction in one particularly narrow context. This specificity of context in conversation analysis approach restricts its capability of generalising the research findings to other contexts. Third, conversation analysis is also criticised for its randomness in selecting the extracts used in illustration of analysis. The selection of extracted examples may appear idealised for illustrating a particular point with little or no attempt of positioning their relation to the overall interactional process.

From the review of the three approaches to classroom discourse analysis, it can be found that they all have their distinctive features, but conversation analysis seems to be more fine-tuned compared with other analytical approaches. Nevertheless, it still has its own disadvantages, in particular its limitation to interpretation within a rather narrow context and the randomness in selecting extracts which may neglect the overall interactional process as mentioned above. In an attempt to complement with this restrictions, many researchers have introduced metadiscourse approach to the study of classroom discourse. Combining a descriptive and prescriptive methods, it goes beyond the content level of discourse to explore the functional categories which constitute how the content is constructed. As a study specifically focusing on the investigating speaker's/ writer's organisation of discourse and their attitude towards the discourse and

Chapter 3 An overview of research in classroom discourse

the listeners/readers, metadiscourse offers new insights to the study of classroom discourse. Although it is a relatively new field of research and little research has been conducted, it has shown its robust analytical power, which will be reviewed in the next section.

3.4 Overview of metadiscoursive research in classroom discourse

Metadiscourse plays a far more significant part in spoken discourse than in written discourse, as there is greater "need to manage spoken interaction in real time" (Mauranen, 2010, p. 37). Nevertheless, few studies have been carried out in spoken discourse compared to those in written discourse. Most scholars in this area so far have focused on the comparison between written and spoken academic discourse, comparison between different genres within spoken academic discourse, or focused on specific metadiscoursal features of spoken academic discourse. The remainder of this section will set out to review these aspects of metadiscourse research. First of all, following the metadiscourse research in written discourse presented above, its comparison with spoken academic genres is reviewed here. Following this transitional part, metadiscourse research in one-way spoken academic genres is presented. And finally, the emerging comparison of metadiscourse research across monologic and dialogic academic genres is overviewed.

3.4.1 Metadiscourse research across classroom discourse and written discourse

In addition to research into the comparison within various written genres, metadiscourse study goes beyond this to incorporate the comparison between written and spoken genres. One prominent model adopted for both spoken and written genres was proposed by Ädel (2010). In this model, she identified two major categories of metadiscourse. One is metatext, which is primarily oriented toward the code/discourse itself. The other is audience orientation, which is primarily oriented toward the audience. Metatext is divided into three different subcategories: metalinguistic comments (e.g. repairing, as in the sentence *Maybe I should have said the possibility ...*), discourse organisation (e.g. introducing topic, as in the sentence *What we're gonna do, in today's lecture, is ...*) and speech act labels (e.g. arguing, as in the sentence *I was arguing to you that the different ...*). Audience interaction involves one subcategory labelled reference to the audience (e.g. managing audience discipline, as in the sentence *All right, can I get your attention please?*). These four categories incorporate altogether 23 types of concrete discourse functions. This lumping approach is characterised by applying the same functional model of metadiscourse to both spoken and written data. As such, it "enables easy comparison across spoken and written types of discourse, pinpointing not only how they differ, but also what they have in common" (Ädel, 2010, p. 73).

Based on the above model, Ädel (2012) compared the use of metadiscourse across three genres—advanced student writing, published academic prose and spoken lectures. Specifically, the metadiscourse functions of audience orientation involving second person *you* is examined. After analysing a randomly selected dataset of 150 examples from each of the three genres, the results show that the three registers share similarities in the distribution of discourse functions. However, spoken lectures are found to have a higher frequency of metadiscourse than in the written modes. This research is claimed to have potential implications for EAP classroom teaching and learning in that the use of Ädel's (2010) taxonomy and the examples appropriate for a specific target genre would help raise students' awareness of audience orientation.

In a recent article, Ädel (2017) made a more integrated comparison of metadiscourse use in teachers' written feedback with her own previous studies investigating metadiscourse in other types of academic discourse, both written (i.e. university student proficient L1 writing and university student L2 writing) and spoken (i.e. university lectures). It was observed that compared with student writing, teacher feedback makes much more frequent use of metadiscourse, with abundant representation of both writer/reader visibility and text/language visibility. On the other hand, the spoken lecture data makes much greater use of first person plurals *we* than the written feedback, which may suggest an *us*-versus-*them* attitude in teachers' feedback genre. Through this comparison, the previous view of metadiscourse function as prototypically discourse organising is reconceptualised as problem/solution-oriented in feedback, serving the metalinguistic function of solving communication problems. This research extends the previous metadiscourse research and sees the roles of writer, audience and text as multidimensional instead of one-dimensional.

3.4.2 Metadiscourse research in one-way classroom discourse

Research into metadiscourse focusing specifically on spoken academic discourse ranges from studies of metadiscourse in student presentations to certain metadiscoursal aspects of university lectures by teachers or dialogic discourse contributed by both teachers and students. Drawing on a broad approach of metadiscourse (Hyland, 2010), Godó (2012) investigated the metadiscursive realisation strategies of interactional acts in English major novice presenters' speeches and their correlation with raters' holistic perceptions of presentation quality. She highlighted the implication of this study in that making such strategies explicit and recognisable can raise awareness, foster self-reflection and create confidence in students to convince them that interactive skills are learnable, which are key to individual development.

Compared with metadiscourse study of students discourse in classrooms, much more research is devoted to teachers' metadiscourse features in university lectures (Lee & Subtirelu, 2015). Some of these studies focused on particular discourse markers functioning as discourse signalling cues in discourse structuring process, for example, *so, OK, I am just saying* ... Specifically, they investigated whether these discourse markers affect the comprehension of lectures. Although Dunkel and Davis (1994) claimed that there is no obvious positive correlation between discourse markers and lecture comprehension, the majority of studies have suggested that devices explicitly signalling text structure have an important effect on both first- and second-language listening comprehension (e. g. Pérez & Maciá, 2002; Kintsch & Yarbrough, 1982; Kuhi et al., 2014; Chaudron & Richards, 1986; Flowerdew, John & Tauroza, 1995; Heshemi et al., 2012; Jalilifar & Alipour, 2007; Jung, 2003).

Among them, Chaudron & Richards (1986) investigated how various categories of discourse markers influence the degree to which EFL students can understand university lectures. The finding shows that teachers' use of signals of major segments and emphasis can be conducive to students' construction of appropriate schematic models of the lecture, "even if they lack sophisticated understanding of the content or the rhetorical structure of expository speech" (p. 123). Swales's (2001) research into academic spoken discourse in both British and North American variants observed that university lectures are "heavily signalled and signposted" (p. 35). Through these signalling and signposting devices, teachers make explicit their organisation of classroom discourse and the relationships between ideas presented. These discourse signalling cues can benefit students by helping them to form a coherent *mental map* of discourse organization, thus facilitating their information processing of lengthy classroom discourse (Thompson, 2003).

Other studies have investigated certain interpersonal characteristics in university lectures under various guises of terms similar to those in metadiscourse. For example, some research has focused on teacher's use of marking asides (local breaks in topicality, one type of metadiscourse function in text organisation as noted above by (Ädel, 2010) to increase global semantic coherence and pragmatic consistency, as well as to evoke in students a variety of interpretive frames (Strodt-Lopez, 1991). Some investigated the use of personal pronouns in building rapport and promoting students engagement, thus facilitating students learning (Fortanet, 2004; Lee, 2009; Morell, 2004). Others devoted themselves to exploring the rhetorical, display, and referential questions in university lectures (Crawford, 2005; Morell, 2007). Although findings have been mixed, the majority of these studies show the importance of such rhetorical and interactive features in facilitating listeners' understanding and involvement in lengthy discourse conducted in real time.

In addition to the above study on students and teachers' metadiscourse features in university lectures, research also focuses on the dialogic types of classroom teaching, such as discussion or seminars. In an attempt to "open other new avenues" compared with previous comparative study of lectures to speech as was done by Ädel (2010), Mauranen (2010) investigated the discourse reflexivity (alternative name of metadiscourse in the narrow approach) in spoken dialogue occurring in classrooms. She found that discourse reflexivity seems to be crucial to successful spoken interaction, as it "enables fluent management of interaction in even complex multi-party discussions, and promotes communicative clarity and precision" (p. 36). She also observed that dialogic classroom teaching involves a large amount of *other-oriented* metadiscourse, which are speakers' monitoring of others' talk rather than their own. This observation is contrary to earlier perception of metadiscourse in which "speakers" monitoring of their own talk is more finely attuned than their monitoring of other talk (Schiffrin, 1987, p. 124). She also noted the tendency of discourse reflexivity to collocate with hedges. This may explain the relatively large amount of research in hedging devices as opposed to other metadiscourse subcategories in existing research.

3.4.3 Metadiscourse research across monologic and dialogic modes of classroom discourse

In this part, the comparative study of metadiscourse use in monologic and dialogic types of classroom discourse will be presented. Very few studies of this type have been found so far, except the following three. Based on data from the Michigan Corpus of Academic Spoken English corpus (MICASE), Pérez-Llantada (2006) quantified the frequency variation of metadiscourse use across primarily monologic and primarily dialogic speech events. The finding indicates that textual metadiscourse occurs less frequently in dialogic speech events but more frequently in monologic ones, in which the speaker, typically the teacher, manipulates discourse organization and seeks optimal understanding from the audience. Results also provide the evidence that in interpreting textual metadiscourse in classrooms, we need to take into account particular contextual parameters such as discourse mode, speakers' discourse role, pedagogical purpose(s), background knowledge of the audience and institutional expectations.

Based on Ädel's (2010) taxonomy of metadiscourse, Zare & Talakoli (2017) compared the functions of personal metadiscourse in academic monologic and dialogic speech, which were represented respectively by classroom lectures and discussions. Findings of the comparative analysis show that speakers use more metatext, or discourse organisation metadiscourse in monologic academic lectures, which may be attributed to the vital role of topic and phoric management in this type of speech. On the other hand, speakers make more frequent use of reference to audience, or audience interaction metadiscourse in dialogic speech. This may be explained by the "presence of an audience whose active understanding and contribution is vital" (Zare & Tavakoli, 2017, p. 173).

Based on Hyland's (2005) interpersonal model of metadiscourse, Lee and Subtirelu (2015) made a comparison between teachers' use of metadiscourse in EAP lessons and academic lectures. It was found that teachers' use of metadiscourse in the classroom has a close bearing on the pedagogical context. EAP teachers make more frequent use of linguistic expressions to explicitly engender student engagement, while university lecturers are more concerned with establishing relationships between ideas in the unfolding arguments of lectures to assist students gaining disciplinary knowledge. Furthermore, they also find that for some interactional metadiscourse features such as hedges, boosters, attitude markers and self-mentions, the real-time spoken environment of the classroom situation seems to exert greater influence than the pedagogical focus and approach.

It can be found that the above three comparative studies of metadiscourse use in monologic and dialogic types of classrooms all share rather similar conclusions. They all show that interactive metadiscourse is used more frequently in monologic speech events, while interactional metadiscourse is more common in dialogic ones due to their respective discourse functions in two pedagogical contexts. This sheds new lights on our understanding of metadiscourse use in classroom contexts. However, as can be seen, very few studies have been conducted in these aspects and far more research is still needed.

To sum up the above overview of metadiscourse research in classroom discourse, it can be concluded that metadiscourse studies in spoken academic genres mainly focus on exploring teachers' metadiscourse use and its relationship with students' comprehension and learning, monologic or dialogic types of metadiscourse and their comparison, and the comparison of overall spoken academic metadiscourse to written ones. This shows that there is a gap in the comparison of teachers' metadiscourse use across cultural contexts. In order to fill this gap, the present research will be devoted to exploring the cross-cultural comparison between teachers across the British and Chinese educational contexts. Specifically, this research will focus on comparing English language teachers' use of metadiscourse in EAP writing classrooms in British and Chinese universities.

3.5 Rationales for the current research

The rationale for focusing on teachers' classroom discourse resides in the fact that the function of classroom discourse in teachers' professional development has not received due attention. Classroom discourse is claimed to be one of the major means by which students internalise knowledge and negotiate meaning, meanwhile it is also the means by which teachers output their knowledge, ideas and experience (Marton & Tsui, 2004; Mercer, 2004, 2010). However, many foreign language teacher education and development programmes attach great importance to pedagogical theories, disciplinary knowledge and teaching methodology, but pay less attention to directing teachers' perception to the vital role of understanding classroom discourse or interaction, or realising continuous professional development (CPD) through analysing classroom discourse (Walsh et al., 2011; Walsh, 2013, 2006b). Therefore, more attention is needed to improve teachers' general English language proficiency, which is claimed to be closely related to their classroom English proficiency (Kamhi-Stein, 2009; Van Canh & Renandya, 2017).

The rationales for focusing on the comparison of classroom metadiscourse used by native English-speaking language teachers in the British context and non-native Englih-speaking language teachers in the Chinese context are multi-fold. First, as an important rhetorical resource in academic genres (Hyland, 2005; Mauranen, 1993b), metadiscourse, in particular devices explicitly signalling text structure, have an important effect in students' classroom comprehension (e. g. Pérez & Maciá, 2002; Kintsch & Yarbrough, 1982; Kuhi et al., 2014; Chaudron & Richards, 1986; Flowerdew & Tauroza, 1995; Heshemi et al., 2012; Jalilifar & Alipour,

2007; Jung, 2003). China has the largest number of students learning English as a foreign language globally. It would therefore be of great significance to improve the EAP teaching comprehensibilities of the English teachers in China, for which teachers' metadiscourse use is one important point of entry. In an EFL learning context in China, teachers' classroom discourse is by far one of the most important input resources for students, thus justifying its vital role.

Second, focusing on the comparison of the classroom discourse between these two groups of teachers is based on the assumption that they have the similar target students. As is widely acknowledged, an increasing number of Chinese students have been pursuing their undergraduate and graduate studies in the UK due to its prime educational resources, especially in the number of EAP students at postgraduate, in particular Masters level. The current research assumes that Chinese students account for a particularly large proportion of the student cohort in the language programme of most British universities. This is true to the selected classes for observation, some of which are made up entirely of Chinese students. Therefore, focusing on this type of class can enhance the comparability of teachers' classroom discourse by involving the majority of target students from the same or similar pedagogical backgrounds.

The third rationale lies in the reality that teachers can better adjust their teaching activity if they know more about their students' prior knowledge, such as their cultural and educational backgrounds. It is of great significance if teachers in the UK know more about the prior educational backgrounds of their Chinese students, who account for a large proportion of those taught. As mentioned above, teachers' classroom discourse in China is one of the most important aspects of students' input. Teachers' classroom metadiscourse is an important point of entry in getting to know students' classroom input backgrounds. Thus, this research is of great significance to UK teachers as well. Alternatively, the current research is also of great significance for the non-native English-speaking EAP teachers in China. By focusing on the comparative metadiscourse strategies between native and non-native EAP teachers, the diverse variety of metadiscourse strategies used by native EAP teachers in current research may be used to develop language teacher training programmes. That is, non-native EAP teachers may learn a wider variety of metadiscourse devices, which the native English-speaking teachers usually are empowered with, and make more flexible use of metadiscourse strategies based on their specific educational contexts in their English language teaching process.

The rationales for focusing on teacher discourse in EAP writing courses of the two cultural contexts are mainly due to its importance in language pedagogy. First, EAP teaching in general is a "specialized English-language teaching grounded in the social, cognitive and linguistic demands of academic target situations, providing focused instruction informed by an understanding of texts and the constraints of academic contexts" (Hyland, 2006, p. 2). The primary aim of EAP courses is to assist academically oriented L2 learners to gain the literacies and skills necessary to navigate a diverse range of complex academic discourses and be successful participants in the academy. Therefore, EAP instructors have the challenging task of simultaneously developing ESL students' "situated language use" and academic skills (Basturkmen, 2010, p. 8), such as writing academic essays, listening to academic lectures, and taking lecture notes, in order to undertake academic work as university students. Adopting pedagogical practices that simulate academic tasks, and at the same time developing students' linguistic and communicative competence, EAP teachers assist such learners in unpacking, navigating, and practicing academic discourse.

Second, EAP writing courses are especially important for EAP students' upcoming academic performance. Students of this stage are still in the process of developing necessary linguistic repertoires to become successful participants in the academy. In such type of writing courses, teachers can assist EAP students in acquiring many transferrable skills. That is, EAP writing teachers can help students not only adapt to academic writing conventions, but also develop other aspects of academic skills, such as listening, reading and speaking. Moreover, choosing EAP writing courses is decided based on an initial survey and comparison of all types of EAP courses, including writing, reading, speaking and listening. The comparative analysis made explicit the fact that more teacher discourse in classrooms is found only in EAP writing courses. Therefore, teachers' classroom discourse in EAP writing courses fits the purpose of the current research, which is aimed at finding comparable discourse types and then analysing both native and non-native EAP teachers' classroom discourse features.

Furthermore, a cross-cultural study of metadiscourse also has its own advantages. It can 1) shed light on the nature of metadiscourse, universality, suitability application cross languages; 2) call attention to linguistic phenomena which go unnoticed when studied separately; 3) help us better understand the nature of rhetoric and rhetoric device (Crismore et al., 1993, p. 41). In this sense, metadiscourse is a "crucial aspect of human communication, which deserves to be studied in its own right" (Mauranen, 2010, p. 37). More specifically, contrastive analysis aims to compare ways of using linguistic items to serve certain functions. Individual items are comparable only based on their function, in this particular study on the similarity of their functions in metadiscourse. Instances of metadiscourse have to be identified and functions analysed separately for each set of data. The present study is designed to be exploratory, with a view to extending the research scope of metadiscourse research and concomitantly shedding some light on English language pedagogy. To the above ends, the following research questions are proposed for the current research:

(1) What are the frequencies and distributions of teachers' metadiscourse use in classrooms by native English-speaking EAP teachers in the UK and non-native English-speaking EAP teachers in China?

(2) What are the similarities and differences between the classroom metadiscourse use of native English-speaking EAP teachers in the UK and that of non-native English-speaking EAP teachers in China?

(3) What are the possible reasons for these similarities and differences?

3.6 Summary

This chapter has presented the literature concerning approaches to the study of classroom discourse and then a detailed description of existing metadiscourse research in classroom teaching contexts. By attempting such a review, the gaps and rationales for the current research were outlined, based on which the research questions were proposed. In the following chapter, a detailed illustration of the analytical framework for the metadiscourse use in the current research will be provided.

CHAPTER 4

An analytical framework for teachers' classroom metadiscourse

4.1 Introduction

This chapter provides an illustration of the two-layered analytical framework that integrates corpus linguistics with Hyland's (2005) interpersonal model of metadiscourse in the current research. First, the adapted framework for the analysis of metadiscourse use for the current research is presented. Altogether, two broader categories, including nine subcategories of metadiscourse are classified. After illustrating these categories and subcategories of metadiscourse for the current research, the identification method of metadiscourse markers is also pointed out. The next section presents the framework for corpus linguistic analysis. It first reviews the basic concepts related to corpus linguistics and the three categories of corpus linguistic research. Then, the corpus-based method is integrated into the study in metadiscourse use by outlining related corpus tools for the current research. In particular, the concordance tool is used for the analysis of the frequencies, lexical types and ranges of metadiscourse markers. The final section ends with a brief summary of this chapter.

4.2 Interpersonal model of metadiscourse analysis

This section introduces the framework for metadiscourse analysis employed in the current research. First, the adapted model of metadiscourse derived from Hyland (2005) is presented, as it is the basis for the categorisation of metadiscourse in the current research. Specifically, two broader categories, including nine subcategories, are classified. They are described and exemplified in the following two sections. After illustrating these categories and subcategories of metadiscourse, the identification method of metadiscourse markers is also illustrated. The detailed information of these two aspects will be described in what follows.

Adapted from Hyland's (2005) interpersonal model of metadiscourse, metadiscourse in teachers' classroom discourse in the current research is mainly divided into two cateogories, that is, interactive metadiscourse and interactional metadiscourse. As shown in Table 4.1 below, interactional metadiscourse includes hedges, boosters, attitude markers, engagement markers and self-mentions. In addition, interactive metadiscourse consists of four subcategories, which are transition markers, frame markers, endophoric markers and code glosses. The evidential category is omitted from the current research as no instance of this metadiscourse category is found through the whole corpus. These subcategories will be illustrated in more detail in the following sections.

Table 4.1 Interpersonal model of metadiscourse for the current research

Categories	Functions	Examples
Interactional resources	Involve the addressee in the argument	
Hedges	Withhold addresser's full commitment to statements	*might, perhaps, it is possible, about*

Chapter 4 An analytical framework for teachers' classroom metadiscourse

continued

Categories	Functions	Examples
Boosters	Emphasize force or addresser's certainty in message	*in fact*, *definitely*, *it is clear*, *obvious*
Attitude markers	Express addresser's attitude to propositional content	*surprisingly*, *I agree*, *X claims*
Engagement markers	Explicitly refer to or build relationship with addressee	*frankly*, *you can see*, *note that*
Self-mentions	Explicit reference to addresser(s)	*I*, *we*, *my*, *mine*, *our*
Interactive resources	**Help to guide addressee through the text**	
Transitions	Express semantic relation between main clauses	*in addition*, *but*, *therefore*, *thus*, *and*
Frame markers	Explicitly refer to discourse acts, sequences, or text stages	*finally*, *to repeat*, *our aim here*, *we try*
Endophoric markers	Refer to information in other parts of the text	*noted above*, *see Fig. 1 below*
Code glosses	Help addressees grasp meanings of ideational material	*namely*, *in other words*, *e. g.*, *such as*

4.2.1 Interactional metadiscourse

Interactional metadiscourse is the means by which the addressers express their perspective towards the proposition and engage with the addressees. In formal instructional contexts, interactional metadiscourse is used to display teachers' awareness of involving students in the process of constructing an ongoing classroom discourse. In particular, the use of interactional metadiscourse may help the teacher to draw students' attention, to engage with students in certain activities, acknowledge students' uncertainties, pulling them along with teachers' viewpoints, and guiding them to appropriate interpretations. The five functional categories of interactional metadiscourse will be described in detail in what follows.

In the first place, hedges are linguistic devices such as *possible*, *might* and *perhaps*, which indicate teachers' decision to recognise alternative viewpoints and thus withhold their complete commitment to a proposition. They stress the "subjectivity of a position by allowing information to be presented as an opinion rather than a fact and therefore open that position to negotiation" (Hyland, 2005, p. 52). Linguistic realisations of hedging devices will be examined in terms of their specific lexical categories. To be specific, hedges in the current research entail five types of lexical categories: adverbs (e.g. *just*, *maybe*, and *sometimes*), modal auxiliaries (e.g. *would*, *could*, and *might*), verbs (e.g. *think*, *seem*, and *feel*), adjectives (e.g. *possible*, *likely*, and *probably*), and multi-word expressions (e.g. *kind of*, *a little bit*, and *more or less*).

Secondly, boosters are linguistic items, such as *clearly*, *obviously* and *demonstrate*, which allow addressers to close down alternatives views and express their certainty in what they say (Hyland, 2005). By doing so, boosters emphasise certainty and construct rapport by marking involvement with the topic and solidarity with an audience, taking a joint position against other voices (Hyland, 2000). That is to say, in contrast to the softening effect to propositions of hedges, boosters can strengthen the illocutionary force of propositions they modify. As is the case with hedges, boosters will be examined in terms of the lexical categories of their linguistic realisations. Resembling hedges, boosters are also realised by five types of linguistic units, namely adverbs (e.g. *actually*, *very*, and *always*), modal auxiliary verbs (e.g. *must*), main verbs (e.g. *know*, *show*, and *demonstrate*), adjectives (e.g. *clear*, *obvious*, and *definite*), and multiword expressions (e.g. *have to*, *in fact*, and *of course*).

Thirdly, attitude markers are linguistic devices used to convey the addresser's affective attitude, such as surprise, agreement, importance, obligation, frustration to certain propositions (Hyland, 2005). As with the above cases of hedges and boosters, attitude markers are investigated in terms of the lexical categories of their linguistics realisations. Differing from hedges and boosters that entail five types of linguistic units, attitude markers are primarily realised by three lexical categories, that is, verbs (e.g. *agree* and *prefer*), adverbs (e.g. *even*, *correctly*, and *hopefully*) and adjectives (e.g. *important*, *right*, and *interesting*).

Fourthly, engagement markers are linguistic devices to highlight the addressee's presence in the discourse, either to explicitly draw their attention or to involve them into the interaction. Distinct from the previous three metadiscourse categories, engagement markers are not examined in terms of their lexical categories, but primarily in relation to their pragmatic functions, and then the linguistic realisations of these pragmatic functions. This is due to the particular characteristics of the linguistic realisations of engagement markers, which are realised not by specific lexical markers, but rather mainly by particular sentence units in which the metadiscourse markers are embedded. Overall, engagement markers in this study are divided into three sub-functional categories: directives (e.g. *let's think about this question*, and *listen!*), addressee-oriented mentions (e.g. *you*, *we*, and *student name*), and questions (e.g. *what is the controlling idea* ↑, *right* ↑, and *okay* ↑).

Finally, self-mentions represent the explicit presence of the addresser. It is arguably the most powerful means of displaying personal projection or authorial identity (Hyland, 2001; Ivanic, 1998). Within the interactional metadiscourse category, self-mentions are the fourth most frequent category in both sub-corpora. As with other cases mentioned above, self-mentions are also examined in terms of their constituting lexical categories. Notably, self-mention markers are realised by just one type of lexical category, namely pronoun, including the first person pronouns *I* and *we*, their respective accusative forms *me* and *us*, adjectival forms *my* and *our*, and nominal forms *mine* and *ours*.

4.2.2 Interactive metadiscourse

Interactive metadiscourse serves to guide the addressee(s) through the interaction. In the specific context of classroom instructions, interactive metadiscourse used by teachers can guide the students through the classroom teaching and learning process. In general, classroom teaching lasts for more than one hour. Such lengthy and information intensive classroom instruction may be mentally challenging for students, who are normally required to understand the hierarchical and semantic relations of knowledge points (Thompson, 2003) so as to form a "sequential-hierarchic network structure" (Givón, 1995, p. 64). Previous research has demonstrated the role of structuring and organising information in students' comprehension, in particular in English as a second/foreign language contexts (e.g. Chaudron & Richards, 1986; Flowerdew & Tauroza, 1995). Generally speaking, interactive metadiscourse may contribute to binding together pieces of information, signposting stages and achieving a cohesive and coherent discourse in the classroom teaching process. The four categories of metadiscourse functions will be described in detail in the following section.

The first category of interactive metadiscourse is transitions markers. It refers to the conjunctions and adverbial phrases that help listeners/audiences to comprehend the pragmatic connections of individual parts of a discourse, or the different steps of an argument. They mainly mark three types of transitional relations, namely additive, causative and contrastive. Following Martin & Rose (2003, p. 127), Hyland (2005) elaborates on these three types of transitional relations. Among them, additive relation or addition generally adds some elements to an argument (e.g. *and*, *furthermore*, *moreover* and *by the way*). Causative relation or consequence refers to cases in which a conclusion is being drawn or justified (e.g. *thus* and *therefore*), or an argument is being rejected (e.g. *nevertheless* and *admittedly*). Contrastive relation or comparison indicates the relations between elements of arguments which are similar to (e.g. *likewise* and *similarly*) or different from (e.g. *in contrast*, *however* and *on the other* hand) each other.

The second interactive metadiscourse category is frame markers, which are expressions indicating the textual boundaries or the elements of schematic text structure. Specifically, linguistic items in this category can generally perform four functions, that is, marking sequences, labelling stages, anticipating goals and shifting topics. Marking sequences refer to the functions of frame markers which arrange the sections of a discourse or an argument in certain order, roughly serving as some explicit additive relations, such as *first*, *then* and *next*. Frame markers can also be used to label stages of arguments that are generally introduced by phrases such as *to sum up* and *in conclusion*. They can announce goals of a discourse, for example, *my purpose is*, *the research proposes* and *there are several reasons why*. And they can also be employed to indicate the shifts of topics, as exemplified by linguistic items *okay*, *now*, *well* and *right*.

The third interactive metadiscourse category is endophoric markers. These are the linguistic expressions that indicate other parts of the teachers' ongoing classroom discourse which can be referred to. Endophoric markers can refer to preceding material which may help the audience to recover the speaker's intended meanings. They can also refer to subsequent arguments or predict something yet to come. As such, endophoric markers can guide the audience through the discourse and facilitate comprehension. By making the additional ideational information more salient, they thus help steer the audiences to a possible interpretation of discourse preferred by the addresser. Endophoric markers are realised by three types of lexical category, that is, nouns (e.g. *page*, *class* and *handout*), adverbs (e.g. *before*, *later* and *earlier*) and multi-word expressions (e.g. *just now*, *that part* and *this lesson*).

The fourth interactive metadiscourse category is code glosses. They are primarily employed to provide additional information to what has already been addressed by means of rephrasing, explaining or elaborating. The major purpose of code glosses is to assist the audience to recover the addresser's intended meaning. The use of code glosses reflects the addresser's consideration or evaluation of the audiences' existing knowledge base. Code glosses are mainly realised by three types of linguistic expressions, that is, verbs (e.g. *like* and *call*), adverbs (e.g. *namely* and *specifically*), and multi-word expressions (e.g. *for example*, *I mean* and *in other words*),

4.2.3 The list of metadiscourse items

Although the current research is mainly based on Hyland's (2005) interpersonal model, the identification of metadiscourse markers also takes into account the findings from other relevant research as well. This is due to the aforementioned fact that Hyland's research of metadiscourse use mainly focuses on written discourse. Due to the differences of linguistic features between written and spoken genres (Ädel, 2010), also mentioned above, there are inevitably some instances of metadiscourse markers specific to spoken discourse but not included in Hyland's (2005) metadiscourse list. Therefore, when dealing with metadiscourse use in spoken discourse for the current research, it warrants the close examination of specific contexts to involve new instances of metadiscourse markers specific to spoken genres. Therefore, the present study also makes reference to reported instances from other metadiscourse research into spoken academic discourse, for example, Yan's (2010) research into Chinese EFL teachers' classroom and Lee and Subtirelu's (2015) research into metadiscourse use by EAP teachers and lecturers. After referring to this literature and examining the data for the current research, the metadiscourse list for the present study was identified (see Appendix 1).

On the whole, this section has presented the framework for metadiscourse analysis in the current research. Hyland's (2005) interpersonal model of metadiscourse forms the basis of the current research in categorising metadiscourse and identifying metadiscourse markers. However, differing from previous research (e.g. Yan, 2010; Lee & Casal, 2014) that follows Hyland's (2005) interpersonal metadiscourse model which compromises ten categories of metadiscourse, the current study identified a total of nine categories of metadiscourse functions in EAP teachers' classroom discourse in both the ET and CT sub-corpora, leaving out evidentials. This is not surprising considering the fact that evidentials are the typical characteristics of academic writing discourse, in which reference to community-based literature is of great significance in supporting research arguments and situating them in a broader academic context (Hyland, 2005). This is evidenced by Lee and Subtirelu (2015), who also found no instances of evidentials in EAP teachers' classroom discourses from their second language classroom discourse corpus (L2CD). Other pertinent research, such as Yan (2010), although involving evidentials, find that it is rather rarely used. The absence of evidentials in EAP classroom teaching contexts might also be explained by the fact that, similar to the textbook genres, teachers in formal instructions normally report a body of established facts without much necessity of exposition (Crismore, 1984). In the next section, a framework for corpus linguistic analysis will be presented.

4.3 Integration of corpus linguistics with metadiscourse analysis

This section introduces the framework for corpus linguistic analysis employed in the current research. First, the basic concepts related to corpus linguistics are presented. Then, three major categories or levels of corpus-based research are illustrated in order to situate the current research into the broader position of corpus linguistics. Finally, the corpus-based method is integrated into the study in metadiscourse use by outlining related corpus tools for the current research. These three aspects will be spelled out in detail in what follows.

4.3.1 Overview of basic concepts in corpus linguistics

Before moving to further exploration of corpus linguistics, it is vital to determine the fundamental definitions of this notion. The term *corpus* refers to a large and principled collection of natural texts (Biber, Conrad & Reppen, 1994), which is distinct from a text archive. Specifically, a corpus is purposefully constructed throughout the data collection and corpus building process (Hunston, 2002; Sinclair, 1991), whereas a text archive is normally a large scale of randomly accumulated text files devoid of systematic design or planning (Kennedy, 2014). Corpus linguistics is defined by McEnery & Hardie (2012, p.1) as "dealing with some set of machine-readable texts which is deemed an appropriate basis on which to study a specific set of research questions". From this definition, it should be noted that there are two essential points. The first point is "machine-readable texts". It implies that a corpus is composed of a set of texts, which denote "a file of machine-readable data" (McEnery & Hardie, 2012, p.2). Each file of texts can represent certain types of data, such as written research articles or transcriptions of spoken discourse. However, with the advance of computer technology, in particular the simultaneous presentation of texts with audio or video, some audio or video data files are also incorporated into a corpus. The second point is "research questions", which means that the corpus data compiled "must be well-matched to that research question" (McEnery & Hardie, 2012, p.2).

Nevertheless, what the above definition of corpus linguistics fails to point out is whether it is a branch of linguistics or a methodology. This also reflects the current debate in the nature of corpus linguistics in relation to these two options (e.g. Baker, 2010; McEnery & Wilson, 2001). There seems to be a tendency in recent research to conceive of corpus linguistics as a methodology, as it is not directly related to the study of any particular aspect of language but rather focusing on a set of procedures or methods of studying language (McEnery & Hardie, 2012). Based on these procedures, a corpus-based approach can be exploited in a range of areas of linguistic research. It can facilitate and promote the exploration of new theories of language by enabling the examination of large-scale data that were difficult to deal with prior to the introduction of corpus.

In addition, the study of two comparative corpora usually makes reference to another important notion, namely log-likelihood value. Log-likelihood value is used to refer to the product of the probability density functions, and it is evaluated at the estimated parameter values. In the current research, a statistical analysis was performed using a log-likelihood ratio test to observe the extent to which the frequency difference is between the ET and CT sub-corpora. Log-likelihood value was proposed by Dunning (1993) as an alternative to Pearson's chi-squared test for relatively smaller texts, and since then it has been used as a statistical method in corpus analysis to determine how significant a difference is (Baker, 2010). In recent years, the log-likelihood ratio test has been increasingly used to compare the frequencies between two corpora, taking into account the sizes of both corpora and the raw frequencies of the linguistic units under scrutiny. For instance, Lin (2012) compares the frequencies of pragmatic force modifiers in lectures based on the BASE and MICASE corpora to identify their similarities and differences potentially associated with academic cultures and lecturing styles. In her recent study, Lin (2017) compares the frequency of pragmatic force modifiers used by the candidate and committee sub-corpora in a thesis defence context. Friginal et al. (2017) compared the frequencies of hedges and boosters used by teachers and students in classroom teaching context. Bychkovska & Lee (2017) compare the frequency of L1-English and L1-Chinese undergraduate students' use of lexical bundles in English argumentative essays. All these studies have employed the log-likelihood statistic in their frequency comparisons.

In the current research, the log-likelihood ratio test is run by Rayson's (n. d.) Log-likelihood Calculator. By importing the corresponding raw frequencies of the linguistic units or categories being investigated and the total word number of each sub-corpus, the log-likelihood value or score was produced to determine whether the discrepancies of their frequencies are statistically significant. The higher the log-likelihood value, the more significant is the difference between the two frequency scores. To be specific, a log-likelihood value of 3.84 or higher is significant at $p<0.05$ level; a log-likelihood value of 6.63 or higher is significant at $p<0.01$ level; a log-likelihood value of 10.83 or higher is significant at $p<0.001$ level; and a log-likelihood value of 15.13 or higher is significant at $p<0.0001$ level (Bychkovska & Lee, 2017). That is to say, if the log-likelihood value for a result is 3.84 or more, the probability of the result happening by chance is less than 5%. If the log-likelihood value is 6.63 or more, the probability of it happening by chance is less than 1%. If the log-likelihood value is 10.83 or more, the probability of it happening by chance is less than 0.1%. If the log-likelihood value is 15.13 or more, the probability of it happening by chance is less than 0.01%.

4.3.2 Three categories of corpus linguistic research

Following Simpson-Vlach (2013), the corpus-based analysis of spoken academic discourse to date can be largely divided into three main categories or levels, namely, research on vocabulary or phraseology, research on grammar, and research on discourse patterns. For the first category, research on vocabulary mainly involves finding the most important or frequent word lists in one specific corpus. One typical example is the proposition of an Academic Lecture Word List (ALWL) by Thompson (2006), based on the analysis of the one million words of lectures in the BASE corpus. This word list incorporates 230 word families, which is relatively fewer than the 570 word families in the Academic Word List

(AWL) proposed by Coxhead (2000) in a comparable written academic corpus which consists of three million words. This analysis may empower teachers to identify those words or word families which are common in spoken academic discourse as opposed to written academic genres. Another piece of research by Biber (2006) focusing specifically on classroom speech found some word types with a higher frequency than for the same example in written academic texts, such as *get, say* and *think.*

Research on phraseology generally focuses on recurrent multi-word expressions, sometimes also called lexical bundles. This line of inquiry has also followed the focus on the occurrence or frequency of multi-word phrases as they appear in written or spoken academic discourse, or the comparison between them in spoken and written discourse. For example, Biber's (2006) research in lexical bundles uncovers that there are more recurrent multi-word phrases in classroom speech than in other spoken registers such as general conversations. Another more recent example relates to the Academic Formulas List (AFL) project (Simpson-Vlach & Ellis, 2010), which produces three lists, namely a spoken list, a written list, and a core list including both spoken and written discourse. These three lists are claimed to be statistically more frequent in academic discourse than other non-academic genres. The above analyses of vocabulary and phraseology have informed our understanding of the lexical features of classroom speech, in particular compared with the spoken academic discourse in general or the broader scope of written academic discourse.

For the second category, research on grammar in spoken academic discourse generally centres on the frequency and distribution of parts of speech and types of clauses. For example, Biber (2006) explores the frequencies of nouns and verbs in a given genre of the TOEFL 2000 Spoken and Written Academic Language (T2K-SWAL), and finds that spoken academic registers have roughly the same frequencies of nouns and verbs as written registers, which are heavily loaded with nouns. By examining the classroom teaching separately from other spoken academic registers, he concludes that nouns in classroom spoken interaction are slightly more frequent than verbs, thus showing that this kind of speech is much closer to academic writing than other spoken academic registers in that respect. In terms of the features of clause types, adverbial clauses, such as conditional adverbial clauses (e. g. *if*-clauses) and causative adverbial clauses (e. g. *because*-clauses), are more common in spoken academic discourse than in written ones, although causative adverbials are less frequent than conditionals. Another clause type, complement clauses, mainly *that*-clauses, are also more common in spoken than in written discourse. These findings help to provide a baseline for investigating the lexico-grammatical and clausal features of academic speech, which in turn could inform us about the linguistic comparison between various genres and the compilation of EAP teaching materials.

The third category, research on discourse patterns of spoken academic corpora, primarily studies the discourse and pragmatic features. Most corpus-based analyses of spoken academic discourse fall into this category, despite their sometimes simultaneously involving studies on vocabulary or grammar. Among those analyses, hedging is one of the common features under investigation. For example, one study (Poos & Simpson, 2002) probes into the use of *kind of* and *sort of* across different disciplines and finds that these hedges occur more frequently in humanities and social science disciplines than in the physical and biological sciences. They also further propose that this disciplinary discrepancy may attribute to the fact that the content in humanities and social sciences is by nature more open to multiple interpretations than that in the hard sciences. This conclusion was later supported by Simpson-Vlach (2006) in her cross-disciplinary exploration of lexical and phraseological distinctions in academic speech.

Another piece of research on hedging conducted by Lindemann & Mauranen (2001) focuses on the discourse-pragmatic features of the word

Chapter 4   An analytical framework for teachers' classroom metadiscourse

just and shows that *just* is among the most frequently used lexical items in spoken academic discourse as opposed to written texts. In addition, it distinguishes the temporal function of *just* (as in *He has just arrived.*) with its mitigating roles (as in *So let me just talk about those a little bit more.*), and points out that the latter is far outnumbered by the former function. Other studies have also dealt with the role of discourse markers or their clusters, such as *okay so now*, in signalling topic transitions or discourse management (Swales & Malczewski, 2001), or *I mean, you know* in creating interactivity in spoken academic discourse (Carter & McCarthy, 2006; O'Keeffe et al., 2007).

In light of the above three traditional subcategories of corpus-based analysis of spoken academic discourse, the current research will principally incorporate the latter two subcategories. To be specific, the current study will examine the lexico-grammatical characteristics of relevant metadiscourse markers in the first place, followed by their discourse and pragmatic functions in the EAP classroom discourse contexts. This is also roughly in line with the latter two of the three strata, or levels of language proclaimed by Lamb (Cf. Halliday, 1977), that is, lexico-grammatical level and semantic level. According to Lamb (1998), a linguistic system is not simply a *unified system* but consists largely of three closely related sub-systems, each with its own units and patterns of arrangement. The three sub-systems include phonological, lexico-grammatical and semantic levels. The relationship between these sub-systems can be called *realisation*, that is, the semantic level is realised by the lexico-grammatical level, and the lexico-grammatical level can then be realised by the phonological level. The phonological level, however, is beyond the scope of the current research, but will be referred to whenever is necessary or relevant in the analytical process.

4.3.3 Integrating corpus-based analytical method into metadiscourse research

Metadiscourse research seems to have a naturally close relationship with a corpus-based approach. Throughout the more than thirty-year history of metadiscourse research, a number of studies in this area involve the use of corpus. Nonetheless, in the early years of metadiscourse-related research, although researchers adopted some sort of dataset for their research, the term *corpus* was not explicitly used (e.g. Crismore et al., 1993; Mauranen, 1993a). In recent years, with the development of many well-known large-scale corpora, such as the British National Corpus (BNC), the British Academic Spoken English (BASE) corpus, Michigan Corpus of Academic Spoken English (MICASE) corpus, more and more researchers have adopted a corpus-based method in their studies. Among them, Mauranen (2001) is one of the earliest to adopt a corpus-based approach in metadiscourse research, in particular based on the MICASE corpus (Simpson et al., 1999).

The advance of computer technology has greatly promoted the application of a corpus linguistic approach to metadiscourse analysis. The corpora used in research are normally of larger sizes than could be dealt with manually within a reasonable timeframe. For example, some quantitative analysis nowadays in particular has its data made up of millions of words, which would be impossible or extremely difficult and time-consuming to work with by mere hand and eye. Thus far, various types of corpus software have been used in the study of metadiscourse, such as Wordsmith (Aull & Lancaster, 2014; Ho, 2016), Antconc (Hyland & Jiang, 2016; Lee & Casal, 2014) and Sketch Engine (Deroey, 2012).

For the current research, AntConc is adopted to identify related metadiscourse items and analyse their usage. Antconc has a list of tools that can facilitate data analysis, such as concordance, concordance plot and

Chapter 4 An analytical framework for teachers' classroom metadiscourse

collocates. Among the large body of existing research, the most frequently employed corpus tool is concordance. A concordance is a collection of the occurrences of a selected word or phrase. Each instance of the searched words or phrases is presented in the centre of a computer screen, with the words that come before and after it to the left and right side. The selected word or phrase which appears at the centre of the screen is known as the node word (Hunston, 2002). An instance of the node word *just* and its concordance line is exemplified in Figure 4.1 below.

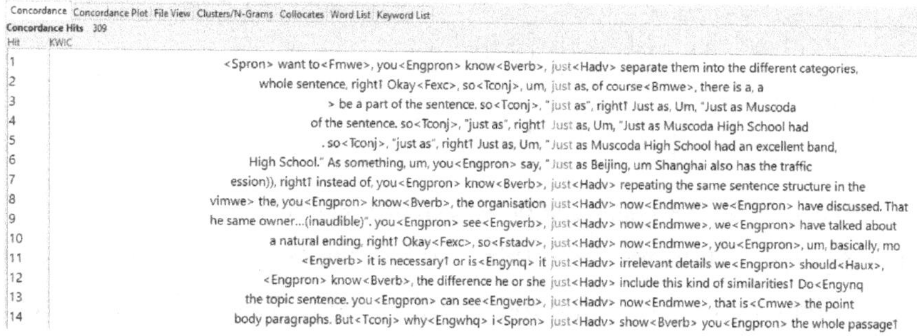

Figure 4.1 An example of the concordance tool in AntConc

To begin with, by clicking on relevant metadiscourse items, the expanded concordance lines of these metadiscourse items can be generated. These concordance lines are then examined to ensure that they express metadiscourse meanings in their specific context, and to eliminate instances which do not fall into the category of metadiscourse. As such, relevant metadiscourse instances can finally be identified. The concordances can facilitate qualitative analysis by displaying the contextual information of the word or phrase being searched (Adolphs et al., 2004). Moreover, concordance lines can also be used for selecting exemplar extracts for qualitative functional analysis and interpretation of the metadiscourse use in the broader contexts.

Apart from generating concordance lines, the corpus-based approach can also provide a concordance plot. By clicking the concordance plot, the number of hits, or frequency of the searched word *just*, in each file of the corpus can be generated. Moreover, the distribution of the searched word or phrase can be visualised. As is displayed in Figure 4.2 below, there are altogether 47 hits of *just* in the file named CT1. This means the frequency of *just* used by the teacher CT1 is 47 instances. These instances of *just* scatter rather evenly in many parts of the teacher CT1's classroom teaching process. For another teacher CT2, only nine instances of the searched word *just* occur. The instances of *just* mainly distribute in the central part of this teacher's classroom instructional process.

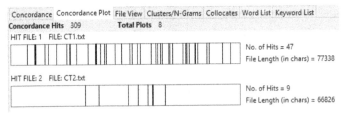

Figure 4.2 An example of the concordance plot tool in AntConc

In addition, collocates can display the "tendency of words to be biased in the way they co-occur" (Hunston, 2002, p.68). This can be calculated by taking a node word and counting the instances of all the words occurring within a specified span, for example, five words to the left of the node word and five words to the right, as is demonstrated in Figure 4.3 below. Moreover, the collocates tool also enables researchers to summarise some information found in concordance lines and therefore allowing more instances of a word to be considered than is feasible with concordance lines. For instance, if a word has 10,000 occurrences in a corpus, it may be possible to look only at 500 concordance lines, but collocational software can make calculations of all the 10,000 occurrences and so offer information that is more reliable in relation to selecting the instances for further analysis or interpretation. Overall, it should be borne in mind that these functions of the corpus tools are merely presenting data information, but not interpreting it. Interpretation of the data information requires the insights and intuition of the researcher, for example, either to distinguish between categories or to generalise the association between the way a word is used and its meaning (Hunston, 2002).

Chapter 4 An analytical framework for teachers' classroom metadiscourse

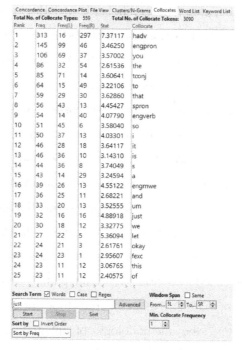

Figure 4.3 An example of the collocates tool in AntConc

Overall, the above section has presented the basic concepts and three traditions related to corpus-linguistics. It has also illustrated the integration of corpus-based method into metadiscourse analysis, in particular by means of the concordance and collocates tools of the corpus software AntConc. As noted by Sinclair (1991), some of the results from current corpus approach in linguistic use have challenged and even conflicted with our intuition towards certain linguistic phenomena. The use of these corpus tools can greatly facilitate our analysis and consequently build up our understanding of metadiscourse phenomenon. In the current research, the concordance tool is first used to assist the analysis of the frequencies, lexical types and ranges of metadiscourse markers.

4.4 Summary

To sum up, this chapter has introduced the two-layered analytical framework for the current research into metadiscourse use. First, a framework for metadiscourse analysis employed in the current research was presented. Based on Hyland's (2005) interpersonal model of metadiscourse, the current research identified two broader categories, including nine subcategories of metadiscourse. After illustrating these categories and subcategories of metadiscourse, the identification method for metadiscourse markers was also presented. Second, this chapter also described the framework for corpus linguistic analysis employed in the current research. Basic concepts related to corpus linguistics, three major categories or levels of corpus-based research were illustrated, situating the current research into the broader position of corpus linguistics. Following this, the corpus-based method was integrated into the study in metadiscourse use by outlining related corpus tools for the current research. In the next chapter, the methodology of integrating this two-layered analytical framework will be illustrated in terms of data preparation, treatment and analysis phases.

CHAPTER 5

Methodology

5.1 Introduction

This chapter illustrates the overall research design, the data preparation, treatment, analysis, and ethical issues related to the current research. Structurally, it consists of eight sections. The first section describes the general content of this chapter. The second section recaps the research questions for the current research, serving as the point of departure for the overall research design in the third section. The fourth section introduces the data preparation, including the rationales for the data collection methods, recruitment of participants and the recording of those teacher participants' classroom teaching. Section 5 deals with the data treatment, ranging from the data transcription, identification of metadiscourse markers and elimination of irrelevant ones, to the compilation and coding of corpus for subsequent data analysis. Section 6 presents the major data analysis process and related corpus tools serving to facilitate the analytical process. Following the above introduction of research design, data preparation, treatment and analysis process, research ethical issues are clarified in Section 7. This chapter ends with a brief summary of the whole chapter in Section 8.

5.2 Research questions

Chapter 2 has demonstrated that metadiscourse is a ubiquitous linguistic device employed in both written and spoken academic contexts. Metadiscourse plays an important part in organising discourse in a cohesive and coherent way, guiding addressees through the discourse and signalling addressers' attitudes and evaluations towards discourse and addressees. The thorough overview of literature in related fields has identified the following gaps. Firstly, previous studies into metadiscourse use primarily focus on written discourse, whereas those in spoken discourse, particularly in spoken academic discourse, are still rarely explored. Secondly, a plethora of research has investigated metadiscourse use from a comparative perspective, between either different disciplines, languages, or cultural backgrounds of the text producers. Nonetheless, these comparative studies have also been conducted in relation to the written texts, or sometimes between written and spoken texts. The relatively few studies on teachers' metadiscourse use in classroom contexts mainly focus on different class types, such as between monologic university lectures and dialogic seminars (e.g. Lee & Subtirelu, 2015). No metadiscourse research has been conducted on the metadiscourse use by teachers, in particular EAP teachers, from different cultural backgrounds in classroom teaching contexts. Thirdly, the majority of existing studies in classroom discourse have centred on teacher and students' interactions. However, the extent to which teachers' metadiscourse use may contribute to the organisation of and interaction in classroom teaching is still underexplored, particularly in the instructional context where teachers' monologue is dominant.

Based on the gaps and rationales described above, Chapter 3 proposed three research questions with a view to exploring the classroom metadiscourse use between native EAP teachers in the UK and non-native

EAP teachers in China. Specifically, classroom discourses used by native English-speaking teachers who teach EAP writing courses in the pre-sessional or in-sessional language programme in the UK and non-native English-speaking teachers who teach EAP writing courses to English majors in China are compared as the data for analysis. These research questions of the current research are revisited here to act as the point of departure for the research design in the following section:

(1) What are the frequencies and distributions of teachers' metadiscourse use in classrooms by native English-speaking EAP teachers in the UK and non-native English-speaking EAP teachers in China?

(2) What are the similarities and differences between the classroom metadiscourse use of native English-speaking EAP teachers in the UK and that of non-native English-speaking EAP teachers in China?

(3) What are the possible reasons for these similarities and differences?

5.3　Overall research design

The function of a research design is to ensure that the evidence obtained enables us to answer the initial questions as unambiguously as possible. Based on the above research questions, the current research adopts a mixed-method approach, involving quantitative and qualitative methods in analysing classroom metadiscourse features of native EAP teachers in the UK and non-native EAP teachers in China. At the quantitative analytical stage, the frequency and distribution of metadiscourse markers used by the two groups of teachers will be examined and compared. Following this, at the qualitative stage, the specific use of certain metadiscourse markers and their co-occurrence with other metadiscourse items will be investigated, with a view to exploring the function of metadiscourse use in specific classroom contexts. Then, the possible reasons for the similarities and differences between metadiscourse use across these two groups of teachers will be discussed. This mixed quantitative and qualitative research method also falls into the category of content analysis, which is usually considered a typical aspect of qualitative approach. To be more specific, it can be categorised as a mixed quantitative and qualitative content analysis, or it can be referred to by one integrative term as summative content analysis. In order to have a clearer view of these easily confused methodological terms, it will be illustrated briefly in what follows.

Different researchers have presented varied classification categories in relation to content analysis. For example, Schreier (2012) distinguishes quantitative content analysis and qualitative content analysis. She notes that quantitative content analysis is one of the simplest and most objective forms of quantitative analysis. It usually considers the word frequencies of certain texts. Typical quantitative content analysis sets up a list of categories derived from the frequency list of words and explores the distribution of words and their respective categories over the texts. The objective of this quantification is not to infer meaning, but rather to explore usage. It transforms observation of found categories into statistical data. Quantitative content analysis constitutes early forms of content analysis, one typical example being the research conducted by Speed (1893). He carried out a diachronic study of the theme components in early newspapers from a comparative perspective, and concluded that the coverage of themes such as gossip and scandal had increased at the expense of religious and scientific content over the years. On the other hand, qualitative content analysis centres more on intentionality and implications, that is, the latent meaning in a text. There are strong parallels between qualitative content analysis and thematic analysis, such as cutting across data, and searching for patterns and themes.

The above quantitative and qualitative content analyses together resemble the summative content analysis put forward in another piece of research by two other researchers Hsieh & Shannon (2005). They propose three approaches to content analysis, which are conventional content analysis, directed content analysis and summative content analysis. In conventional content analysis, the coding categories are derived directly from the text data. With regard to directed content analysis, the analysis starts with a theory or relevant research findings as a guidance for initial codes. In the summative approach to content analysis, data analysis usually starts with a quantitative content analysis, which identifies occurrences of certain words or content in a text by hand or computer with a view to understanding the contextual use of the words or content. This type of analysing for the appearance of a particular word or content in a text is referred to as literal or manifest content analysis (Potter & Levine-Donnerstein, 1999). Nevertheless, summative content analysis goes beyond mere word counts to include latent content analysis, which refers to the process of interpretation of content (Holsti, 1969). It allows for interpretation of the context associated with the use of the word or phrase. Researchers of this approach attempt to explore the word usage or discover the range of meanings that a word can have in normal use.

 Both of the above pieces of research by Schreier (2012) and Hsieh & Shannon (2005) have pointed out that analysis of simple word frequencies is limited because the meaning of a word depends on its surrounding text. This warrants a qualitative content analysis and forms the rationale for the current research design to adopt mixed quantitative and qualitative methods. In the data coding stage under the guidance of the metadiscourse classification, classroom metadiscourse items are allocated to pre-determined categories. However, the coding schemes are normally static, which usually cannot reflect the dynamic nature of classroom discourse and how the meanings are constructed through classroom interaction. It is in this sense that Mercer (2004) argues the actual data of classroom discourse may be lost in this analytical process. However, metadiscourse is sometimes multifunctional (Hyland, 2017; Ädel, 2006). One metadiscourse item may perform variable functions. Meanwhile, several metadiscourse items can also come together to perform one particular function. The mere quantitative analysis of classroom metadiscourse items, that is, the measurement of the relative frequencies of occurrence, cannot reflect the holistic picture of what actually happens in the real classroom. Therefore, the current research is complemented with a qualitative exploration of functions of metadiscourse use in the broader classroom contexts, followed by the exploration of possible reasons.

However, Hsieh & Shannon (2005) also indicate that a summative approach to quantitative content analysis has its advantages and shortcomings. On the one hand, it is an unobtrusive and nonreactive way to study the phenomenon in question (Babbie, 1992). It can provide basic insights into how words are actually used. On the other hand, the findings of the summative approach to quantitative content analysis could be limited as a result of their inattention to the broader meanings present in the data. As evidence of trustworthiness, this type of study relies on credibility. A mechanism to demonstrate credibility or internal consistency is intended to show that the textual evidence is consistent with the interpretation (Weber, 1990). However, this can be complemented through validation by experts on the usage of the linguistic phenomenon in question or check with their participants as to their intended meaning through the process of member check (Lincoln & Guba, 1985). In light of the above illustration, the analysis and interpretation of the results of the current research were sent to relevant participating teachers for member check in order to confirm that whether it was a true reflection of the actual circumstance. Appropriate changes were made when necessary.

A mixed methods approach is generally claimed to have advantages over pure quantitative or qualitative approach. A single method study would normally fail to depict the multi-functional nature of metadiscourse markers, whereas a mixed methods approach may offer the opportunity to present the overall landscape from multiple perspectives and thus develop comprehensiveness or completeness in research (Creswell & Poth, 2018; Dörnyei, 2007; Morse, 2003). Specifically, the overall research design of the present study can be divided into three broad phrases, that is, data preparation, data treatment and data analysis. In the following sections, these three phases will be described in detail.

5.4 Data preparation

5.4.1 Rationales for data collection methods

The major instrument of data collection in the present study is video recording of teachers' classroom teaching, which is complemented with slides, course books and classroom handouts. As mentioned in the above section, the current research focuses on the classroom discourse used by teachers who teach EAP writing courses in either pre-sessional or in-sessional language programme in the UK, and those who teach EAP writing courses to the English majors in China. Therefore, classroom discourse would be employed as the major data source for analysis. However, the current research chooses classroom video recordings as its major source of datasets and then transcribes them into texts for analysis, rather than using existing transcription data from existing spoken language database, such as British Academic Spoken English (BASE) and Michigan Corpus of Academic Spoken English (MICASE).

The reasons for the above decision are twofold. First and foremost, there do exist large corpora commonly used in classroom discourse analysis, such as the use of the above MICASE in exploring teachers' metadiscourse in university lectures (e.g. Lee & Subtirelu, 2015). Nevertheless, there are very few language courses, especially EAP writing courses in existing corpora. After a general survey of the above-mentioned BASE and MICASE corpora, it was found that there was only one course named "Essay Writing and Scholarly Practice" in BASE and one named "English Composition Seminar" in MICASE respectively. This lack of systematic series of EAP writing courses makes it impossible to use these corpora in the current research. The second reason for this research to collect data from video recordings lies in the internal advantage of recording teachers' classroom discourse. As noted by Liddicoat (2011), conducting a recording of the data to be analysed "allows for the possibility of playing and replaying the interaction both for transcribing and developing an analysis, permits rechecking of the analysis against full detailed material and makes it possible to return to the data with new interests" (p.9).

In addition, although collecting and transcribing material for building a spoken discourse corpus is widely acknowledged to be time-consuming (e.g. Tsui, 2008), the present research chooses to start from video recording the data or collecting the existing video data and then transcribe them. This is largely because many existing transcriptions may not necessarily appropriate for the current analytical purpose, as some linguistic or contextual features may have been missing compared with the original recordings. Some researchers claim that transcripts are by no means simply objective and neutral representations of naturally occurring talk (Green et al., 1997). The transcription of recordings is based on relevant research purposes and questions, which may cause the transcription to make prominent some features whilst obscuring others. For example, by using the data example from the Hansard report, transcripts of parliamentary debates produced in the UK, Mollin (2007) points to the shortcomings of using existing transcripts. He notes that these transcripts may omit certain interpersonal and situation references, such as some procedure information of whether the utterances are "stretches of speech addressing another person or dedicated to turn-taking" (Mollin, 2007, p.195).

Furthermore, it is noteworthy that the data collection methods adopted for the two datasets are not exactly the same. With regard to the data collection in the UK, I chose to collect the video recordings of the EAP courses by myself. However, the online courses from the Massive Open Online Courses (MOOCs) website were used as the dataset for the Chinese context. On the one hand, the reason why I chose to collect teachers' classroom discourse data in the UK by myself instead of using existing databases lies in two aspects. First, although certain EAP writing courses in the UK can be found online, especially from YouTube, their number and length seem not to be appropriate for creating a corpus for a systematic research. A preliminary survey revealed that very few of such EAP writing course videos could be found online. In addition, these scanty course videos vary considerably in length, with most of them being several minutes in length and very few lasting up to one or two hours. Moreover, they are not presented in a systematic way, but uploaded sporadically by individuals or social institutions. As a result, it is not appropriate to be used for a systematic analysis.

The second reason for me to collect data by myself in the UK is due to the fact that the process of collecting data in field may empower me as a learner of English as a Foreign Language (EFL) to have a better knowledge of the authentic circumstance in the British pedagogical context. This reason can also explain the above aspect on the reason I use recordings rather than existing text corpus. Although an increasing number of researchers have shifted from using a self-compiled corpus to using a larger scale and technologically advanced online corpus available to a wide scope of audiences (McEnery & Hardie, 2012), these online corpora often do not necessarily provide the "fuller recoverability of the contextual information of matched text" (Hasebe, 2015, p.174). Going into the authentic classrooms, approaching the teachers and the students in person, even from the initial contact with them and getting their approvals, enabled me to perceive gradually in more depth the situational and sociocultural contexts in which teachers' classroom instruction resides. This systematic data collection process is a very good learning process for me as well. Through this integrative process of getting authentic data, I practiced the ways of how to get along with participants, which is expected to further benefit my future academic career.

On the other hand, in terms of teachers' classroom discourse data from China, I chose to use the existing online videos. This is because there are large amounts of online EAP writing courses which are presented in a systematic way. By *systematic*, here is meant they are often shown online with a holistic course being composed of a series of coherently related modules. These systematic online courses are created by the national education reform of China to embrace the Massive Open Online Courses as a typical way of presenting some quality courses. Before conducting this research, I had been educated in the Chinese pedagogical system. I also worked in a Chinese university for seven years, and taught EAP writing as one of the major subjects for Chinese EFL students. Through my previous understanding and especially the survey process, I found that these online courses were recorded in the real contexts of their classroom teaching, which are conducted by the teachers with a serious attitude and usually recorded in a formal way by specific divisions in the universities. This strict recording procedure could mean that these recordings are comparable to the videos recordings that I did by myself in the UK.

Furthermore, although the two datasets are collected in different ways, this may not affect much of their comparability, as they are both video recorded from the back of the classroom, with the recorders trying to minimise the interferences to related teachers and students. These two datasets are made rather comparable also because of the similar length of self-collected data in the UK context and the online MOOCs in the Chinese context. For those video recordings I recorded in the UK, the length generally ranges from one and a half hour to two hours. Specifically, the pre-sessional writing EAP courses typically last for one and a half hour. And the in-sessional EAP writing courses usually last for two hours, sometimes with five to ten minutes' break in between. Whereas the online videos in China normally last for one and a half hour. These inherent similar lengths in time may help to enhance their comparability.

5.4.2 Recruitment of participants

One of the crucial aspects to consider in gaining access to participants is teachers' unwillingness to be recorded. Previous research has noted that research sometimes results in a large number of teachers "feeling guilty about the nature of communication in their classrooms, and being suspicious of researchers wanting to record their lessons" (Gil, 2002, p. 273; Cf. Strobelberger, 2012, p. 38). Nevertheless, this is not to say that there is no chance of getting access to such participants. Responding to the above issue, Allwright & Bailey (1991, p. 69) point out that "you can always hope to find a willing and welcoming teacher who likes visitors". However, it should be born in mind that there is the possibility that such teachers might be uncommon. Allwright and Bailey also note that those teachers' lessons "may be unrepresentative of the sort of teaching provided by their less welcoming (and perhaps less self-assured/self-confident) colleagues" (ibid). Due to the difference of my familiarity with the two research contexts in the UK and China, the effort needed to get access to related participants varied as well. As I am a student who came from China to study in the UK at the beginning of my PhD programme, my relative lack of familiarity with this pedagogical context and its native English-speaking EAP teachers made it much more difficult to find participants for my research. The overall data collection process resembles a method of snowball sampling.

During the systematic recruiting of research participants, recommended by my supervisors, I began to look through the website of relevant universities in the UK, searching for the webpages and email addresses of the directors of language centres. Then I emailed them with the general information about my research and requested their assistance to forward my email to relevant EAP tutors. For some universities, I sent emails to their university offices, providing them with the purpose and a general introduction to my research, and then requesting their assistance in forwarding my emails to the directors or relevant participants. However, I got no effective reply after sending a large number of emails to a number of universities.

In this severe situation of finding relevant participants, it is again my supervisors who offered me great assistance and encouragement. Fortunately, then, through the written recommendation of one of my supervisors, I was able to get into contact with the director of the Language Centre in one university. This Language Centre is the department specifically delivering the EAP language programmes to international students. I emailed the director of the language centre my letter for recruiting potential participants and other relevant materials, including the participant information sheet and consent form, as is shown in Appendixes 2 – 4. This director forwarded my email to the tutors in the language centre and then recommended me to email relevant tutors directly to get their agreement to participate in my research. Then I emailed the EAP tutors separately the participant information sheet and consent form for their reference, in order to get their signature before recording their classroom teachings. Luckily, one tutor showed her interest in participating in my research. After answering all of her questions and concerns by exchanges of emails, she agreed to be video recorded. I made an appointment with her for us to meet. Then I conducted a brief preliminary interview with her and we agreed upon an appropriate time that I could video record her classroom teaching. I also requested this EAP tutor to recommend other EAP tutors who could participate in my research and finally I was able to access another participant.

Moreover, the director of the language centre in the above-mentioned university also recommended me two other EAP programme directors at other universities. Then I proceeded to contact them and requested them to forward my email to EAP tutors in their respective department. After they forwarded my email to relevant EAP tutors, I received a reply from one EAP tutor. In the similar way as above, I emailed her relevant documents and tried to answer all of her possible questions and concerns through several exchanges of emails, made appointments for mutually agreed time, conducted a semi-structured interview and got access to her classes. After ensuring that she was comfortable enough to be recorded, we made an appointment for an appropriate time for me to record her classroom teaching. Finally, I got access to this EAP tutor from another university in another city in the UK.

In addition to the above method of getting access, I also took every possible opportunity to attend some conferences in the UK and tried to present my research if possible to meet and recruit potential participants. I attended the BAAL Language Learning and Teaching (LL & T) Special Interest Group (SIG) conference on 31st June to 1st July 2016. Thanks to the organising committee, I was fortunate to get the opportunity of presenting the preliminary ideas of my PhD research in this conference. Many attendees at that conference attended my presentation, and surprisingly one EAP tutor was greatly interested in my research and agreed to be my participant after listening to my presentation. I really appreciated this good fortune and shortly after returning from the conference, I got to contact this EAP tutor and went to the tutor's university to record her classroom teaching.

Overall, the recruitment process of potential participants in the UK lasted for around one year. It was affected by many factors, for example, most of the participants are reluctant to be video recorded. Sometimes it was also constrained by the availability of the course. The time for relevant EAP courses is generally in the summer holidays or during the terms. Therefore, it was necessary to wait for the proper teaching time of the EAP tutors who would be willing to participate in this research.

The above-mentioned process is about the way of getting access to EAP tutors in UK universities, in what follows I will present briefly how I got access to the EAP tutors in China. As noted above, I used open online EAP writing courses as the data source for non-native English language teachers in China. Thus, this could be relatively easier to get the approval from related teachers. First, I got the emails or telephone numbers of relevant EAP teachers from the Internet or from my friends or colleagues. Then similar to the above process with accessing EAP tutors in the UK, I contacted these teachers in China and sent them the general introduction of my research and relevant participant information sheet and consent forms to get their approval for using their classroom teaching videos and the materials used in their classroom instructions.

5.4.3 Data recording

As only the native English-speaking teachers were recorded in the field, data recording here only refers to those which took place in the UK. Each of the four teachers' classroom teachings was recorded for two sessions, totalling seven hours. Each of the two pre-sessional EAP writing courses lasted for one and a half hours or two, while each of the two in-sessional EAP writing courses are two hours. In order to reduce the Howthorne effect, that is, the possible effect of being studied on the behaviour of the participants, every effort was made not to interfere with the classroom interaction and I restricted my role to that of a passive observer, being an operator of the video camera. The camera was positioned at the back or side of the classrooms to record the teachers' linguistic and non-linguistic features when they were at the front of the classrooms. Meanwhile, I put another audio recorder in front of the classrooms to capture the teachers' speech. Nonetheless, since the teachers did not wear a clip-on lavalier microphone, it was difficult to capture their voices when they moved around the classroom and interacted with students to offer assistance and check on their progress during individual, pair or group tasks. Therefore, the recordings are mostly of instructor speech directed to the whole class, and the analysis is constrained to teachers' contributions to classroom discourse.

However, as for the video data of the non-native English-speaking EAP teachers in China, I used the online video recordings from the MOOCs website. Since these video recordings are online courses, viewing is limited by the network conditions. In addition, these videos are not downloadable in a direct way. Therefore, in order to make the data more accessible, I used the Apowersoft online screen recorder to record the online data and saved them to the local file of my computer. In this way, these video data are more easily replayed and positioned according the need of the current research. After making these above data preparations, the next step was the transcription of the data, which will be elaborated in what follows.

5.5 Data treatment

5.5.1 Transcription

After collecting the data, the next step is to transcribe it. For any type of discourse analysis, it is vital that the transcription should be a faithful representation of the speaker's utterances and includes as much information relevant to the analysis as possible (Mercer, 2004). The purpose of transcribing spoken data is to make explicit what was said and how it was said to facilitate subsequent analysis (Ten Have, 2007). As the current research attempts to explore the functions of certain metadiscourse markers in their specific contexts, contextual information will be presented in a detailed way. Therefore, a more detailed transcription of the dataset was made for discourse analysis. Specifically, the transcription of teachers' classroom discourse for the present study is mainly enlightened by the conversation analytical transcription system first developed by Gail Jefferson (2004), with some minor modifications (see Appendix 5). Jefferson is the pioneer in conversation analysis study, most well-known for her endeavour in developing a comprehensive conversation analysis system used for transcribing the early works by conversation analysts such as Sacks, Schegloff and Jefferson (1974).

Nevertheless, it is worth noting that a transcript is not an objective or neutral account of the utterances and the way it is carried out often reflects and facilitates particular forms of analysis (Peplow et al., 2015). As noted by Green, Franquiz and Dixon (1997, p.172), a "transcript is a text that represents an event; it is not the event itself. Following this logic, what is represented is data constructed by a researcher for a particular purpose, not just talk written down". A transcript is always a subjective representation of the utterance based on the decisions about what features to include or exclude from the transcription (Liddicoat, 2007). These decisions are in large part determined by the research questions and the claims which are supposed to be made on the basis of the analysis. In this sense, it is arguable that "no one particular convention for transcribing speech is intrinsically better than another" (Mercer, 2004, p. 147). In a similar vein, although it is complex, the transcription convention of conversation analysis is not intended to capture all the interactional details, but to reveal the sequential features of talk by visualising the interactional progression complemented by prosodic features such as intonation and stress.

Guided by the above principle, the current research is transcribed verbatim by taking into account a range of prosodic features in the transcription process which are considered to be relevant to the questions to be addressed. For example, the obviously perceivable length of pause, stress, intonation are included in this transcription. Non-verbal aspects of utterances such as *um/ah* are included when they are judged to have a communicative function (e.g. to show agreement or to extend a speaker's turn when facing possible interruptions). Features of written discourse, such as standard punctuation which marks sentence boundaries, were avoided. They are marked with arrows " ↑ / ↓ " or capitalisation of words wherever necessary. Words translated from one language to another are italicised. Simultaneous utterances are shown by putting them into square brackets "[ ]". Where the accurate transcription of a word is in doubt, it is included in parentheses "( )". Utterances that cannot be understood are marked "(unintelligible)".

5.5.2 Identification of potential metadiscourse markers

A corpus-based method is employed in the current research to retrieve potential items of metadiscourse, complemented by a manual analysis of each metadiscourse marker to sift out those irrelevant linguistic items. Firstly, an integrated corpus that contains eight text files was compiled and stored. Each file represents one individual teacher's classroom metadiscourse but excludes the students' talk. This corpus serves as the basis for the calculation of teachers' classroom metadiscourse frequencies. Secondly, two formats of each teacher's classroom discourse including the student contributions, that is, one in Word format and the other in text format, were compiled and stored separately. The text files are compiled for conducting corpus analysis using the AntConc software, as only text file formats can be imported into this corpus software. Alternatively, the word files are used as a reference for the broader contexts of specific metadiscourse markers when necessary, as the word files can keep the original format of the data being transcribed, thus facilitating subsequent review and observation.

Thirdly, the text format files containing the eight teachers' classroom teaching discourse were then imported into the analytical software AntConc. Fourthly, by referring to the metadiscourse items adopted in this research, as is shown in Appendix 1, each item on the metadiscourse list was input one by one into the *Search Term* box of the AntConc software. Then, by clicking on the *Start* button and then the *Concordance* tool, the overall occurrences of each searching term can be generated automatically in their correspondent concordance lines, as exemplified in Figure 5.1 below in relation to the search item *about*. Meanwhile, the overall distributions of the occurrences of the search term used by individual teachers can also be found by clicking on the *Concordance Plot* tool, as shown in Figure 5.2 below.

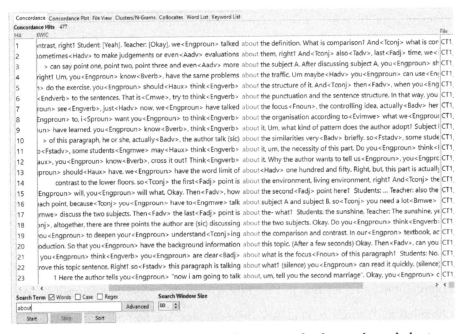

Figure 5.1 The overall raw number of occurrences by the search word *about*

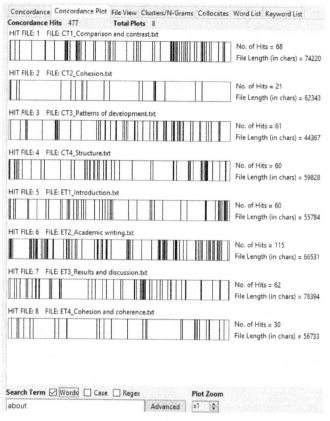

Figure 5.2　The raw occurrences of the search word *about* in each sub-corpus

Fifthly, based on the above search results from AntConc, the metadiscourse markers were further identified with reference to concordance lines, that is, their immediate contextual information before or after that concordance word. This was carried out because metadiscourse markers are context-dependent, that is, some linguistic items that function as metadiscourse markers in one context probably do not in another context. Thus, this warrants the manual identification of metadiscourse items in the overall corpus. For the items that cannot be adequately identified, the detailed and longer stretch of information from the corresponding word files was referred to and it was then decided whether they are metadiscourse items based on a broader contextual information. Then, the metadiscourse markers were coded in the corresponding word files. The reason for coding the metadiscourse markers in the word files is due to the fact that the text files cannot be edited directly in the AntConc software. After these word files have been coded with all the metadiscourse markers, they are once again copied and stored separately in individual text files for further quantitative retrieval and later functional analysis. During this process, a former colleague was requested to crosscheck part of the identified instances of metadiscourse markers, until a final agreement was achieved concerning the disagreed linguistic items.

5.5.3 Elimination of irrelevant metadiscourse items

It is noteworthy that the number of above occurrences shown in the software in Figure 5.2 above is merely the preliminary raw frequency of each search term. A number of generated linguistic items do not fall into the category of metadiscourse markers in their specific contexts. In view of the context-dependent nature of metadiscourse markers, some linguistic items that function as such in one context might not in another. First of all, whether a searching item is a metadiscourse marker or not largely relies on its specific meaning and function in specific contexts. For example, using the search word *about* in the hedge subcategory of metadiscourse list can bring out 477 instances, representing the overall number of the word *about* in the complete corpus. However, based on the defining characteristics of hedges as "words whose meaning implicitly involves fuzziness" (Lakoff, 1973, p. 471), only when *about* is used as an adverb and in front of a numeral to show the inexactness of the number, can it be conceived as a metadiscourse marker. Consider the following three extracts for an illustration of this point.

Extract 5.1 (CT1)

Teacher: ... you know, to write this kind of paragraph, um, we should have, we have the word limit of **about** one hundred and fifty. Right, but, this part is actually necessary if you have much more space to develop your paragraph, because in this kind of paragraph, remember your purpose …

Extract 5.2 (CT3)

Teacher: If you don't have it with you, that is OK. If you don't have that thick book, that is OK. Um, you listen carefully, I will read this part, and show what a logic-, what a good logic is. OK. "On the average, **about** half a minute is devoted to a story". This is um, what we discussed we last time, actually, is once over likely local TV news, the author talked **about** un, how the (news ↑ sacrifice solid news for their personalities and ↑ impact), still remember that ↑?

Extract 5.3 (CT3)

Teacher: Now you need to catch the readers' attention, so write interesting introduction, **about** five minutes, **about** five minutes and then we'll look at it. We'll listen to your I-, your introduction later on.

As shown in Extract 5.1 above, the teacher is talking about the organisation of a paragraph. Specifically, the paragraph is about the differences between living on the top floor and the lower floor, whether it would be necessary to talk about the similarities of living in the two places. The teacher goes on to say that in the students' writing, they may omit this part because of the limit space. She then told the students about the 150-word limit, modifying it by using a hedging lexical item *about*. This shows that the word limit is not strictly 150 words, but can be somewhat more or less than this number, as it would not be possible for a student to count the exact number when he or she writes the composition. This lexical item indicates a sense of inexactness. Therefore, it can be counted as a hedge in this case.

Moreover, following Ädel (2010), quoted materials and dysfluencies are excluded from the metadiscourse markers. In Extract 5.2 above, the teacher is trying to read one sample paragraph from the textbook and show the students what a good logic is. In the third line of this example, *about* in the sentence "On the average, about half a minute is devoted to a story" does express a sort of vagueness. However, as this is a sentence quoted from the book, rather than an utterance made by the current speaker, *about* will not be deemed as a metadiscourse marker in the current research. In another sentence in line four of this same example, there is another instance of *about*. This word is not a quoted one as the above one was. However, the meaning of this *about* is not related to vagueness or approximation, but concerns the concrete content of talk, that is, the *local TV news*. Therefore, it will also be excluded from metadiscourse markers in the current research. In case of dysfluencies, such as repetition of the metadiscourse markers, only one occurrence is counted if the same metadiscourse marker is repeated by the speaker. Therefore, in Extract 5.3 above, in which the teacher is assigning the time to the students for them to accomplish a writing task, although both instances of *about* are hedging metadiscourse markers, the occurrence of *about* in such cases will be counted only once.

5.5.4 Compilation of corpus

As indicated above, the current research focuses on classroom metadiscourse use across native EAP teachers from the UK and non-native EAP English teachers from China. In order to achieve a more in-depth analysis overall, as well as for individual groups of teachers, two separate sub-corpora were compiled. One sub-corpus involves classroom discourse used by native English-speaking EAP teachers from the UK (hereafter abbreviated as ET sub-corpus), and the other non-native EAP teachers from China (CT sub-corpus). Notably, the current research is aware of the fact that a wealth of existing research uses NESTs and NNESTs as the abbreviations for native and non-native English-speaking teachers respectively. Nevertheless, although the participants for this study are selected based preliminarily on the NESTs and NNESTs criterion, they may not necessarily be representative of or generalizable to the universal features of NESTs and NNESTs due to the relatively small-scale corpus used for this study. In addition, the current research also attempts to use abbreviations that may ease the identification of these two groups of teachers in their respective sub-corpus.

Therefore, the current research made up two abbreviations specifically for the sample participants in the two groups of teachers in the UK and China. For each of these two sub-corpora, a separate version which removes students' contribution and incorporates only the teachers' classroom discourse is created in order to calculate the frequency of teachers' metadiscourse use. However, it is the two sub-corpora which involve both teachers' and students' classroom discourse that are referred to when examining the contexts and functions of metadiscourse markers. This may situate teachers' classroom discourse in the broader classroom interactional contexts, thus facilitating subsequent qualitative analysis of the functions of metadiscourse markers in the related classroom language instructional process.

With regard to the size of corpus for the current research, it is a small-scale self-compiled corpus due to time limits. It is acknowledged that the larger the size of the data, the more generalizable the conclusion would be (Walsh, 2006b). The judgement of the adequacy of the data size can be made with reference to previous researchers. As Seedhouse (2004) put it, "it seems, then, that recent classroom research into communication in both L1 and L2 classrooms has considered between five and ten lessons a reasonable database from which to generalise and draw conclusion" (p.87). However, it is also essential in each case to relate the size and nature of the database to its pertinent research questions and methodology (Seedhouse, 2004). That is to say, the suitability of the data cannot merely be decided by the amount of data. It must also be considered whether they can answer the proposed research questions.

Based on previous research into classroom discourse (e.g. Seedhouse, 2004) and the availability of accessible data, the overall dataset of the current research encompasses 16 sessions of classroom teaching with about thirteen hours in total. There are altogether eight EAP teachers, with four native English-speaking EAP teachers in the UK and four in China. Each was recorded two sessions, each of which being around 45 minutes to one hour. In the UK, generally the two sessions are successive without any break in-between. In the Chinese context, there are generally two successive sessions, with 45 minutes in each session and altogether 90 minutes. The data in the current research has roughly the same time span for the classroom teaching in the UK and that in China. The overall amount and distribution of data in each sub-corpus is shown in Table 5.1 below.

Table 5.1 Overall amount and distribution of data in each sub-corpus

ET sub-corpus	Time	Word count		CT sub-corpus	Time	Word count	
		Before*	After**			Before	After
ET1	90min	7,851	6,551	CT1	90min	10,146	9,950
ET2	90min	9,242	8,522	CT2	90min	8,966	8,881
ET3	120min	10,986	10,170	CT3	90min	5,858	5,605
ET4	120min	8,197	7,617	CT4	90min	8,827	8,739
Total	420min	36,276	32,860	Total	360min	33,797	33,175
Total time	780min						
Total word count of the two sub-corpora	Before	70,073 words					
	After	66,035 words					

Notes: Before* means the word count of both teachers and students' classroom discourse before subtracting students' classroom discourse. After** means the word count of teachers' classroom discourse after students' classroom discourse. The unit for word count is word.

5.5.5 Coding of corpus

Corpus coding or mark-up "is the practice of adding extra information to raw data" (Leech, 2004; Cf. Yang 2013, p. 85). Metadiscourse markers in the current research are coded by combining their subcategories with their lexicogrammatical categories for subsequent analysis. For example, the hedging device *might* in the utterance "So time and space might <Haux> be the necessary elements" is marked with "might <Haux>", representing the metadiscourse category of hedges followed by its part of speech, *auxiliary modal verb* in this case.

5.6 Data analysis

After compiling and coding the two sub-corpora for the current research, the next step is data analysis. The procedure of data analysis is followed on the basis of pertinent research questions. For the first research question, that is, the frequencies and distributions of metadiscourse used by teachers in the two sub-corpora, a quantitative analysis is carried out. The AntConc software is adopted to assist the analysis of frequencies and ranges. Specifically, the raw frequencies and ranges of certain metadiscourse items can be generated by importing the coded texts into AntConc, and inputting the metadiscourse markers into the search term tool.

For example, in Figure 5.3 below, the metadiscourse item *might*, together with its coding mark <Haux>, is searched by clicking the "start" button. And then by clicking the Concordance Plot tool at the upper part of the software, an overall landscape of the total number of instances, number of instances used by individual teachers, and the ranges of this metadiscourse item are generated. This example shows that the number of total instances of *might* is 95 (Concordance hits). And the range is 6, that is, *might* as a metadiscourse item occurs in six teachers' classroom discourse. In particular, the concordance tool is used to generate the frequencies of related metadiscourse markers. However, the number of total instances generated above is the raw frequency of *might*. It is not the raw frequency, but the normalised frequency, or the frequency of specific metadiscourse item against one thousand words for the current research, that make all the metadiscourse items comparable to each other. In order to generate the normalised frequency, the raw frequency of each item is input into the excel file, and then a formula for the number of raw frequencies per thousand words is run to calculate their respective normalised frequencies. Each of these metadiscourse items and their frequencies are then listed based on their lexical categories (e.g. adv., verb, and modal auxiliary) or pragmatic functions (e.g. sequencing, labelling stages and shifting topics) for detailed quantitative analysis.

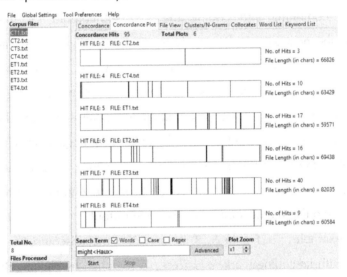

Figure 5.3   Proportions of metadiscourse categories used by teachers in the ET sub-corpus

5.7   Research ethics

As a piece of research conducted in the classroom setting, the research ethics of protecting the rights of participants are of paramount importance. All possible efforts were made to ensure that the current research followed relevant research ethics. Before conducting the data collection, I applied to the Research Ethics and Governance Committee of the College of Arts and Social Sciences at the University of Aberdeen for ethical approval of my research. All the research activities in my research strictly adhere to the College Policy and Procedure for the Ethical Review of Research. This is in accordance with the College policy of the university to ensure that relevant researchers shall have received appropriate ethical approval for research activity and all high ethical standards are maintained. In addition, this research also follows the Recommendations on Good Practice in Applied Linguistics (BAAL, 2016b) and Recommendations for good practice in Applied Linguistics student projects (BAAL, 2016a) developed by the British Association of Applied Linguistics (BAAL). The following section lists the policies common to all the above research practice, which are abided by in the current research: Research should be designed, reviewed and undertaken to ensure integrity quality and transparency.

(1) Research staff and subjects must normally be informed fully about the purpose, methods and intended possible uses of the research, what their participation in the research entails and what risks, if any, are involved. Some variation is allowed in very specific and exceptional research contexts for which detailed Guidance is provided.

(2) The confidentiality of information supplied by research subjects and the anonymity of respondents must be respected.

(3) Research participants must take part voluntarily, free from any coercion.

(4) Harm to research participants and researchers must be avoided in all instances.

(5) The independence of research must be clear, and any conflicts of interest or partiality must be explicit.

　　—Extracted from the checklist of good research practice, College of Arts and Social Sciences, University of Aberdeen (University of Aberdeen, 2016)

Strict procedures are followed in the specific data collection process, with some variations based on specific contexts. As the present study collected data from two cultural contexts with slightly different methods, that is, one from my own video-recording of teachers' classroom teaching the UK and the other from Massive Online Open Courses in China, the ethic procedures also vary to some extent from each other. For teachers in the UK, I sent to individual teachers the participant information sheets and consent forms by email and collect these files when we met. On the other hand, for teachers in China, their classroom teachings were recorded by specific university divisions and have been accessible to anyone. I got to contact these teachers through the recommendation of my friends in academia. Then I sent them the participant information sheets and consent forms, and got their signed and scanned copy as an approval for me to use their videos for my current research.

Notably, although the current research mainly focuses on teachers' classroom discourse and endeavours to capture teachers' images and/or voices, students' images and/or voices will also inevitably appear in my video and/or audio recorder. In order to protect the rights of related students, research ethics approvals from students were also requested by the Social Science Research Ethics and Governance Committee of the College of Arts and Social Sciences at the University of Aberdeen. First, during the process of recruiting potential participants, I sent relevant participant information sheets and consent forms for both teachers and students to prospective participating teachers, and request the teachers to send these files to their students. Then, through the teachers' introduction and recommendation of my research to their students, I got the approval from their students for me to go into their classrooms to do the video and audio recording activity. Furthermore, every time I went into the classes, I would arrive in advance of the class and hand out the printed participant information sheets and consent forms to the students, allowing them sufficient time to read relevant information about my research and their rights, and get their written approvals before I began to record their classes. However, as for the students in the Chinese context, I didn't get the students' approval mainly due to the fact that their images were generally recorded from their back and there were no instances in which their names were called by the teachers. Moreover, those online teaching courses were recorded several years ago, and it would be impossible to get in touch with all the students and get their signified approval in view of the time limit.

5.8 Summary

So far, this chapter has provided a detailed description of the overall research design, the data preparation, treatment and analysis process. The detailed research design process was categorised into three phases, that is, data preparation, data treatment, and data analysis. Nevertheless, data analysis in its broad sense was carried out in all of these three stages. In the data preparation phase, EAP writing course teachers' classroom discourse was chosen as the subject of my research. This was determined after an initial survey and comparison of all types of EAP courses, including writing, reading, speaking and listening. The comparative analysis made explicit the fact that more teacher discourse in classrooms is found in EAP writing courses. Therefore, teachers' classroom discourse in EAP writing courses fits the purpose of the current research, which is aimed at finding comparable discourse types and then analysing both native and non-native EAP teachers' classroom discourse features. In the data treatment phase, the level of detail in transcribing data was also adjusted based on the research questions, which may change with the iterative viewing of the data. Consequently, it can be argued that each phase of the research design is an analysis of the data. In the next chapter, the quantitative analysis will be carried out to examine the detailed frequencies, lexical types and ranges of metadiscourse markers used by the two groups of teachers.

CHAPTER 6

A corpus linguistic analysis of metadiscourse use across native and non-native EAP teachers

❋ 6.1 Introduction

This chapter presents in detail the quantitative corpus linguistic analysis of metadiscourse markers as employed by both native and non-native EAP teachers, focusing specifically on the frequency and distribution of each metadiscourse category employed by the two groups in general and individual members of each group in particular. Structurally, this chapter first outlines the overall result of the interactional and interactive metadiscourse use between teachers in both sub-corpora, and then examines these two broad categories respectively. The interactional category involves five subcategories, that is, hedges, boosters, attitude markers, engagement markers and self-mentions. Meanwhile, the interactive category encompasses four metadiscourse categories, namely transitions, frame markers, endophoric markers and code glosses. Some of these subcategories are realised by certain lexical categories, such as hedges, boosters and attitude markers, whereas other subcategories are realised in a more straightforward way by certain pragmatic functions, such as questions or directives. Therefore, these nine metadiscourse categories will be spelled out in relation to their linguistic realisations or pragmatic functions. In each of these categories, the analysis begins with an outline of the overall result, then moves on to an examination of individual lexical categories or pragmatic functions. The chapter then ends with a summary of the major findings.

6.2 Overall result of metadiscourse markers in both ET and CT sub-corpora

As mentioned above, there are altogether eight EAP writing teachers selected for the current research, with four native English speakers in the UK and four non-native English speakers of Chinese. Each teacher was video-recorded for two sessions of their classroom teaching, ranging from 90 to 120 minutes. The total verbatim transcript of their classroom discourse amounts to 70,073 words. By sifting out student talk, the total amount of teacher discourse is 66,035 words, accounting for 92% of the total classroom discourse. Among them, 32,860 words constitute the teacher discourse in the ET sub-corpus, and 33,175 words in the CT sub-corpus. After importing the metadiscourse list for potential metadiscourse markers into the AntConc software, 28,794 instances of metadiscourse markers are generated. Through the concordance tool of AntConc, these metadiscourse markers are then manually examined by referring to the contexts in which they occur. Finally, the total number of raw frequency (RawFrq.), that is, 16,731 instances of metadiscourse markers, including 8,663 instances in the ET sub-corpus and 8,068 instances in the CT sub-corpus, are obtained. The normalised frequency (NmlFrq.) of each instance is calculated against per thousand words (ptw).

Table 6.1 below offers an overview of the frequency and distribution of metadiscourse markers used by teachers in the ET and CT sub-corpora. Overall, teachers in the ET sub-corpus employ significantly more metadiscourse markers than those in the CT sub-corpus do at $p < 0.0001$ level. In terms of the two broad metadiscourse categories, teachers in the ET sub-corpus use significantly more frequently interactional metadiscourse markers than those in the CT sub-corpus. However, there is no significant difference in the use of interactive metadiscourse markers across the two sub-corpora. Within the interactional metadiscourse markers, both groups of teachers use engagement markers the most, attitude markers and self-mentions are the two least frequently used metadiscourse categories. However, the two teacher groups differ in their use of hedges and boosters. That is, teachers in the ET sub-corpus use significantly more hedges but less boosters than those in the CT sub-corpus do. As for the interactive metadiscourse markers, endophoric markers and code glosses are the two least frequently employed categories in both sub-corpora. However, teachers in the ET sub-corpus use transitions with the highest frequency and frame markers are the second most frequent category, while teachers in the CT sub-corpus employ frame markers with the highest frequency and then followed by transitions.

Table 6.1 Overall frequency and distribution of metadiscourse markers in both sub-corpora

MD categories		ETs		CTs		Log-likelihood value*
		RawFrq.	NmlFrq.	RawFrq.	NmlFrq.	
Interactional MD	Hedges	972	29.58	450	13.56	201.19 ****
	Boosters	601	18.29	827	24.93	-33.79 ****
	Attitude markers	156	4.75	120	3.62	7.42 **
	Engagement markers	3,535	107.58	3,687	111.14	-1.91
	Self-mentions	543	16.52	186	5.61	186.01 ****
	Total	5,807	176.72	5,270	158.86	31.42 ****
Interactive MD	Transitions	1,377	41.91	935	28.18	89.29 ****
	Fame markers	1,165	35.45	1,484	44.73	-35.53 ****
	Endophoric markers	64	1.95	92	2.77	-4.79 *
	Code glosses	250	7.61	287	8.65	-2.21
	Total	2,856	86.92	2,798	84.33	1.28
	Total	8,663	263.63	8,068	243.19	27.22 ****

Note: * = significant at $p<0.05$ level; ** = significant at $p<0.01$ level; *** = significant at $p<0.001$ level; **** = significant at $p<0.0001$ level.

Figures 6.1 and 6.2 below demonstrate the proportions of metadiscourse categories employed by teachers in the ET and CT sub-corpora respectively. It can be seen that engagement markers are the most frequently used metadiscourse category by both groups of teachers. This may be attributed to genre-related factors that involve the asymmetrical power relations between teachers and students. This result resonates with Lee and Subtirelu (2015), who note that engagement markers are the most frequent category among all metadiscourse resources in teachers' classroom discourse in both EAP courses and university lectures. Moreover, this high frequency of engagement markers also corroborates previous finding by Hyland (2009) who claims that instruction in language-oriented classrooms involves "high levels of involvement and interactivity" (p. 102). Next to engagement markers, frame markers and transition markers also account for relatively larger proportions compared with other categories. This may reflect the phenomenon that signposting is common in classroom instructions and can contribute to signalling changes in teachers' discourse trajectory (Crawford, 2005; Swales, 2001). In addition, two other metadiscourse categories, hedges and boosters take up quite large proportions as well. They are then followed by code glosses and self-mentions. Finally, endophoric markers and attitude markers are used with the lowest frequencies.

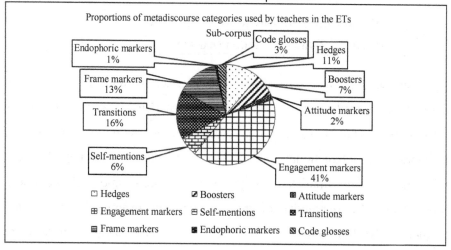

Figure 6.1 Proportions of metadiscourse categories used by teachers in the ET sub-corpus

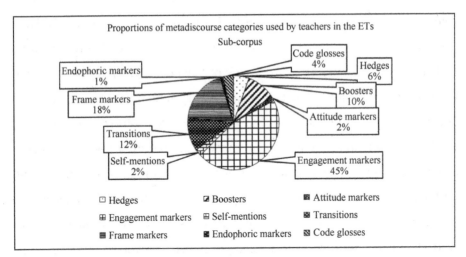

Figure 6.2 Proportions of metadiscourse categories used by teachers in the CT sub-corpus

In short, the above section has outlined the overall landscape of the frequency and distribution of all the metadiscourse categories used by teachers across the two sub-corpora. In what remains, these nine metadiscourse categories, which fall into two broader categories, will be examined in terms of the frequency and distribution of their linguistic realisations, either lexical categories or pragmatic functions. In each lexical category or pragmatic function, particular attention is paid to the frequencies, types and ranges of relevant lexical items.

6.3 Interactional metadiscourse markers in both ET and CT sub-corpora

This section will investigate the frequency and distribution of interactional metadiscourse markers used by teachers across the ET and CT sub-corpora. As made explicit in previous sections, there are altogether five categories of interactional metadiscourse markers, including hedges, boosters, attitude markers, engagement markers and self-mentions. Specifically, the remainder of this section will examine in detail the frequency and distribution of individual metadiscourse categories in terms of their respective lexical categories (such as adverbs and adjectives in hedges) or pragmatic functions (such as directives and questions in engagement markers). In each lexical category or pragmatic function, attention is mainly focused on the comparison of the frequencies, types and ranges of specific lexical items across the two sub-corpora. By this means, salient lexical items stand out in the two sub-corpora.

Moreover, as the data for analysis in this research is from a self-compiled corpus, the size is relatively small due to the practical time limits associated with the research conducted. Nonetheless, this small-scale corpus allows for in-depth examination of the characteristics of individual teachers in each of the two sub-corpora, which is unprecedented in the large corpus analysis conducted by previous research. This comprehensive intra- and inter-group analysis provides us deeper insights into the possible individual variations that may skew the result of the whole group as is compared with a counterpart corpus. Therefore, the current research will also take into account the frequency and distribution of these five metadiscoursal categories in terms of their usage by each individual teacher. In the following five metadiscourse categories, an overall result of each metadiscourse category is first presented, then followed by the examination of individual lexical categories or pragmatic functions, and finally by a brief conclusion of metadiscourse use in that category.

6.3.1 Hedges

This section reports the frequency and distribution of hedging devices in both the ET and CT sub-corpora. As mentioned above, hedges are linguistic devices such as *possible*, *might* and *perhaps*, which indicate teachers' decisions to recognize alternative viewpoints and thus withhold their complete commitment to a proposition. They stress the "subjectivity of a position by allowing information to be presented as an opinion rather than a fact and therefore open that position to negotiation" (Hyland, 2005, p.52). Linguistic realisations of hedging devices are examined in terms of their specific lexical categories. To be specific, hedges in the current research entail five types of lexical categories: adverbs, modal auxiliaries, verbs, adjectives, and multi-word expressions. These lexical categories and their coding examples are shown in Table 6.2 below.

Table 6.2 Linguistic realisations of hedges

MD markers		Linguistic realisations	Examples with codes*
Interactional MD	Hedges	Adverbs	Just < Hadv >
		Modal auxiliaries	Might < Haux >
		Verbs	Suppose < Hverb >
		Adjectives	Possible < Hadj >
		Multiword expressions	Kind of < Hmwe >

*Note: metadiscourse markers are coded and annotated based on the initials of subcategory followed by abbreviations of word class and sentence type. To avoid ambiguity, "Eng" and "End" are used to represent engagement markers and endophoric markers respectively.

6.3.1.1 Overall result of hedges

This subsection outlines the frequency and distribution of hedges used by teachers in the ET and CT sub-corpora. Based on the first research question which is concerned with the frequency and distribution of metadiscourse use across the two groups of teachers, this section will present the results of hedges from two perspectives. One aspect concerns the frequency and distribution of hedges employed by individual teachers within each of the two sub-corpora in particular and by the individual groups of teachers across both sub-corpora in general. The other aspect focuses on the frequency and distribution of hedges in terms of individual lexical categories. Figure 6.3 below illustrates an overall landscape of the normalised frequency and distribution of specific hedging lexical categories employed by individual teachers in the two sub-corpora.

Chapter 6 A corpus linguistic analysis of metadiscourse use across native and non-native EAP teachers

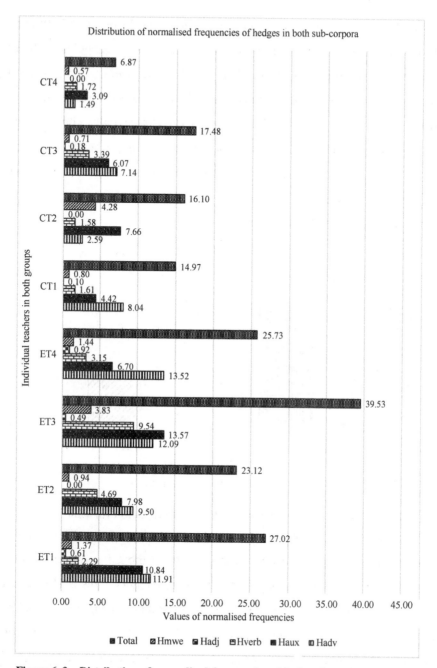

Figure 6.3 Distribution of normalised frequencies of hedges in both sub-corpora

It is interesting to note from Figure 6.3 above that each teacher in the ET sub-corpus uses hedges more frequently than any of the teachers in the CT sub-corpus. Specifically, the frequencies of hedges range from 23.12

ptw to 39.53 ptw in the ET sub-corpus, whereas 6.87 ptw to 17.48 ptw in the CT sub-corpus. Figure 6.4 below presents the frequencies of hedges used by the two groups of teachers in the two sub-corpora. Overall, teachers in the ET sub-corpus make more frequent use of hedges than non-native EAP teachers in the CT sub-corpus do. Specifically, hedges occur 29.58 times per thousand words in the ET sub-corpus, whereas they occur 13.56 times per thousand words in the CT sub-corpus. That is to say, teachers in the ET sub-corpus employ over twice as many hedges as their non-native counterparts in the CT sub-corpus.

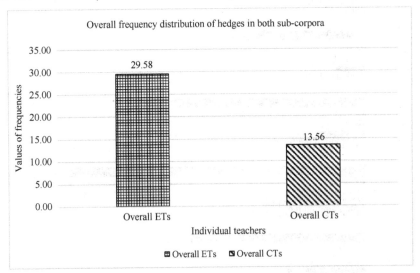

Figure 6.4 Overall frequency distribution of hedges in both sub-corpora

The above paragraph has indicated that teachers in the ET sub-corpus make more frequent use of hedges than those in the CT sub-corpus do, in terms of both the overall group and individual teachers. This is also true for each of the five lexical categories. As demonstrated by Figure 6.5 below, teachers in the ET sub-corpus employ higher frequencies than their counterparts in the CT sub-corpus in all the five lexical categories. In relation to the distributional pattern of these five lexical categories, the two groups of teachers present roughly the same tendency, except that they differ in their most frequently used lexical categories. Native EAP teachers use adverbs most frequently, while the non-native ones employ the highest frequency of modal auxiliary verbs. Nevertheless, the following three types of lexical categories, that is, verbs, adjectives and multiword expressions, present the same tendency for both groups of EAP teachers. Main verbs represent the third most frequently used type, followed by multi-word expressions and adjectives. In the following five subsections, the five lexical categories realising hedges will be investigated in detail.

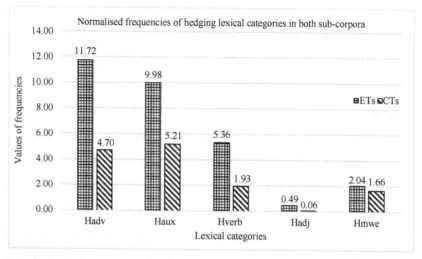

Figure 6.5 **Normalised frequencies of hedging lexical categories in both sub-corpora**

6.3.1.2 Adverbs

Adverbs constitute one of the four major lexical categories or word classes, along with verbs, adjectives and nouns. According to *Oxford English Dictionary* (2018), *adverb* refers to the word or lexical unit that modifies the meaning of a verb, adjective, or another adverb, expressing manner, place, time, or degree. It is probably due to its broad range of functions and great flexibility to modify other lexical categories that it is extensively used in hedging devices. As will be illustrated in the following sections, hedging adverbs in both of the ET and CT sub-corpora are used relatively more frequently compared with other lexical categories. Based on previous metadiscoursal research on academic lectures (Yan, 2010), adverbs for hedges are mainly divided into four subcategories, namely adverbs of approximation, adverbs of degree, adverbs of frequency, and adverbs of probability. The frequency and distribution of each subcategory of adverbs and the individual lexical items for hedging used by teachers in the two sub-corpora will be presented in the next section.

Table 6.3 below presents the frequencies, types and ranges of hedging adverbs used across the two sub-corpora. In terms of the frequencies, teachers in the ET sub-corpus use hedging adverbs twice as frequently as their non-native counterparts. The log-likelihood value (102.26) indicates that teachers in the ET sub-corpus employ significantly more hedging adverbs than those in the CT sub-corpus at $p<0.0001$ level. In terms of the sub-categories of hedging adverbs, it can be found that both groups of teachers share a similar pattern in their use of the subcategories of adverbs for hedging. Both groups employ adverbs of approximation with the highest frequency, followed in sequence by adverbs of probability, adverbs of frequency and adverbs of degree. As for the types of hedging adverbs, more types of lexical items are shared by individual teachers in the ETs (21 types) than the CTs (12 types). In relation to the ranges of hedging adverbs, the most prominent feature is the prevalence of the lexical item *just*. *Just* is used by every individual teacher and with the highest frequencies in both ET and CT sub-corpora. Consider the following Extract 6.1 on the use of the most frequent and differentiated hedging marker *just* for a detailed illustration.

Table 6.3 Summary of individual hedging adverbs in both sub-corpora

Lexical subcategories	No.	Lexical items	ETs RawFrq.	ETs NmlFrq.	ETs Ranges	CTs RawFrq.	CTs NmlFrq.	CTs Ranges	Log-likelihood value*
Adverbs of approximation	1	just	214	6.51	4	71	2.14	4	76.48****
	2	about	1	0.03	1	11	0.33	3	-9.66**
	3	mainly	1	0.03	1	0	0.00	0	1.40
	4	almost	1	0.03	1	1	0.03	2	0.00
		Total	217	6.60		83	2.50		63.31****
Adverbs of probability	1	maybe	52	1.58	4	29	0.87	3	6.84**
	2	probably	18	0.55	4	3	0.09	2	12.03***
	3	perhaps	8	0.24	3	0	0.00	0	11.17***
	4	possibly	2	0.06	2	1	0.03	1	0.35
	5	presumably	3	0.09	1	0	0.00	0	4.19*
		Total	83	2.52		33	0.99		22.75***
Adverbs of frequency	1	often	14	0.43	4	8	0.24	4	1.72
	2	usually	10	0.30	3	3	0.09	1	4.04*
	3	sometimes	11	0.33	3	15	0.45	4	-0.58
	4	frequently	0	0.00	0	2	0.06	1	-2.75
	5	generally	8	0.24	4	1	0.03	1	6.26*
		Total	43	1.30		29	0.87		2.87

continued

Lexical subcategories	No.	Lexical items	ETs			CTs			Log-likelihood value*
			RawFrq.	NmlFrq.	Ranges	RawFrq.	NmlFrq.	Ranges	
Adverbs of degree	1	quite	29	0.88	4	11	0.33	2	8.57**
	2	slightly	4	0.12	2	0	0.00	0	5.58*
	3	technically	3	0.09	1	0	0.00	0	4.19*
	4	rather	1	0.03	1	0	0.00	0	1.40
	5	fairly	2	0.06	1	0	0.00	0	2.79
	6	pretty	2	0.06	1	0	0.00	0	2.79
	7	mostly	1	0.03	1	0	0.00	0	1.40
		Total	42	1.27		11	0.33		19.64****
Total			385	11.72		156	4.70		102.26****

Note: * = significant at $p<0.05$ level; ** = significant at $p<0.01$ level; *** = significant at $p<0.001$ level; **** = significant at $p<0.0001$ level.

Extract 6.1 (ET2)

Teacher: Great, so I think, I think all these problems you were having, questions you had last night, and you can ask me them now. alRIGHT ↓. But let's start *just* thinking about citations. And I'll *just* keep checking if you know this information or not, because I don't want to repeat things I think you've already known … OK, so, let's *just* remind ourselves um what the essay should look like. So what is the first part of your essay, the first paragraph ↑?

The above extract takes place at the beginning of a class session. The teacher is attempting to engage the student in reviewing related knowledge they covered in the last session. The first and third instances of *just* serve to soften the command for the students to think about previous knowledge, without intimidating the students with an imposing tone at the beginning of a class. The second *just* mainly functions to tone down the teacher's action of checking students' mastering of what they had learned. These instances of the adverb of approximation *just* tone down the illocutionary force, avoid being impolite or offensive to the students and contribute to the harmonious interaction between the teacher and students in class.

6.3.1.3 Modal auxiliaries

The frequencies, types, and ranges of hedging modal auxiliaries in the two sub-corpora can be illustrated by Table 6.4 below. First, it can be seen that teachers in the ET sub-corpus use significantly more modal auxiliaries than teachers in the CT sub-corpus at $p<0.0001$ level. In relation to types, seven types of modal auxiliaries are used by teachers in the ET sub-corpus, whereas five types are used by teachers in the CT sub-corpus. Regarding the ranges of these lexical items, the auxiliaries with a comparatively stronger hedging degree such as *would/wouldn't*, *could/couldn't* and *might* are used by each of the four teachers and they are used more than others. In particular, *would* that is used with the highest frequency in the ET sub-corpus. In contrast, the auxiliaries *should* and *may* which have a relatively weaker degree of hedging, or some sense of boosting, are the two most frequent modal auxiliaries employed by all the four teachers in the CT sub-corpus. This may be contributable to many factors. One possible explanation might be the relatively more authoritative role of teachers in China, which is likely to be influenced by the ingrained traditional Confucianism (Hinkel, 1995, 1997). Therefore, such a discrepancy in their use of modal auxiliaries may reflect the influence of sociocultural constructs on teachers' online pedagogical decisions in the classroom instructional activities (Ho, 2006). The following three extracts illustrate the uses of some salient hedging auxiliaries.

Table 6.4　Summary of individual hedging auxiliaries in both sub-corpora

No.	Lexical items	ETs			CTs			Log-likelihood value*
		RawFrq.	NmlFrq.	Ranges	RawFrq.	NmlFrq.	Ranges	
1	would	117	3.56	4	25	0.75	3	65.57****
2	wouldn't	10	0.30	4	0	0.00	0	13.96***
3	could	71	2.16	4	41	1.24	3	8.42**
4	couldn't	1	0.03	1	0	0.00	0	1.40
5	might	82	2.50	4	13	0.39	2	56.51****
6	should	42	1.28	4	59	1.78	4	-2.72
7	may	5	0.15	3	35	1.06	4	-25.02****
	Total	328	9.98		173	5.22		50.24****

Notes: RawFrq.* stands for raw frequencies of related metadiscourse markers. NmlFrq.** stands for normalised frequencies of related metadiscourse markers against per thousand words.

Extract 6.2　(ET4)

Teacher: Good, okay, I think we will just go through that ... okay, so, the point about this is that, as we saw in the previous example, the second word is the key word, um, so, it's a warehouse owned by a brewery. So, here, it's about for safety, or for improving safety. And so it's the purpose, we knew that. Roof timbers, um, so it's timbers in the roof. So that tells location ... okay, so that's quite a useful summary of some of the purposes that we use noun phrases. These are just the kind of the simple um functions that are very commonly recognised.

Student: Um. ((one student tries to initiate a question)).

Teacher: Yeah.

Student: For the timbers, um I think we could say the roof made of timbers.

Teacher: A roof made of timbers. Um, you **wouldn't** then use that structure to express that idea, because the key word as we saw before is the last word, so it's the timbers which are found in the roof. Um-

Student: I thought the expanded phrase is the roof is made of timbers.

Teacher: Well, it sounds that the roof-. But I can't ever see an example for you **would** want to narrow it down just two words to express that idea. £££

Extract 6.3 (ET1)

Teacher: So you are- are your, you are saying that the possible is the focus ↑?

Student A: Yeah, and I think um without the development of the Internet and telecommunication is the limitation.

Student B: Not the topic ... ((there are also some other students respond to this student's answer))

Student A: Ho, globalisation is the topic.

Teacher: I mean I understand, I can understand what you are trying to say, because we're- we're-, well, are we only looking at the Internet ↑, are we only looking at the Internet ↑, that's-that's what you have decided, um you **might** want to say there are other factors (1) okay ↑ you **might** want to say there are other factors that contribute to globalisation, so that **might** not be the limitation, that **might** be the focus, okay ↑ ?

Extract 6.4　(CT1)

Teacher: Then ... subject by subject pattern, or block pattern. Yeah, that's the first method to organize your ideas. Then in this paragraph, you can see, um, you **should** have to present your topic sentence clearly at the very beginning. And then, you first begin with Subject A, right ↑ ? Subject A. Then, you can say Point One, Point Two, Point three and even more about the Subject A. After discussing Subject A, you **should** come to Subject B. Of course, you need the connectors. OK. Then, Subject B, still, you **should** discuss the same points in the same order. That is Point One, Point Two, Point Three and even more. Right ↑ ? Okay, then after the discussion of all the subjects, two subjects here, and then you come to the last part, the concluding sentence of your whole paragraph. Right ↑ ? That is the, um, subject by subject pattern. Then, let's see organising by points. Still, in this paragraph, you **should** provide your topic sentence. But different from the subject by subject method, you **should** begin with the points, yeah, the first, Point One.

In Extract 6.2 above, the teacher is checking the answers to an exercise concerning the extended forms of expressing the two-word noun phrase "roof timber". Following the teacher's answers, one student provides a different opinion by saying "I think we could say the roof made of timbers". However, the teacher's response shows that she does not agree with the student's alternative answer by saying "you wouldn't then use that structure to express that idea" and gives the reason "because the key word as we saw before is the last word". Here the teacher denies the student's contribution with a more mitigating tone by using the modal auxiliary verb "wouldn't". This serves to save face for the student. In the following turn, the teacher's response of "but I can't ever see an example for you *would* want to narrow it down just two words to express that idea" shows the reason why the student's contribution is unacceptable from a different viewpoint. This has a similar function to the above use of *wouldn't*.

In Extract 6.3 above, the teacher and the students are carrying out the exercise of categorising the different components of a sentence. That is, which part is the focus, and which part is the limitation or topic. Reacting to students' different answers, the teacher introduces the correct answer gradually by using "you might want to ..." to offer a tentative alternative suggestion and prompt the students to think about the reasons behind it, rather than directly telling the students the answer. The frequent use of "might" in teacher's talk in this part indicates the teacher's attempt to negotiate with the students. This may serve to redress the power distance between the teacher and the students, helping them to engage more readily, and thereby reach the correct answers. Then following this, the teacher's use of *might* in "that might (not) be" shows her decision to withhold her commitment, which may avoid "overstating an assertion which later proves to have been in error" (Hyland, 2005, p. 80). On the other hand, the frequent use of *should* in Extract 6.4 above may reflect the way the teacher tends to deliver her command in a rather direct manner to the students.

6.3.1.4 Verbs

The frequency, types and ranges of hedging lexical verbs in the two sub-corpora are illustrated by Table 6.5 below. Concerning the overall frequency, native EAP teachers use hedging verbs more frequently than their non-native counterparts do (5.33 ptw versus 1.92 ptw). The log-likelihood value (55.43) reveals that teachers in the ET sub-corpus employ significantly more hedging verbs than those in the CT sub-corpus at $p < 0.0001$ level. With respect to the types of hedging verbs, more types of lexical items are used by teachers in the ETs (19 types) than those in the CTs (12 types). In relation to the ranges of hedging verbs, it is most typically characterised by the most frequent use of *think* by each teacher in the ET sub-corpus. Although *think* has the highest frequency in the CT sub-corpus, it is only used by three of the four English teachers from China. Let us consider the following Extract 6.5 on the use of the most frequent and differentiated hedging marker *think* and its variant form *thought* for a detailed illustration.

Table 6.5 Summary of individual hedging verbs in both sub-corpora

No.	Lexical items	ETs			CTs			Log-likelihood value*
		RawFrq.	NmlFrq.	Ranges	RawFrq.	NmlFrq.	Ranges	
1	think	116	3.53	4	19	0.57	3	78.38****
2	seem	11	0.33	4	4	0.12	1	3.46
3	seems	8	0.24	2	9	0.27	3	-0.05
4	thought	6	0.18	3	0	0.00	0	8.38**
5	guess	6	0.18	1	0	0.00	0	8.38**
6	argue	5	0.15	2	8	0.24	1	-0.67
7	suggesting	4	0.12	2	0	0.00	0	5.58*
8	feel	4	0.12	1	14	0.42	4	-5.79*
9	suggested	3	0.09	2	1	0.03	1	1.07
10	suggest	3	0.09	2	2	0.06	2	0.21
11	assume	2	0.06	1	2	0.06	1	0.00
12	claim	1	0.03	1	0	0.00	0	1.40
13	indicate	1	0.03	1	2	0.06	2	-0.33
14	suppose	1	0.03	1	0	0.00	0	1.40
15	supposed	1	0.03	1	1	0.03	1	0.00
16	appears	1	0.03	1	0	0.00	0	1.40
17	feels	1	0.03	1	1	0.03	1	0.00
18	felt	1	0.03	1	0	0.00	0	1.40
19	suggests	1	0.03	1	0	0.00	0	1.40
20	assumes	0	0.00	0.00	1	0.03	1	1.40
	Total	176	5.33		64	1.92		55.43****

Note: * = significant at $p < 0.05$ level; ** = significant at $p < 0.01$ level; *** = significant at $p < 0.001$ level; **** = significant at $p < 0.0001$ level.

Extract 6.5 (ET2)

Teacher: OK, so, today, the timetable says we maybe could have a scenario, but I am not going to do that. I I think we need to concentrate on the writing. Yeah, so we are going to have both sessions this morning until 10:50. Both of the sessions are about writing. So I ***thought*** um I would give you some information about citations and referencing.

Extract 6.6 (ET3)

Teacher: ... which IELTS skill in his study was most related to success in TESOL ↑?

Student: Reading.

Teacher: ... reading, yeah, does that make sense ↑ £££ (2) given the amounts of-, I was ***thinking*** the amounts of reading that you'll have to do. So I guess, we always, I mean, we always assume that it would be writing, because you have to write your assignments. So I ***thought*** that was actually quite interesting, um, quite an interesting finding. Um, but I ***think*** you can't write well if you don't understand well what you read.

In Extract 6.5 above, *thought* may be used to imply that it is the teacher's plan before the class, or the teacher's careful preparation prior to the beginning of the class. Moreover, *thought*, instead of the more common way of using *think* in this case, may indicate the speaker's view was in the past, whereas the view she currently holds is not necessarily the same. Thus, this may protect the speaker from possible objections. Moreover, in Extract 6.6 above, the teacher is talking about a finding in the literature the students are reading which shows that reading was mostly related to the person's IELTS success, a view that is contrary to the common intuition as the teacher says "we always assume that it would be writing". She uses *was thinking* and *thought* to indicate that this was the view she held when she read the literature. On the other hand, *think* shows the speaker's current state of mind. In the above sentence, it forms a contrast with the above uses of *thought* to show the teacher's current personal viewpoint that "you can't write well if you don't understand well what you read".

6.3.1.5 Adjectives

According to *Oxford English Dictionary* (2018), an adjective is a word or lexical unit that designates an attribute and qualifies a noun or pronoun to describe it more fully. Table 6.6 below presents the frequencies, types and ranges of hedging adjectives used by teachers in the two sub-corpora. As mentioned above, hedging adjective is the least frequent category in both sub-corpora. Despite their relatively lower frequencies in both sub-corpora, the log-likelihood value indicates that teachers in the ET sub-corpus employ significantly more instances of hedging adjectives than their counterparts in the CT sub-corpus do at $p<0.0001$ level. As for the types of hedging adjectives, five types occur in the ET sub-corpus, while only two types are found in the CT sub-corpus. As for lexical ranges, except that *possible* is used by three of the four ETs teachers, no instances of individual adjectives are found to be used commonly by the four teachers in either of the two sub-corpora. The above analysis demonstrates that adjectives are not a typical resource for hedging in the classroom teaching context, which differs from Hyland (1994) who reports that adjectives are used relatively frequently as a hedging device in academic and scientific writings. Extract 6.7 below demonstrates the use of the hedging adjective *possible* for a detailed illustration.

Table 6.6 Summary of individual hedging adjectives in both sub-corpora

No.	Lexical items	ETs			CTs			Log-likelihood value*
		RawFrq.	NmlFrq.	Ranges	RawFrq.	NmlFrq.	Ranges	
1	possible	8	0.24	3	1	0.03	1	6.26*
2	likely	5	0.15	2	1	0.03	1	2.95

continued

No.	Lexical items	ETs			CTs			Log-likelihood value*
		RawFrq.	NmlFrq.	Ranges	RawFrq.	NmlFrq.	Ranges	
3	pretty	3	0.09	2	0	0.00	0	4.19*
4	unlikely	2	0.06	1	0	0.00	0	2.79
5	probable	1	0.03	1	0	0.00	0	1.40
	Total	19	0.57		2	0.06		16.07****

Note: * = significant at $p < 0.05$ level; ** = significant at $p < 0.01$ level; *** = significant at $p < 0.001$ level; **** = significant at $p < 0.0001$ level.

Extract 6.7 (ET3)

Teacher: ... How is the findings chapter organised ↑? What do you say ↑, yeah ↑, Cathy ↑?

Student: ... (Does it relate to the literature review?)

Teacher: Well, ah, OK, so relating it to literature review. £££ I'm not sure, because I don't have in front of me, it's **possible**. um, yeah, it's kind of by theme, isn't it ↑?

In Extract 6.7 above, the teacher and the students are working on an exercise about evaluating several sample structures of a thesis. The teacher attempts to elicit the student's opinion on how "the findings chapter" is organised. Responding to one student's answer, the teacher indicates that she was not sure of its correctness because this exercise merely shows the general structure, rather than the details of each chapter. By using the hedging adjective *possible*, it attenuates the teacher's speculative assumptions about the proposition under discussion (Yan, 2010). This may serve to save face for the teacher in case the judgement is proved to be wrong. In addition, the lexical item *possible* here also resonates with the above expression "I'm not sure", which makes the teacher's feedback cohesive and coherent.

6.3.1.6 Multi-word expressions

Some multi-word expressions such as *kind of*, *a little bit* and *tend to* are commonly used by teachers in both groups. The frequencies, types and ranges of hedging multi-word expressions used by the two groups of teachers are shown in Table 6.7 below. In the first place, teachers in the ET and CT sub-corpora employ hedging multi-word expressions 2.03 and 1.66 times per thousand words respectively. The log-likelihood value indicates that there is no significant difference in the use of hedging multi-word expressions across the two sub-corpora. As for the number of types of multi-word expressions, eleven types are used in the ET sub-corpus, while six types in the CT sub-corpus. In terms of ranges, it can be observed that *kind of* occurs with the highest frequency. It is also the only linguistic unit used by all the teachers in the two sub-corpora. This supports the findings of Poos & Simpson (2002) and Simpson-Vlach (2006) that the use of *kind of* is a common feature of academic speech. The use of *kind of* can be illustrated by Extract 6.8 below.

Table 6.7 Summary of individual hedging multi-word expressions in both sub-corpora

No.	Lexical items	ETs			CTs			Log-likelihood value*
		RawFrq.	NmlFrq.	Ranges	RawFrq.	NmlFrq.	Ranges	
1	kind of	25	0.76	4	43	1.30	4	-4.65*
2	a little bit	17	0.52	4	7	0.21	2	4.39*
3	a bit	10	0.30	2	0	0.00	0	13.96***
4	sort of	4	0.12	3	0	0.00	0	5.58*
5	in my opinion	3	0.09	1	0	0.00	0	4.19*
6	tend to	2	0.06	1	2	0.06	1	0.00
7	a little	2	0.06	1	0	0.00	0	2.79
8	in general	1	0.03	1	1	0.03	1	0.00
9	tends to	1	0.03	1	0	0.00	0	1.40
10	tended to	1	0.03	1	0	0.00	0	1.40
11	a quick bit	1	0.03	1	0	0.00	0	1.40
12	in most cases	0	0.00	0	1	0.03	1	-1.38
13	more or less	0	0.00	0	1	0.03	1	-1.38
	Total	67	2.03		55	1.66		1.30

Note: * = significant at $p < 0.05$ level; ** = significant at $p < 0.01$ level; *** = significant at $p < 0.001$ level; **** = significant at $p < 0.0001$ level.

Extract 6.8 (ET3)

Teacher: So, I'll leave you to, I'll leave you to look at the last pages yourselves. They are about discussing qualitative findings. And there are (sic) some helpful advice from Dörnyei. Well, it's **kind of** helpful, but it also says. It says, it says in qualitative research writing, there are no fixed formats or templates. It is **kind of** easier to tell people how to write a quantitative finding than a qualitative one.

In Extract 6.8 above, the teacher leaves the student to look at some parts of the reading tasks, and then she comments on the content of the reading material. By using the multi-word expression *kind of*, she mitigates the degree of the helpfulness of Dörnyei's advice. Later in the following section, she uses another *kind of* to soften the claim that telling people how to write a quantitative finding is easier than a qualitative one. By using this softening lexical unit, the teacher acknowledges the tentativeness of the claim, opening up alternative opinions from the students.

6.3.2 Boosters

This section presents the frequency and distribution of boosting devices in both of the ET and CT sub-corpora. Boosters are linguistic items such as *clearly*, *obviously* and *demonstrate*, which allow addressers to close down the alternative views and express their certainty in what they say (Hyland, 2005). By doing so, boosters emphasize certainty and construct rapport by marking involvement with the topic and solidarity with the audience, taking a joint position against other voices (Hyland, 2000). That is to say, in contrast to the softening effect to propositions of hedges, boosters can strengthen the illocutionary force of propositions they modify. As is the case with the hedging devices discussed above, boosters are examined in terms of the lexical categories of their linguistic realisations. Resembling hedges, boosters are also realised by five types of linguistic units, namely adverbs, modal auxiliary verbs, main verbs, adjectives, and multiword expressions. The linguistic realisations and their coding examples are given in Table 6.8 below.

Table 6.8 Linguistic realisations of boosters

MD markers		Linguistic realisations	Examples with codes*
Interactional MD	Boosters	Adverbs	Actually < Badv >
		Modal auxiliaries	Must < Baux >
		Verbs	Know < Bverb >
		Adjectives	Sure < Badj >
		Multiword expressions	Of course < Bmwe >

*Note: metadiscourse markers are coded and annotated based on the initials of metadiscourse subcategory followed by abbreviations of word class and sentence type. For example, *actually* < Badv > means that the metadiscourse marker *actually* belongs to booster and it is an adverb in terms of lexical category.

6.3.2.1 Overall result of boosters

This subsection reports briefly the frequency and distribution of boosters employed by teachers in the ET and CT sub-corpora. As with hedges, this section will present the results of boosters from two perspectives, in light of the first research question which concerns the frequency and distribution of metadiscourse use across the two groups of teachers. The first perspective focuses on the frequency and distribution of boosters in terms of teachers in the ET and CT sub-corpora, and the other relates to the frequency and distribution of boosters in terms of individual lexical categories. Figure 6.6 below presents an overall landscape of the normalised frequency and distribution of specific boosting lexical categories used by teachers in the two sub-corpora.

Chapter 6 A corpus linguistic analysis of metadiscourse use across native and non-native EAP teachers

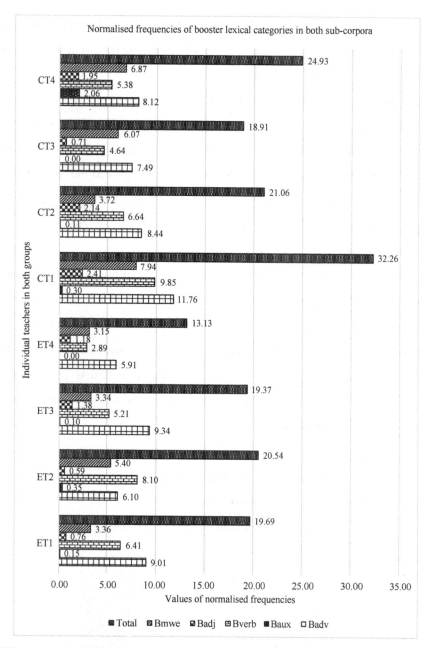

Figure 6.6 Normalised frequencies of booster lexical categories in both sub-corpora

Figure 6.6 above shows that three of the four EAP teachers in the CT sub-corpus, that is CT1 (32.26 ptw), CT2 (21.06 ptw) and CT4 (24.93 ptw), use comparatively higher frequencies of boosters than all the four teachers in the ET sub-corpus. It is interesting to note that boosters are least frequently used by ET4 (13.13 ptw), who was teaching a group of PhD students. These PhD level students are, at least to a certain extent, supposed to have a higher proficiency level of English compared with master students. Such relatively limited expression of certainty by ET4 may indicate the teacher's greater endeavour to open up dialogue with students, and narrow down the power distance between the students and herself in formal classroom instructions (Hyland, 2009). In contrast, CT1 uses the highest frequency of boosters, with a fairly high frequency of 32.26 instances per thousand words.

Figure 6.7 below indicates the normalised frequencies of boosters employed by the two groups of teachers in the ET and CT sub-corpora. It can be seen that teachers in the ET sub-corpus (18.29 ptw) use boosters less frequently than those in CT sub-corpus (24.9 ptw). Concerning the above analysis of hedges, it can be concluded that native EAP teachers generally employ a higher frequency of hedges but a lower frequency of boosters than their non-native EAP counterparts. This is in line with previous research in written academic discourse by Hyland (2005) that native English speakers' essays show a higher frequency of hedges but lower frequency of boosters than non-native English speakers' essays.

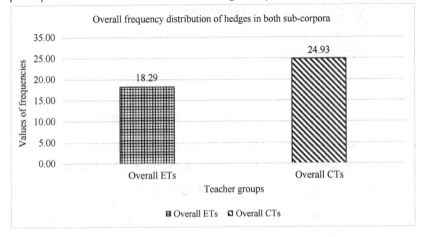

Figure 6.7 **Overall frequency distribution of boosters in both sub-corpora**

Figure 6.8 below presents the frequency and distribution of boosters in terms of their lexical categories. It can be found that the frequency and distribution of the lexical categories employed by the two teacher groups exhibit a similar pattern. Both groups make rather frequent use of adverbs, verbs and multiword expressions to serve boosting function in classroom teaching. Among these lexical categories, adverbs are the top ranked metadiscourse markers in ET and CT sub-corpora, with normalised frequencies of 7.62 and 9.18 instances per thousand words respectively. The second most frequent lexical category used by the two groups is verbs (5.65 ptw in ETs versus 6.93 ptw in CTs). This is followed by multiword expressions, which occur 3.84 and 6.20 times per thousand words in ET and CT sub-corpora. In addition, two other lexical categories, adjective and modal auxiliaries are employed with comparatively lower frequencies than the above three categories. In particular, modal auxiliaries are the least frequently used lexical category, which may be attributed to the fact that only one type of modal auxiliary, namely *must*, functions as a booster. In the following five subsections, the five lexical categories which made up boosters will be spelled out.

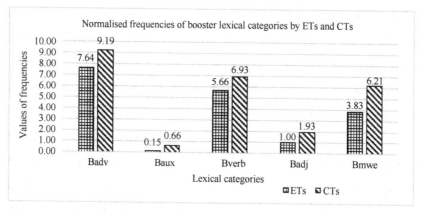

Figure 6.8 Normalised frequencies of hedging lexical categories in both sub-corpora

6.3.2.2 Adverbs

As noted above, adverbs account for the highest frequency in achieving hedging functions. Similarly, adverbs also represent the most frequently used lexical category in fulfilling boosting functions. Differing from previous research (e. g. Yan, 2010) which involves only two types of lexical subcategories for adverbs, that is adverbs of certainty and frequency, the current research advocates Lee & Subtirelu (2015) and Friginal et al. (2017) in that it adds the adverbs of degree (mainly including *too*, *very* and *so*) to the original classification. This is because after a thorough examination of the dataset for the current research, it is found that these adverbial lexical items for expressing degree are a prominent feature used for strengthening the propositions being conveyed. That is to say, the adverbs of approximation and probability for hedges are replaced by the adverbs of certainty for boosters to strengthen the illocutionary force of relevant propositions. The frequency and distribution of these three subcategories of boosting adverbs used by individual members of the ETs and CTs will be investigated in detail in what follows.

Table 6. 9 below illustrates the frequencies, types and ranges of boosting adverbs in the two sub-corpora. As for the frequencies, teachers in the CT sub-corpus employ significantly more boosting adverbs than those in the ET sub-corpus at $p < 0.05$ level. Regarding the three subcategories, adverbs of certainty such as *really*, *obviously* and *definitely* occur more frequently in the ET sub-corpus, whereas adverbs of degree such as *very* and *too* are used with higher frequencies in the CT sub-corpus. There is no significant difference between the frequencies of adverbs, the least frequent subcategory of boosting adverbs, between the two sub-corpora. This may manifest the core conception of boosters in intensifying the certainty, degree and frequency of the propositions being conveyed (Yan, 2010). In relation to the types of boosting adverbs, thirteen types are used in the ET sub-corpus, while eleven types in the CT sub-corpus. With respect to ranges, *actually*, *very* and *always* are used by all the teachers across the two sub-corpora, in particular the first two lexical items which are used with relatively high frequencies. See the following Extract 6.9 for a detailed illustration.

Chapter 6 A corpus linguistic analysis of metadiscourse use across native and non-native EAP teachers

Table 6.9 Summary of individual boosting adverbs in both sub-corpora

Lexical subcategories	No.	Lexical items	ETs RawFrq.	ETs NmlFrq.	ETs Ranges	CTs RawFrq.	CTs NmlFrq.	CTs Ranges	Log-likelihood value*
Adverbs of certainty	1	actually	56	1.70	4	71	2.14	4	-1.64
	2	really	51	1.55	4	10	0.30	3	30.53****
	3	obviously	13	0.40	4	1	0.03	1	12.32***
	4	definitely	8	0.24	3	0	0.00	0	11.17***
	5	clearly	5	0.15	4	18	0.54	4	-7.68**
	6	certainly	4	0.12	2	0	0.00	0	5.58*
	7	totally	3	0.09	2	4	0.12	3	-0.13
	8	apparently	1	0.03	1	0	0.00	0	1.40
	9	indeed	0	0.00	0	2	0.06	1	-2.75
		Total	141	4.28		106	3.19		5.32*
Adverbs of degree	1	very	77	2.34	4	130	3.92	4	-13.22***
	2	too	10	0.30	3	34	1.02	4	-13.60***
	3	so	5	0.15	4	16	0.48	3	-5.95*
		Total	92	2.79		180	5.42		-28.16****
Adverbs of frequency	1	always	15	0.46	4	14	0.42	4	0.04
	2	never	3	0.09	2	5	0.15	2	-0.49
		Total	18	0.55		19	0.57		-0.02
		Total	251	7.62		305	9.18		-4.75*

Note: * = significant at $p < 0.05$ level; ** = significant at $p < 0.01$ level; *** = significant at $p < 0.001$ level; **** = significant at $p < 0.0001$ level.

Extract 6.9 (ET1)

Teacher: Okay, to analyse. Yes, I mean a lot of these have a component of evaluation in them yes.

Student: So what is the exact difference between evaluate and analyse↑?

Teacher: We:ll, I mean, probably there is not a lot of difference between analyse something and evaluate, because you-you would be looking in detail and with an element of evaluation. There tends to **always** be an element of evaluation in academic writing, yeah, um you **very** rarely get an essay that has description only, because it's not a **very** academic way to look at something describing, so **very** often you have a combination of these two words.

In Extract 6.9 above, the teacher and the students are carrying out the exercise of identifying whether the given sentence is an evaluation or analysis. One student initiates the question of what the exact difference between evaluate and analyse is. The teacher tries to explain this to the student. She uses the adverb of frequency *always* to highlight the certainty of using evaluation in academic writing. However, here the teacher combines the frequency booster *always* with one hedge "tends to" to soften her view on the absoluteness of involving evaluation in academic writing. It shows that although the teacher intends to emphasize the general correctness of involving evaluation in academic writing, she also realises that there might be some exceptions in specific conditions. This may indicate the teacher's endeavour to create a "cohesive and close-knit ambience in the discourse community" (Lin, 2010, p. 1177) by balancing the use of hedges and boosters. However, these two types of metadiscourse markers work closely together primarily for the purpose of strengthening the proposition following them, instead of going in two totally opposite directions. This necessitates the interpretation of metadiscourse markers in terms of their co-occurrences in the broader contexts that has aroused sparse attention from researchers in this field (Lin, 2010; Yan, 2010).

Moreover, the adverb of degree *very* appears three times in Extract 6.9 above. Following her claim that academic writing tends to always have an element of evaluation, the teacher elaborates this further from an opposite perspective. By using the first adverb of degree *very*, she intensifies the unlikelihood of involving only description in an essay. Then she provides the reason for this. Through combining the negation marker of "not" with another booster metadiscourse marker *very*, the teacher conveys a kind of hedging meaning and implies that it might be reasonable to incorporate description in academic writing, but this is "not a very academic way". The third *very* is used when the teacher comes to the conclusion of using a combination of the two words, that is, analysis and evaluation. Here *very* is used to modify the frequency adverb *often* to stress the likelihood or certainty of having a combination of the analysis and evaluation elements. It may reveal that the teacher in this extract makes a tactful balance of boosters and hedges in explaining her statement to the students.

6.3.2.3 Modal auxiliaries

Modal auxiliaries are generally used for giving information about the function of the main verbs they modify. As noted above, among the five types of lexical categories realising boosters, modal auxiliary verbs are used with the lowest frequency. This might be due to the limited types of modal auxiliaries, as only the modal auxiliary verb *must* is observed to perform the boosting metadiscourse function in the data of the current research. It can be found from Table 6.10 below that the only modal auxiliary *must* is used with rather rare instances across both sub-corpora, except that it is employed with a comparatively high frequency by CT4. Although the log-likelihood value (−11.39) indicates that CTs employ significantly more modal auxiliaries for boosters than ETs at <0.001 level, it is obvious that the reason lies in the predominantly high frequency by CT4.

Table 6.10 Summary of individual boosting modal auxiliaries in both sub-corpora

Lexical item	Teachers	RawFreq.	NmlFreq.	Teachers	RawFreq.	NmlFreq.	Log-likelihood value
must	ET1	1	0.15	CT1	3	0.30	
	ET2	3	0.35	CT2	1	0.11	
	ET3	1	0.10	CT3	0	0.00	
	ET4	0	0.00	CT4	18	2.06	
Overall		5	0.15		22	0.66	−11.39***

Note: * = significant at $p<0.05$ level; ** = significant at $p<0.01$ level; *** = significant at $p<0.001$ level; **** = significant at $p<0.0001$ level.

6.3.2.4 Verbs

Within the booster metadiscourse category, verbs rank as the second most frequent lexical category after adverbs in both ET and CT sub-corpora. Table 6.11 below shows the frequencies, types and ranges of boosting verbs in the two sub-corpora. Regarding the overall frequency of boosting verbs, they are used significantly more often by teachers in the CT sub-corpus (6.93 ptw) than those in the ET sub-corpus (5.66 ptw) at $p<0.05$ level. In relation to the two lexical subcategories of verbs, both sub-corpora have more tentative cognition verbs than factive reporting verbs for boosters in their classroom discourse. Teachers in the ET sub-corpus employ more tentative cognition verbs but less factive reporting verbs than those in the CT sub-corpus do. As for the types of boosting verbs, twelve types occur in the ET sub-corpus, whereas six types occur in the CT sub-corpus. In terms of ranges, it is characterised by the prevalent use of the most frequent boosting verb *know* across all individual teachers in both sub-corpora. Extract 6.10 below illustrates the use of this lexical category.

Chapter 6 A corpus linguistic analysis of metadiscourse use across native and non-native EAP teachers

Table 6.11 Summary of individual boosting verbs in both sub-corpora

Lexical categories	No.	Lexical items	ETs			CTs			Log-likelihood value
			RawFrq.	NmlFrq.	Ranges	RawFrq.	NmlFrq.	Ranges	
Tentative cognition verbs	1	know	106	3.23	4	161	4.85	4	−10.89***
	2	find	21	0.64	4	38	1.15	3	−4.81*
	3	found	3	0.09	1	3	0.09	2	0.00
	4	believe	1	0.03	1	0	0.00	0	1.40
	5	known	2	0.06	2	0	0.00	0	2.79
	6	realise	0	0.00	0	1	0.03	1	−1.38
	7	realised	1	0.03	1	0	0.00	0	1.40
		Total	134	4.08		203	6.12		−13.58***
Factive reporting verbs	1	show	34	1.03	3	24	0.72	4	1.83
	2	shows	9	0.27	3	1	0.03	1	7.44**
	3	showed	2	0.06	2	0	0.00	0	2.79
	4	shown	1	0.03	1	0	0.00	0	1.40
	5	showing	5	0.15	2	2	0.06	2	1.36
	6	demonstrate	1	0.03	1	0	0.00	0	1.40
		Total	52	1.57		27	0.81		8.29**
Total			186	5.65		230	6.93		−4.25*

Note: * = significant at $p < 0.05$ level; ** = significant at $p < 0.01$ level; *** = significant at $p < 0.001$ level; **** = significant at $p < 0.0001$ level.

Extract 6.10　(ET1)

Teacher: LISTEN, listen that you won't have problems in the exam, £ it will be a very simple question. £

Student: £ Because we just can't answer that question £ =

Teacher: = NO it-i mean it is- it is a fact that, you **know**, people agonise over these interpretations, you **know**, questions are difficult to interpret, and you **know**, you have got to analyse them very carefully, and you **know**, what is it asking us to do ↓ and (1) so you have to decide here, globalisation was it possible with or without the Internet yeah, do you agree Jason ((student name)) ↑?

Student: Yeah.

In Extract 6.10 above, the teacher and the students are carrying out an exercise on finding the topic and focus of the sample passage. Prior to this extract, the students and the teacher differed in their opinion. The students have a heated discussion in explicating their rationales and this lasts for a few minutes. At the beginning of this extract, the teacher uses a higher volume of the utterance "LISTEN, listen" to stop their discussion on this question by assuring them this disagreement will not affect their performance in the final exam. In what follows, the teacher further explains the acceptability of this disagreement in one question. She uses booster markers *know* four times together with the engagement marker *you* to constitute the phrase *you know*, which may be assigned the function of prefacing shared knowledge (He & Lindsey, 1998) or mutual experience (Hyland, 2005) that is needed to draw the same conclusion between the addresser and the addressees. The co-occurrence of engagement marker *you* and the booster marker *know* work together here to emphasise that the teacher acknowledges what the students know. Her explanations to the disputed answers bring the issue in question to a reasonable solution.

6.3.2.5 Adjectives

Of the five lexical types realising booster functions, adjectives are the second least frequently used type next to the modal auxiliary verbs in both sub-corpora (see Figure 6.8 above). Table 6.12 below indicates the frequencies, types and ranges of boosting adjectives in the two sub-corpora. Firstly, teachers in the CT sub-corpus use significantly more boosting adjectives than their counterparts in the ET sub-corpus do at $p<0.01$ level. Secondly, it is found that resembling the case of other lexical categories, teachers in the ET sub-corpus use more types of lexical categories of adjectives than those of the CT sub-corpus (six versus four types). The discrepancy is more obvious if we take the main lexical verbs and their inflectional forms as one major type (five types in the ET sub-corpus versus two types in the CT sub-corpus). Thirdly, the most frequent boosting adjective *clear*, together with its inflectional forms *clear(er/est)*, is used extensively by each teacher in both sub-corpora. Extract 6.11 below provides a detailed illustration of the use of *clear(ly)*.

Table 6.12 Summary of individual boosting adjectives in both sub-corpora

No.	Lexical items	ETs			CTs			Log-likelihood value
		RawFrq.	NmlFrq.	Ranges	RawFrq.	NmlFrq.	Ranges	
1	clear	14	0.43	4	58	1.75	4	-28.46****
2	obvious	5	0.15	2	3	0.09	2	0.52
3	sure	5	0.15	2	0	0.00	0	6.98**
4	definite	4	0.12	2	0	0.00	0	5.58*
5	clearer	2	0.06	2	2	0.06	2	0.00
6	certain	3	0.09	1	0	0.00	0	4.19*
7	clearest	0	0.00	0	1	0.03	1	-1.38
	Total	33	1.00		64	1.93		-9.79**

Note: * = significant at $p<0.05$ level; ** = significant at $p<0.01$ level; *** = significant at $p<0.001$ level; **** = significant at $p<0.0001$ level.

Extract 6.11 (CT4)

Teacher: ... when you reach the last sentence, you know this is another place for you to REGAIN the topic sentence, if you cannot understand the topic sentence **clearly** the topic sentence, then you might have another chance to REgain the idea, in the- in the last sentence, alright ↑ ? So to be a writer is also to be a reader, if you are a good writer, you must be a good reader, and you can read in a **clear** way, and you can read in a very efficient way (2) no matter how evolved the technique that the writer use- has used, you still can find the gist, the main idea of the article, of the paragraph, because you know you where to find what, THEREfore, a **clear** structure is highly important, a **clear** structure an ordered structure only indicates I am an ordered person, a reasonable person, a logical person, a person who knows how to persuade people, a person how- a person who knows how to convey ideas, in a **clear** way, so that other people would just follow him or her, alright ↓ .

In Extract 6.11 above, the teacher is instructing the students on the relationship between the last sentence and the topic sentence in one paragraph. Here the teacher uses the adjective *clear* four times, twice in the phrase "clear way" and twice in "clear structure". She endeavours to stress the importance of writing a paragraph in a way that is easy to understand. In the first instance of *clear*, the teacher uses it together with another booster marker *must* to emphasise that only when you can read in a clear way, can you be a good reader. In the second and third instances, the repetitive use of *clear* in the noun phrase "clear structure" intensifies the teacher's instruction on what a structure should be like. In the last instance of *clear*, the teacher repeats its first instance, the phrase "clear way". By using several paralleled structures of "a ... person", she finally concludes that such a person is the one who can convey ideas in a *clear* way, which is an indispensable feature of reader-friendly writing.

6.3.2.6 Multiword expressions

Among the five types of boosting lexical categories realising booster metadiscourse function, multiword expressions are the third most frequently employed type, following adverbs and verbs. Table 6.13 below presents the frequencies, types and ranges of boosting multiword expressions in the two sub-corpora. In relation to frequencies, teachers in the ET sub-corpus use significantly less boosting multiword expressions than those in the CT sub-corpus at $p < 0.0001$ level. In terms of the number of lexical types, the former employ slightly more types than the latter. Additionally, three relatively frequent lexical items, *have to*, *need to* and *a lot*, are used widely by each teacher in the two sub-corpora. Among them, the most frequent multiword expression *have to* appears significantly more frequently in the CT sub-corpus than the ET sub-corpus. This high frequency of *have to*, together with *must* noted above, may further support the previous claim that Chinese teachers tend to exhibit a more authoritative role in their classroom teaching. Extract 6.12 below illustrates the usage of *have to*.

Table 6.13 Summary of individual boosting multiword expressions in both sub-corpora

No.	Lexical items	ETs			CTs			Log-likelihood value
		RawFrq.	NmlFrq.	Ranges	RawFrq.	NmlFrq.	Ranges	
1	have to	49	1.49	4	97	2.92	4	-15.62****
2	need to	41	1.25	4	49	1.48	4	-0.64
3	a lot	14	0.43	4	34	1.02	4	-8.40**
4	lots of	12	0.37	3	0	0.00	0	16.75****
5	in fact	7	0.21	2	1	0.03	1	5.12*
6	of course	3	0.09	1	25	0.75	3	-19.54****
	Total	126	3.84		206	6.20		-18.71****

Note: * = significant at $p < 0.05$ level; ** = significant at $p < 0.01$ level; *** = significant at $p < 0.001$ level; **** = significant at $p < 0.0001$ level.

Extract 6.12　（CT1）

Teacher: ... now you have decided on your topic, you **have to** select the details, relevant details. Right ↑? Then, cross out the irrelevant ones, just as we did just now. And since we have too many points, but we have two subjects. Then, still you **have to** organise them in a logical way. So we have talked about it, um, in today's class. You can organise them by subject by subject or point by point method. Right. Okay. Both way, both methods are fine. It depends on you, actually. You **have to** think about which method is better is more appropriate in this paragraph. For me, it's to express my idea clearly, right ↑? Okay. You **have to** think about that. And, also, after that, you **have to** write the outline, you **have to** write clearly the outline. That is also very necessary, because with this kind of outline, you know, you can make it very clear, or you will find some problems. Right ↑?

In Extract 6.12 above, the teacher is talking about how to write an essay after deciding on the topic. It can be seen that the teacher uses the phrase *have to* during every procedure of writing she instructs. This multiword expression has to follow the second person pronoun "you", which functions as a commonly used engagement marker and preceding an action verb. By using this structure, the teacher assertively engages the students to follow her instructions on the stages of writing and stresses the actions the student should take in every procedure.

6.3.3　Attitude markers

This section focuses on the frequency and distribution of attitude markers in both of the ET and CT sub-corpora. Attitude markers are linguistic devices used to convey the addresser's affective attitude, such as surprise, agreement, importance, obligation, and frustration to certain propositions (Hyland, 2005). As with the above cases of hedges and boosters, attitude markers are investigated in terms of the lexical categories of their linguistic realisations. Differing from hedges and boosters that entail five types of linguistic units, attitude markers are primarily realised by three lexical categories, that is, verbs, adverbs and adjectives. The linguistic realisations and their coding examples can be shown in Table 6.14 below.

Table 6.14 Linguistic realisations of attitude markers

MD markers		Linguistic realisations	Examples with codes*
Interactional MD	Attitude markers	Verbs	Agree < Averb >
		Adjectives	Interesting < Aadj >
		Sentence adverbs	Fortunately < Asadv >

*Note: metadiscourse markers are coded and annotated based on the initials of metadiscourse subcategory followed by abbreviations of word class and sentence type. For example, *agree* <Aadv> means that the metadiscourse marker *agree* belongs to attitude marker and it is an adverb in terms of lexical category.

6.3.3.1 Overall result of attitude markers

This section presents the frequency and distribution of attitude markers in the ET and CT sub-corpora. As with hedges and boosters, the overall result of attitude markers in this section will also be presented from two aspects. The first aspect focuses on the frequency and distribution of attitude markers employed by individual teachers within each of the two sub-corpora in particular and then in general, two groups of teachers across both sub-corpora in general. The other aspect examines the frequency and distribution of attitude markers regarding individual lexical categories. Figure 6.9 below displays an overview of the frequency and distribution of the total and specific lexical categories employed by individual teachers in the two sub-corpora.

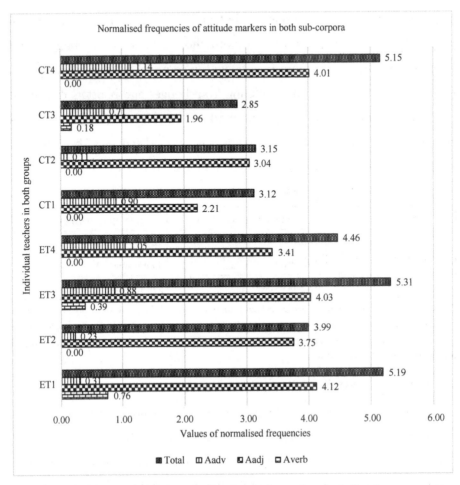

Figure 6.9 Normalised frequencies of attitude markers in both sub-corpora

Overall, Figure 6.9 above shows that three teachers in the CT sub-corpus (not CT4), employ attitude markers with relatively lower frequencies than all the four teachers in the ET sub-corpus. In relation to the frequency and distribution of attitude markers used by the two groups of teachers in both sub-corpora, Figure 6.10 below demonstrates that teachers in the ET sub-corpus employ attitude markers with a slightly higher frequency than those in the CT sub-corpus do (4.75 ptw versus 3.62 ptw). This is roughly similar to hedges, which occur more frequently in the ET sub-corpus than the CT sub-corpus. However, compared with hedges and boosters mentioned above, teachers in both sub-corpora use attitude markers far less often in their classroom instruction. In fact, as can be found by comparing with all the other four interactional metadiscourse categories, attitude markers accounts for the least frequent metadiscourse category in both sub-corpora. This finding is in line with Lee and Subtirelu's (2015) study of teachers' classroom metadiscourse use in both the EAP classrooms and university lectures, in which teachers in both classroom instructional types use attitude markers with the least frequency.

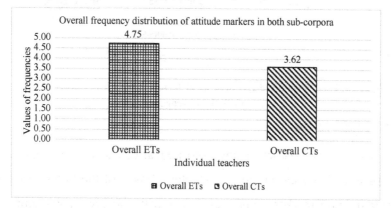

Figure 6.10 Overall frequency distribution of attitude markers in both sub-corpora

Figure 6.11 below shows the frequency and distribution of attitude markers in terms of their lexical categories. As with those of hedges and boosters, the frequency and distribution of the lexical categories in this metadiscoursal category also present a similar pattern in the two sub-corpora. Teachers in both sub-corpora make the most frequent use of adjectives, followed by adverbials and verbs. Specifically, teachers in both ET and CT sub-corpora make the most frequent use of attitude markers, with 3.81 and 2.86 instances per thousand words respectively. The second most frequently used lexical category is adverbs, which occur slightly less in the ET sub-corpus (0.64 ptw) than the CT sub-corpus (0.72 ptw). Accordingly, verbs are employed with the least frequencies by teachers in both ETs (0.27 ptw) and CTs sub-corpora (0.03 ptw). The following five subsections will elaborate on the five lexical categories realising attitude markers.

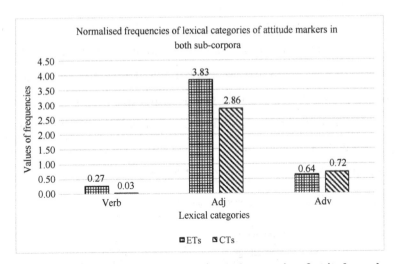

Figure 6.11 Normalised frequencies of lexical categories of attitude marker in both sub-corpora

6.3.3.2 Verbs

Verbs are the least frequently used lexical category to express teachers' attitudes in the two sub-corpora. As noted above, of the three lexical types realising attitude markers, verbs are used with the lowest frequency. This might be due to their limited types, of which merely two types of verbs, *agree* and *prefer*, are observed in the two sub-corpora. Table 6.15 below indicates that these two lexical verbs are used only by ET1 and ET3 in the ET sub-corpus, and only one instance of *prefer* used by CT3. Although the log-likelihood value (7.44) indicates that teachers in the ET sub-corpus employ significant more attitude verbs than their counterparts in the CT sub-corpus do at $p < 0.01$ level, it is clear that this has come about because of the comparatively higher frequency of these two words used by ET1 and ET3.

Table 6.15 Summary of individual attitude verbs in both sub-corpora

Lexical item	Teachers	RawFrq.	NmlFrq.	Teachers	RawFrq.	NmlFrq.	Log-likelihood value*
Agree	ET1	4	0.61	CT1	0	0.00	5.58*
	ET2	0	0.00	CT2	0	0.00	0.00
	ET3	2	0.20	CT3	0	0.00	2.79
	ET4	0	0.00	CT4	0	0.00	0.00
	Overall	6	0.18	Overall	0	0.00	8.38**
Prefer	ET1	1	0.15	CT1	0	0.00	1.40
	ET2	0	0.00	CT2	0	0.00	0.00
	ET3	2	0.20	CT3	1	0.18	0.35
	ET4	0	0.00	CT4	0	0.00	0.00
	Overall	3	0.09	Overall	1	0.03	1.07
Total		9	0.27	Total	1	0.03	7.44**

Note: * = significant at $p<0.05$ level; ** = significant at $p<0.01$ level; *** = significant at $p<0.001$ level; **** = significant at $p<0.0001$ level.

6.3.3.3 Adjectives

Of the three lexical categories constituting attitude markers, adjectives represent the most frequently employed category in the ET and CT sub-corpus. Table 6.16 below demonstrates the frequencies, types and ranges of attitude adjectives in the two sub-corpora. Teachers in the ET sub-corpus use attitude adjectives more often than those in the CT sub-corpus do. The log-likelihood value across the two groups of teachers shows that, as is the case with the above attitude verbs, teachers in the ET sub-corpus employ significant more adjectives as attitude markers than their counterparts in the CT sub-corpus do at $p<0.01$ level. In relation to lexical types, teachers in the ET sub-corpus use 16 types of adjectives, three instances more than those in the CT sub-corpus with 13 types. With regard to the ranges of adjective lexical items, it can be seen that two relatively frequent lexical items, *important* and *right*, are employed extensively by each teacher in both sub-corpora. Extract 6.13 below provides an illustration of the usage of adjectives and verbs as attitude markers.

Table 6.16 Summary of individual attitude adjectives in both sub-corpora

No.	Lexical items	ETs			CTs			Log-likelihood value*
		RawFrq.	NmlFrq.	Ranges	RawFrq.	NmlFrq.	Ranges	
1	important	30	0.91	4	40	1.21	4	-1.34
2	right	34	1.03	4	8	0.24	4	17.57****
3	interesting	12	0.37	3	12	0.36	4	0.00
4	difficult	8	0.24	4	8	0.24	3	0.00
5	wrong	8	0.24	3	4	0.12	1	1.40
6	correct	6	0.18	3	4	0.12	1	0.42
7	easy	5	0.15	2	4	0.12	3	0.12
8	appropriate	2	0.06	2	4	0.12	2	-0.66
9	unusual	5	0.15	1	0	0.00	0	6.98**
10	essential	4	0.12	1	0	0.00	0	5.58*
11	natural	0	0.00	0	4	0.12	2	-5.51*
12	necessary	0	0.00	0	4	0.12	2	-5.51*
13	usual	2	0.06	1	1	0.03	1	0.35
14	straightforward	3	0.09	2	0	0.00	0	4.19*
15	expected	2	0.06	2	0	0.00	0	2.79
16	significant	2	0.06	1	0	0.00	0	2.79
17	fantastic	2	0.06	1	0	0.00	0	2.79
18	unexpected	1	0.03	1	0	0.00	0	1.40
19	practical	0	0.00	0	1	0.03	1	-1.38
20	meaningful	0	0.00	0	1	0.03	1	-1.38
	Total	126	3.81		95	2.86		4.66*

Note: * = significant at $p<0.05$ level; ** = significant at $p<0.01$ level; *** = significant at $p<0.001$ level; **** = significant at $p<0.0001$ level.

Extract 6.13 (ET1)

Teacher: Okay, what would you say is the <TOPIC> ↑ ?

Student: [Face-to-face communication]

Students: [Face-to-face communication]

Teacher: Yeah, it's face-to-face communication, **right** that would be your topic, really because that's what you are looking at here

Student: We cannot say it's the face-to-face kind of communication is limitation ↑ ?

Teacher: Well, you could, you could say that is the communication, that face to face communication is the limitation, you could do that, I- I *agree* with that, or you can just see it as face to face communication =

Student: =That topic is communication or face to face communication, that's what we say quite often.

Teacher: Yeah, (1) so if that's the topic then what is ah the focus ↑ ?

Students: Most effective communication.

Teacher: Yeah, so you are trying to decide if face to face communication is the most effective form of communication, right ↑ ? So that's your actual focus here, °right° ↑ ? So I mean I *agree*. You could decide that face to face is the limitation, yeah, (1) OK, that's good.

In Extract 6.13 above, the teacher is leading the students to identify the arrangement of the sample passage, that is, what can be seen as the limitation, and what can be deemed as the topic of that sample passage. After asking the students what the topic is and getting one student along with other students' responses, the teacher shows her opinion or attitude by using the adjective *right* to confirm the correctness of their answer. Moreover, this confirmation also co-occurs with other confirmation devices, including the most common way of communicating agreement by saying yes, followed by the repetition of the students' answer. Then, in what follows, the students question this answer and try to negotiate with the teacher on other alternative interpretations. In response to these interpretations, the teacher shows her agreement with the students and recognises the rationality of the students' answer by using the verb *agree* in two cases. Notably, much fewer instances of the adjective *right* are used as a confirmation of students' responses to the teacher's questions in CT sub-corpus. This may be due to the fact that there are very few occasions when teachers in the CT sub-corpus attempt to genuinely elicit answers from students. Instead, a thorough examination of the data reveals that, in most cases, when teachers in the CT sub-corpus ask questions, they tend to leave very short wait time, but provide the answers to these questions immediately by themselves, and then check their students' opinions on the answers they provide by using a tag question *right* ↑ or *okay* ↑. This may also explain why in the metadiscourse category of engagement markers, the frequencies of *right* ↑ and *okay* ↑ are much higher in the CT sub-corpus than in the ET sub-corpus.

6.3.3.4 Adverbs

As noted above, among the three lexical categories of attitude markers, adverbs rank the second, following adjectives and followed by verbs in both ET and CT sub-corpora. Table 6.17 below illustrates the frequencies, types and ranges of attitude adverbs in the two sub-corpora. With reference to frequencies of adverbs, teachers in the ET sub-corpus use adverbs slightly less frequently (0.79 ptw) than those in the CT sub-corpus do (0.81 ptw). The log-likelihood value (-0.17) across the two sub-corpora shows that such a difference is not significant. In terms of lexical types, both groups of teachers from the two sub-corpora use the same number of five types of adverbs. As for the ranges of the lexical items, it can be found that *even*, among others, is used more extensively compared with other lexical items across the two sub-corpora. This lexical item is used by four teachers in the ET sub-corpus, whereas three teachers in the CT sub-corpus. Let us see Extract 6.14 below for an illustration of the usage of adverbs as attitude markers.

Table 6.17 Summary of individual attitude adverbs in both sub-corpora

No.	Lexical items	ETs			CTs			Log-likelihood value*
		RawFrq.	NmlFrq.	Ranges	RawFrq.	NmlFrq.	Ranges	
1	even	15	0.46	4	19	0.57	3	-0.43
2	correctly	1	0.03	1	1	0.03	1	0.00
3	essentially	2	0.06	1	0	0.00	0	2.79
4	importantly	0	0.00	0	2	0.06	2	-2.75
5	unfortunately	2	0.06	2	0	0.00	0	2.79
6	appropriately	0	0.00	0	1	0.03	2	-1.38
7	hopefully	1	0.03	1	0	0.00	0	1.40
8	preferably	0	0.00	0	1	0.03	2	-1.38
	Total	21	0.64		24	0.72		-0.17

Note: * = significant at $p < 0.05$ level; ** = significant at $p < 0.01$ level; *** = significant at $p < 0.001$ level; **** = significant at $p < 0.0001$ level.

Extract 6.14 (ET4)

> Teacher: If you had "The student did exceptionally well in their exam", that would be one clause, independent clause, okay. "is the one who chewing gum at the back", that doesn't work as a sentence, does it ↑? Um, because, at this point, we don't have a subject for that. So it **even** not working as a clause. So, um, and if you had the "who chewing", "who chewing gum" ↑? That doesn't work, because it needs to be a finite verb, who is chewing, or you could have "who chews gum". You could also have that, but it needs to be a finite verb. OK, so, let's just put this back into the right order …

In Extract 6.14 above, the teacher and the students are doing an exercise, for which the students are asked to put the given words into the correct order to form meaningful sentences. The teacher first uses a prolonged sound after the first word "the" in the sentence they are working on to elicit students' answers. In response to the teacher's elicitation, one student offers an answer, "The student did exceptionally well in their exam is the one who chewing the gum at the back." which is not grammatically correct. The teacher tries to motivate the students to think about why this sentence does not work. After several turns, the teacher does not get the expected answer, so she gives the reasons by herself. She notes that "is the one who chewing the gum at the back" is lack of one subject. She uses "even" to modify that this does not work as a clause. As is known that a clause constitutes one part of a sentence. Therefore, the use of "even" here implies that since it does not work as a clause, it certainly cannot form a grammatically correct sentence. It shows the explicit attitude of the teacher to the appropriateness of the answer provided by the students.

6.3.4 Engagement markers

This section examines the frequency and distribution of engagement markers in both of the ET and CT sub-corpora. Based on Hyland (2005), engagement markers are linguistic devices to highlight the addressee's presence in the discourse, either to explicitly draw their attention or to involve them in the interaction. Distinct from the previous three metadiscourse categories, engagement markers are not examined in terms of their lexical categories, but primarily in relation to their pragmatic functions, and then the linguistic realisations of these pragmatic functions. This is due to the particular characteristics of the linguistic realisations of engagement markers, which are realised not by specific lexical markers, but rather mainly by particular sentence units in which the metadiscourse markers are embedded. Overall, engagement markers in this study are divided into three functional sub-categories: directives, addressee-oriented mentions, and questions. The pragmatic functions of engagement markers, and the respective lexical categories realising these functions, together with their coding examples, can be illustrated by Table 6.18 below.

Table 6.18 Linguistic realisations of engagement markers

MD markers		Linguistic realisations		Examples with codes*
Interactional MD	Engagement markers	Addressee-oriented mention		you < Engpron >
				Student name < Engnoun >
		Directives		Let's ... < Engverb >
		Questions	*Wh*-questions	What ... ↑ < Engwhq >
			Yes/no questions	Can/Do ... ↑ < Engynq >
			Tag questions	Isn't it ↑ < Engtgq >

* The symbol is in the form of initial letter of each category followed by the abbreviation of word class or sentence type. To avoid ambiguity, special forms "Eng" and "End" are used to stand for engagement markers and endophoric markers respectively.

6.3.4.1 Overall result of engagement markers

This section centres on the frequency and distribution of engagement markers in the ET and CT sub-corpora. As is with other metadiscourse categories mentioned above, the overall result of engagement markers in this section will also be presented from two aspects. The first aspect deals with the frequency and distribution of attitude markers employed by individual teachers within each of the two sub-corpora in particular and by the individual groups of teachers across both sub-corpora in general. The other aspect examines the frequency and distribution of attitude markers regarding individual lexical categories. Figure 6.12 below illustrates an overview of the frequency and distribution of the total and specific lexical categories employed by individual teachers in the two sub-corpora.

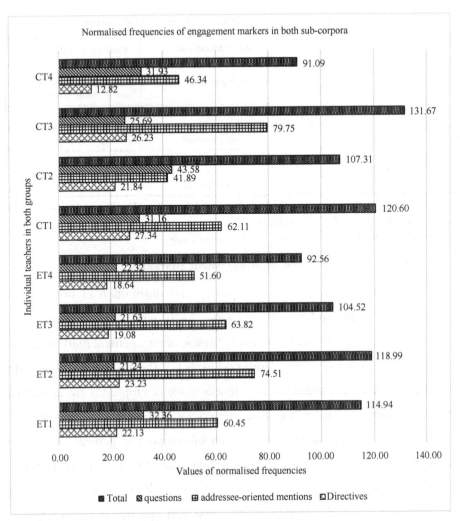

Figure 6.12 Normalised frequencies of engagement markers in both sub-corpora

Figure 6.12 above manifests that six of the eight EAP teachers in both sub-corpora use engagement markers with over 100 instances per thousand words. Comparatively, the remaining two teachers CT4 and ET4 employ engagement markers with relatively lower frequency. This high frequency of engagement markers reflects EAP teachers' effort to create more opportunities for students to participate in teacher-student interaction and to engage student in academic and language tasks (Lee & Subtirelu, 2015). Figure 6.13 below demonstrates that teachers in the ET sub-corpus employ engagement markers less frequently than those in the CT sub-corpus do (111.14 ptw versus 107.58

ptw). Overall, compared with other interactional metadiscourse categories, teachers in both sub-corpora employ a much higher frequency of engagement markers. This result echoes the research by Lee and Subtirelu (2015) that engagement markers are the most frequent category among all metadiscourse resources in both types of classrooms. Moreover, such a finding also evidences Hyland (2009) who claims that instruction in language-oriented classrooms involves "high levels of involvement and interactivity" (p. 102).

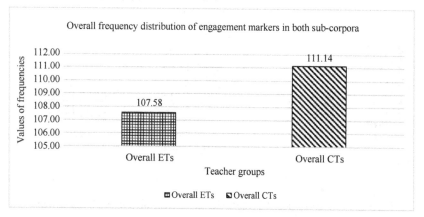

Figure 6.13 Overall frequency distribution of engagement markers in both sub-corpora

Figure 6.14 below illustrates the frequency and distribution of engagement markers in terms of each pragmatic category. It can be seen that among the three types of pragmatic functions realising engagement markers, addressee-oriented mention is employed with the highest frequency. This can be attributed mainly to the relatively higher frequency of the second person pronoun *you* as opposed to other metadiscourse items. Additionally, this result diverges from previous studies that inclusive-*we* is the major pronoun in spoken academic discourse (e. g. Cheng, 2012; Fortanet, 2004). Lee (2009) also notes that using inclusive-*we* and *you* is one of the central ways of establishing and maintaining high levels of student involvement. On the other hand, this result supports the research by Lee and Subtirelu (2015) in that *you* occurs nearly four times as commonly as inclusive-*we*. The second person pronoun *you* is extensively used by EAP teachers to "orientate listeners to the discourse and focus students' attention on the topic" (Hyland, 2009, p. 107), or to "set up pedagogical tasks" (Lee & Subtirelu, 2015, p. 16). Following addressee-oriented mentions, questions and directives rank second and third respectively in realising engagement markers. In the following sections, these three types of pragmatic functions in the ET and CT sub-corpora will be investigated in detail.

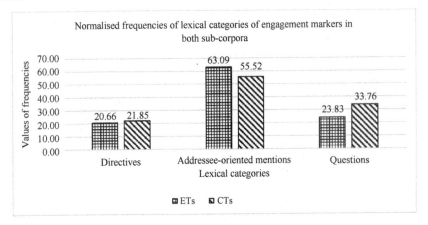

Figure 6.14　Normalised frequencies of lexical categories of engagement markers in both sub-corpora

6.3.4.2　Directives

Directives mainly refer to those speech acts that express the addresser's desire or wish to get the addressee(s) to do something. According to Huang (2009), paradigmatic cases of directives include advice, commands, orders and requests. By using directives, the addresser attempts to elicit some potential actions from the addressee, thus making the world match the word. In other words, the addresser's directive speech may lead to certain actions on the part of the addressee(s) in the real world. In his research into written academic discourse, Hyland (2005) views directives as engagement markers to indicate the writer's intention to guide the reader to perform an action or to understand things in certain ways. Similarly, in spoken academic speech, especially in the classroom instructional context, directives are usually adopted by teachers to express their requirement of students, such as to ask students to achieve certain tasks successfully or answer certain questions. Based on previous research into directives used as engagement markers (Hyland, 2005; Yan, 2010), and other researchers' list of potential directive devices (e.g. Huang, 2009), the present research identifies the potential directives that encompass mainly imperative verbs or verbal phrases to engage students to take some actions such as *Let's* ... and *Listen, listen*.

From the three pragmatic categories, directives are used least often to engage students. However, it has the largest number of lexical types compared with addressee-oriented mentions and questions. As is observed from the data, this is largely due to the extensive use of the lexical verbs. Directives as engagement markers are unanimously realised by verbs or verbal phrases to prompt the students into taking specific actions. Due to the overwhelmingly large amount of directive verbs and verbal phrases in the two sub-corpora, only the top 20 most frequently employed lexical items are selected for a general comparison of the frequency and distribution in the two sub-corpora. Table 6.19 below shows that among the top 20 frequently used directives, 13 lexical items are used by both sub-corpora. Most of these lexical items are widely used by each of the individual teachers. In particular, the lexical items *think*, *(have a) look at*, *let's*, and *see* are among the top four frequently used directives by every teacher in both sub-corpora. See the following Extract 6.15 with a detailed illustration.

Table 6.19 Top 20 frequent lexical items for directives in both sub-corpora

No.	ETs			CTs		
	Lexical items	NmlFrq.	Range	Lexical items	NmlFrq.	Range
1	think	3.23	4	see	3.41	4
2	(have a) look at	2.95	4	let's	3.17	4
3	let's	2.13	4	think	2.68	4
4	see	1.58	4	use	1.84	4
5	do not/don't	1.46	4	try to	1.27	2

continued

No.	ETs			CTs		
	Lexical items	NmlFrq.	Range	Lexical items	NmlFrq.	Range
6	use	1.28	4	do not/don't	0.93	4
7	remember	0.91	4	remember	0.84	4
8	go	0.61	4	(have a) look at	0.60	4
9	have	0.37	3	choose	0.45	3
10	show	0.33	2	follow	0.45	4
11	take	0.33	4	pay attention (to)	0.45	4
12	add	0.30	3	add	0.39	4
13	do	0.30	4	make sure	0.39	2
14	choose	0.27	3	compare	0.27	2
15	agree	0.24	2	give	0.27	1
16	turn	0.24	3	turn	0.27	3
17	make sure	0.24	4	analyse	0.24	2
18	write	0.18	3	select	0.24	2
19	analyse	0.15	1	show	0.24	4
20	evaluate	0.15	2	develop	0.21	2

Extract 6.15 (CT2)

Teacher: OK. Now, after reading, tell me, **what** do **you think** ↑?

Students: (inaudible)

Teacher: It's a mess, right ↑? It seems totally out of order. Ok ↑? And it looks that you don't know what the author wants to tell you, right ↑? And, if **we read** a second time, **we** will come to the idea of the purpose of the writing is-, **what** is the purpose of the writing ↑?

Students: Introduce =

Teacher: Yeah, it's a kind of introduction, right ↑? Introduction to a place or the author wants to describe to the reader what this place looks like, right ↑? OK, so, now, **let's think** about this question, OK ↑? If **we** want to describe a place, OK, **what** kind of method can make the description seem logical and clear and not so messy ↑?

In Extract 6.15 above, the background information is that the teacher is instructing the students on how to write a paragraph in a reasonable order, such as in an emphatic order or chronological order. At present, they are dealing with some exercises on identifying the organisational patterns of some sample paragraphs. After reading one sample paragraph from the student textbook, the teacher attempts to encourage the students to reflect on and elicit their opinions on the organisation of the paragraph. This is achieved by using the action verb *think* following the typical engagement pronoun *you* being integrated into one *wh*-question sentence introduced by the question marker *what*. As is observed from the data, this co-occurrence of the second person pronoun *you* and the action verb *think* is rather commonly used to actively involve students in specific pedagogical tasks. Later, after identifying that the sample sentence is problematic by saying "it seems totally out of order", the teacher uses another co-occurrence of engagement markers, inclusive-*we* and the directive action word *read*, to involve students into further action on the paragraph. She also makes explicit the purpose of this further action by using another *wh*-question sentence introduced by *what*. After solving this question, the teacher tries to engage the students in reflecting on one more in-depth question by using the imperative verbal phrase *let's* plus the action verb *think*. This is followed by a hypothetical condition and another question. From this example, it can be seen that the teacher frequently uses a variety of engagement devices to keep the students on track in the classroom. In addition, the frequent use of inclusive-*we* contributes to building a rapport with the students and to motivating them into better involvement which will be further mapped out in the following sections.

6.3.4.3 Addressee-oriented mentions

Comparatively speaking, addressee-oriented mentions account for the highest frequencies among the three categories that constitute the engagement markers in both ET and CT sub-corpora. Table 6.20 below presents the frequencies, types and ranges of addressee-oriented mentions in the two sub-corpora. It can be seen that teachers in ET sub-corpus use significantly more addressee-oriented mentions as engagement markers than those in the CT sub-corpus at $p<0.0001$ level. In terms of the lexical types of addressee-oriented mentions, teachers in the ET sub-corpus use 14 types, while those in the CT sub-corpus use altogether 10 types. As for the ranges of lexical items in this pragmatic category, the second person pronoun *you* is employed with the highest frequency and by all the eight teachers in both sub-corpora, which leads to the higher frequency of address-oriented mentions than the other two pragmatic categories. This corresponds with previous research in the features of classroom discourse (e. g. Hyland, 2009; Lee & Subtirelu, 2015). In addition to *you*, other lexical items such as the inclusive-*we*, and their respective adjective possessive pronouns *your* and *our* are also used extensively by each of the individual teachers in both sub-corpora.

Table 6.20 Summary of addressee-oriented pronouns in both sub-corpora

No.	Lexical items	ETs			CTs			Log-likelihood value*
		RawFrq.	NmlFrq.	Ranges	RawFrq.	NmlFrq.	Ranges	
1	you	1,286	39.14	4	1,148	34.60	4	9.20**
2	we (inclusive)	330	10.04	4	436	13.14	4	-13.72***
3	your	261	7.94	4	191	5.76	4	11.56****
4	student name	142	4.32	4	1	0.03	1	187.67****
5	anybody	12	0.37	2	0		0	16.75****
6	our (inclusive)	11	0.33	4	41	1.24	4	-18.14****
7	anyone/any one	8	0.24	3	0			11.17***
8	some (of you)	8	0.24	3	1	0.03	1	6.26*
9	us (inclusive)	5	0.15	2	16	0.48	3	-5.95*
10	yours	3	0.09	2	0			4.19*
11	yourself	3	0.09	1	5	0.15	2	-0.49
12	ourselves	2	0.06	2	0			2.79
13	yourselves	1	0.03	1	1	0.03	1	0.00
14	some students	1	0.03	1	2	0.06	1	-0.33
	Total	2,073	63.07		1,842	55.52		15.93****

Note: * = significant at $p<0.05$ level; ** = significant at $p<0.01$ level; *** = significant at $p<0.001$ level; **** = significant at $p<0.0001$ level.

One thing that merits our attention is the lexical item of direct nomination of students by name. This item is rather frequently used in the ET sub-corpus, but very rare in the CT sub-corpus. To be exact, only one instance occurs in the CT sub-corpus, and it is used to group the students to perform a classroom task, as is shown in Extract 6.16 below to perform a classroom task, rather than eliciting answers from the student, as is often the case in the ET sub-corpus. This may reflect the fact that EAP teachers in the ET sub-corpus prefer direct involvement of individual students in the on-site pedagogical tasks in the class.

Extract 6.16 （CT1）

Teacher: But, still, I think, another point, you should pay attention to, is that, you have to think about what is your focus ... you want to focus on the positive side or the negative side, or the one over the other ↑? Right ↑? That means, um, for example, um, **Gao Yang** ((student name)), in your group. You are discussing this topic just now. Then if you are going to write a paragraph like this, you want to say, um, the similarities or the differences of the two ↑?

6.3.4.4 Questions

Next to addressee-oriented mentions, questions are the second most frequently employed category among the three devices for realising engagement markers. Specifically, questions as engagement markers fall into three subcategories: *wh*-question, *tag* question and *yes/no* question. Table 6.21 below evinces the frequencies, types and ranges of questions used in the two sub-corpora. Regarding frequencies, teachers in the ET sub-corpus use significantly less questions than those in CT sub-corpus at $p<0.0001$ level. In terms of frequencies of the three subcategories of questions, teachers in the ET sub-corpus use *wh*-questions most frequently, followed by *yes/no* questions and *tag* questions. Alternatively, teachers in the CT sub-corpus employ *tag* question with the highest frequency, followed by *wh*-questions and *yes/no* questions. In relation to types, teachers in the ET sub-corpus use more types of lexical categories (27) than those in the CT sub-corpus (13). It is obvious that the former group of teachers employ more types of *tag* question than the latter. As for ranges of lexical items, the relatively more frequent marker *what* and *how* are used to introduce *wh*-questions by all the eight teachers in both sub-corpora. Within *tag* questions, *all right* ↑ and *okay/OK* ↑ are used by each individual teacher in both sub-corpora. However, this pragmatic category is also characterised by the vast amount of other types of *tag* questions occurring exclusively in the ET sub-corpus. Finally, the two types of *yes/no* questions, those introduced by auxiliary verbs and those in a statement form but with rising tone, are both extensively used by all teachers in both sub-corpora. Extract 6.17 below provides an illustration of functional category.

Table 6.21 Summary of questions for engagement markers in both sub-corpora

Subcategory	Lexical item	ETs			CTs			Log-likelihood value
		RawFrq.	NmlFrq.	Range	RawFrq.	NmlFrq.	Range	
wh-question	what	194	5.90	4	218	6.57	4	-1.18
	why	20	0.61	4	38	1.15	3	-5.51*
	how	35	1.07	4	60	1.81	4	-6.42*
	who	9	0.27	3	7	0.21	3	0.27
	where	7	0.21	2	3	0.09	2	1.68
	which	21	0.64	4	12	0.36	3	2.57
	how many	2	0.06	2	8	0.24	3	-3.80
	how much	1	0.03	1	0	0.00	0	1.40
	when	0	0.00	0	0	0.00	0	0.00
	whose	1	0.03	2	0	0.00	0	1.40
	Total	290	8.82		346	10.43		-4.42*
tag question	doesn't it ↑	4	0.12	2	0	0.00	0	5.58*
	does it ↑	1	0.03	1	0	0.00	0	1.40
	is it ↑	2	0.06	1	0	0.00	0	2.79
	isn't it ↑	13	0.40	2	0	0.00	0	18.15****
	was it? ↑	1	0.03	1	0	0.00	0	1.40
	wasn't it ↑	2	0.06	1	0	0.00	0	2.79

continued

Subcategory	Lexical item	ETs			CTs			Log-likelihood value
		RawFrq.	NmlFrq.	Range	RawFrq.	NmlFrq.	Range	
	don't you ↑	1	0.03	1	0	0.00	0	1.40
	don't we ↑	1	0.03	1	0	0.00	0	1.40
	shall we ↑	1	0.03	1	0	0.00	0	1.40
	didn't you ↑	2	0.06	2	0	0.00	0	2.79
	aren't they ↑	2	0.06	1	0	0.00	0	2.79
	aren't you ↑	2	0.06	2	0	0.00	0	2.79
	(all) right ↑	32	0.97	4	408	12.30	4	−377.03****
	okay ↑/OK ↑	125	3.80	4	241	7.26	4	−36.31****
	yeah ↑	24	0.73	4	3	0.09	2	18.79****
	yes ↑	10	0.30	3	7	0.21	3	0.56
	Total	223	6.77		659	19.86		−221.16****
yes/no question	auxiliary verbs ↑	188	5.72	4	72	2.17	4	54.74****
	statement ↑	82	2.50	4	43	1.30	4	12.75***
	Total	270	8.22		115	3.47		65.7****
	Total	783	23.81		1,120	33.76		−56.82****

Note: * = significant at $p < 0.05$ level; ** = significant at $p < 0.01$ level; *** = significant at $p < 0.001$ level; **** = significant at $p < 0.0001$ level.

Extract 6.17　（CT4）

Teacher: ... so starting from Sentence One down to Sentence Six, all these sentences are arranged according to a time order, **all right** ↑ ? These are all supporting details to do **what**, to support an idea, > **what** is the idea, **what** is the controlling idea, **what** is with the topic sentence, **what** it is to support the topic sentence < , **can** you generate the topic sentence ↑ ? It seems that the topic is very much relying on mother, and anything related with child is related with mother, the language, **all right** ↑ ? The voice, **right** ↑ ? The words, that the child utters, then we could see, there is a very CLOSE relationship that must be inside here, in the topic sentence, a cause relationship between **WHO** ↑ ?

In Extract 6.17 above, the teacher is leading the students to do an exercise on the organisation of a sample paragraph, including the order of sentences, the topic sentence and supporting sentences. The teacher makes frequent use of various questioning strategies to engage the students in pedagogical tasks. At the beginning, by using *all right* ↑ , the teacher attempts to seek students' agreement on her judgment of sentence order. Then, she engages students in thinking about answers to the following questions by using the interrogative marker *what* five times. Although the teacher poses these questions to the students, she provides her answers immediately. It implies that the teacher does not really want the students to answer her question, but to arouse their attention to think about these questions. Following these eliciting questions, the teacher gives the answer and uses another two confirmation seeking markers, *all right* ↑ and *right* ↑ . Finally, she raises another question concerning the content of the sample paragraph by using the interrogative word *who* ↑ , which has a similar function to her above utterances.

6.3.5 Self-mentions

This section is intended to present the frequency and distribution of self-mentions in the two sub-corpora. As one important component of metadiscourse markers, self-mentions represent the explicit presence of the addresser. It is arguably the most powerful means of displaying personal projection or authorial identity (Hyland, 2001; Ivanic, 1998). Within the interactional metadiscourse category, self-mentions are the fourth most frequent category in both sub-corpora. Notably, self-mention markers are realised by merely one type of lexical category, namely pronoun, including the first person pronouns *I* and *we*, their accusative forms, adjectival forms and nominal forms. As with other cases above, self-mentions are also examined in terms of their constituting lexical categories. The linguistic realisations and their coding examples are shown in Table 6.22 below.

Table 6.22 Linguistic realisations of self-mentions

MD markers		Linguistic realisations	Examples with codes*
Interactional MD	Self-mentions	Pronouns	I < Spron >
			we < Spron >
			me < Spron >
			my < Spron >
			mine < Spron >

Note: metadiscourse markers are coded and annotated based on the initials of metadiscourse subcategory followed by abbreviations of word class and sentence type. For example, *I < Spron >* means that the metadiscourse marker *I* belongs to self-mentions and it is a pronoun in terms of lexical category.

As noted above, self-mentions merely involve one type of lexical category, that is, pronouns, together with their accusative forms, adjectival possessive forms and nominal possessive forms. Therefore, this section will not report the frequency and distribution of metadiscourse markers in terms of their lexical categories, but only explore these features in terms of each of the two sub-corpora as a whole and the individual teachers in each sub-corpus.

Table 6.23 below gives us a birds-eye view of the overall landscape of the frequencies, types and ranges of self-mentions by teachers in the ET and CT sub-corpora. Overall, teachers in the ET sub-corpus employ significantly more self-mentions than their counterparts in the CT sub-corpus do at $p < 0.0001$ level. As for types, five types of lexical items are used by teachers in the ETs, compared with four types by those in the CT sub-corpus. As for ranges, the first and second most frequent lexical items, *I* and its accusative case *me*, are used by all the eight teachers in both sub-corpora. It is interesting to note that six instances of *we* in the ET sub-corpus are used to refer to the teacher herself, instead of the commonly used reference of *we* inclusive of the students. Consider Extract 6.18 below for an illustration of its usage.

Table 6.23 Summary of self-mentions in both sub-corpora

No.	Lexical items	ETs			CTs			Log-likelihood value
		RawFrq.	NmlFrq.	Ranges	RawFrq.	NmlFrq.	Ranges	
1	I	472	14.36	4	151	4.55	4	176.70 ****
2	me	46	1.40	4	24	0.72	4	7.24 **
3	my	17	0.52	2	10	0.30	3	1.90
4	mine	2	0.06	2	1	0.03	1	0.35
5	we	6	0.18	1	0	0.00	0	8.38 **
	Total	543	16.52		186	5.60		186.01 ****

Note: * = significant at $p < 0.05$ level; ** = significant at $p < 0.01$ level; *** = significant at $p < 0.001$ level; **** = significant at $p < 0.0001$ level.

Extract 6.18 (ET3)

Teacher: ... A pie chart or a bar chart is more suitable for comparing and contrasting than, um, than a table would be. So, there is, there is only one more, which I think is in the wrong place. Can anybody spot it ↑?

Student: (the last one ↑ the table may not be so appropriate to describe relationships)

Teacher: Really ↑? Oh, £££ **we, we** thought it was OK, actually.

In Extract 6.18 above, the teacher is doing an exercise together with the students. The exercise is about a graphics use checklist table. There are two columns in the table. The left hand side is the purpose, while the right hand side is the suggested types of graphics used for the corresponding purpose on its left hand side. Two of the suggested types of graphics in the table would not be very suitable for the purpose. The students' task is to spot these two types of graphics. The teacher and the students have already found the first type, and now the teacher is asking the students whether they can spot the second one. Based on the teacher's eliciting question, one student provides an answer by saying "the last one ↑ the table may not be so appropriate to describe relationships". In response to this student's contribution, the teacher negates the student's answer by acknowledging the appropriateness of the graphic type use of table for the correspondent purpose. This is realised by the utterance "Really ↑? Oh, £££ we, we thought it was OK, actually". In this feedback, the teacher uses *we* which is generally used to refer to the teacher and the students in the classroom instructional context, rather than the common expression of *I* to refer to the teacher herself. It would also be possible for the teacher to use this expression *we* to refer to the EAP teacher group. By doing so, she may imply this is the whole teacher groups' opinion, rather than her own. Thus, she may improve the authority or reliability of the opinion, decrease personal responsibility and soften the outcome of possible objections.

In short, the above analysis has demonstrated that teachers in the ET sub-corpus use significantly more self-mentions than those in the CT sub-corpus do at $p < 0.0001$ level. Furthermore, each teacher in the ET sub-corpus also uses self-mentions with a higher frequency than every other teacher in the CT sub-corpus does. With regard to lexical types, five types occur in the ET sub-corpus, but four types in the CT sub-corpus. In terms of ranges, *I* and *me* are pervasively used by each teacher in both sub-corpora. However, the frequencies of these two items used by teachers in ET sub-corpus are higher than those in CT sub-corpus. This finding corresponds with previous research (Hyland, 2005; Ohta, 1991; Scollon, 1994) on written academic discourse, which claims that compared with their Western counterparts, Asian writers tend to avoid self-mentions, in particular the singular form *I*, in showing their identities or viewpoints. Another thing that merits our attention concerning the individual lexical items is the use of *we* to refer to the teacher or teacher groups in the classroom instructional context in the ET sub-corpus.

6.4 Interactive metadiscourse markers in both ET and CT sub-corpora

Generally speaking, interactional metadiscourse refers to the addresser's interaction with the addressee(s), while interactive metadiscourse serves to guide the addressee(s) through the interaction. In the specific context of classroom instructions, interactional metadiscourse relates to the teacher's interaction with the students, whereas interactive metadiscourse serves to guide the students through the classroom teaching and learning process. As made explicit in previous sections, there are altogether four categories of interactional metadiscourse markers, namely transitions, frame markers, endophoric markers and code glosses. The following section will examine the frequency and distribution of these interactive metadiscourse markers used by teachers in the two sub-corpora, and accordingly identify the relatively frequently used metadiscourse categories in the two sub-corpora.

6.4.1 Transitions

This section investigates the frequency and distribution of transition markers in both ET and CT sub-corpora. Transition markers mainly refer to conjunctions or adverbial phrases that assist the addressees to better understand pragmatic connections between steps in an argument. Similar to engagement markers above and frame markers below, the linguistic realisations of transitions are examined in terms of the pragmatic functions in which they are embedded. Specifically, following Hyland (2005), transitions in the current study consist of three pragmatic functions, namely additions, comparisons and consequences. An analysis of the data reveals that the linguistic realisations of transitions are generally represented by the lexical category of conjunctions and multiword expressions. The pragmatic functions of transition markers, and the respective lexical categories realising these functions, together with their coding examples, are illustrated by Table 6.24 below.

Table 6.24 Linguistic realisations of transition markers

MD markers		Linguistic realisations	Examples with codes*
Interactive MD	Transitions	Additions	And < Tconj >
		Comparisons	But < Tconj >
		Consequences	As a result < Tconj >

* Note: metadiscourse markers are coded and annotated based on the initials of metadiscourse subcategory followed by abbreviations of word class and sentence type. For example, *actually* < Badv > means that the metadiscourse marker *actually* belongs booster and it is an adverb in terms of lexical category.

The following section presents the overall result of transitions employed by teachers in the ET and CT sub-corpora. In light of the first research question that relates to the frequency and distribution of metadiscourse use across the two groups of teachers, this section will present the results of transitions from two perspectives. One aspect focuses on the frequency and distribution of transitions employed by individual teachers within each of the two sub-corpora in particular and by the individual groups of teachers from both sub-corpora in general. The other aspect concerns the frequency and distribution of transitions in terms of individual lexical categories. Figure 6.15 below illustrates the overall landscape of the normalised frequency and distribution of the specific pragmatic functions which make up the transitions employed by individual teachers in both the ET and CT sub-corpora.

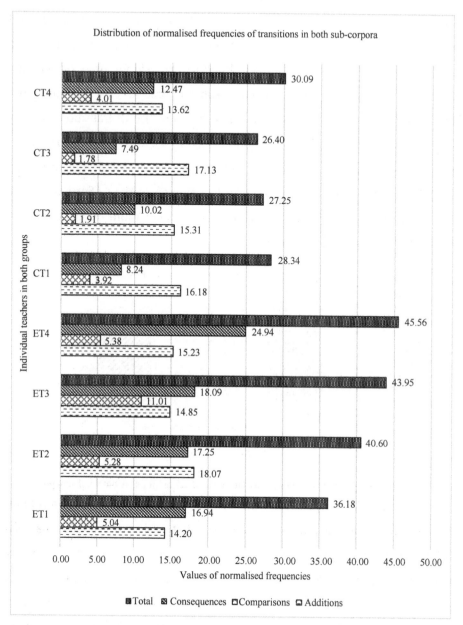

Figure 6.15 Distribution of normalised frequencies of transitions in both sub-corpora

Overall, Figure 6.15 above manifests that each of the four teachers in the ET sub-corpus uses transitions in higher frequencies than any of the individual teachers in the CT sub-corpus do. This may reflect the EAP teachers' perception of the greater need to guide their L2 students, who are in their preliminary stage of entering into the UK, in setting up and reviewing academic tasks (Lee & Subtirelu, 2015). Figure 6.16 below demonstrates the frequency and distribution of transitions used by the two groups of teachers in their respective sub-corpora. It can be found that teachers in the ET sub-corpus make more frequent use of transition markers than their counterparts in the CT sub-corpus do (41.90 ptw versus 28.18 ptw). This is similar to some of the above interactional metadiscourse categories, such as hedges (Section 6.3.1), attitude markers (Section 6.3.3) and self-mentions (Section 6.3.5), which all occur more frequently in the ET sub-corpus than the CT sub-corpus.

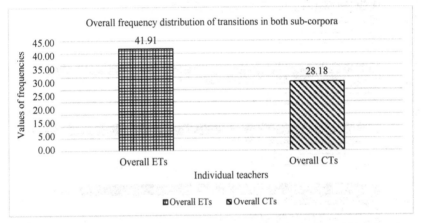

Figure 6.16 Overall frequency distribution of transitions in both sub-corpora

Figure 6.17 below indicates the frequency and distribution of transitions in terms of the three pragmatic functions that realise transitions, namely *additions*, *comparisons* and *consequences*. It can be found that teachers in both sub-corpora overall employ higher frequencies of additions and consequences but a lower frequency of comparisons. Specifically, teachers in the ET and CT sub-corpora employ additions with relatively similar frequencies (15.64 ptw versus 15.43 ptw). As for the pragmatic function of comparisons, they are used with a higher frequency by teachers in the ET sub-corpus than those in the CT sub-corpus (7.03 ptw versus 3.04 ptw). Comparisons are the least frequently used pragmatic function in both sub-corpora. Additionally, teachers in the ET sub-corpus use consequences more frequently than their counterparts in the CT sub-corpus do (19.23 ptw versus 9.71 ptw). In other words, teachers in the ET sub-corpus use consequences with the highest frequency, followed by additions and comparisons. On the other hand, teachers in the CT sub-corpus employ additions with the highest frequency, followed by consequences and comparisons.

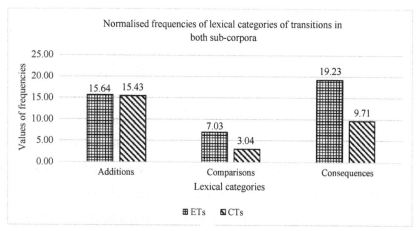

Figure 6.17　Normalised frequencies of lexical categories of transitions in both sub-corpora

Specifically, in relation to frequencies, Table 6.25 below indicates that teachers in the ET sub-corpus make significantly more frequent use of total transition markers, along with comparisons and consequences than those in the CT sub-corpus do at a $p < 0.0001$ level. Nevertheless, no significant difference of addition use is observed between teachers in the two sub-corpora. This may support Lee and Subtirelu (2015) in that EAP teachers in the UK are more concerned with guiding their L2 students, who are at their preliminary stage of entering into the UK, in setting up and reviewing academic tasks.

Regarding the use of transition markers, teachers in the ET sub-corpus use consequences with the highest frequency, whereas those in the CT sub-corpus employ additions most frequently. Comparative transition is the least frequently used pragmatic category in both sub-corpora.

Table 6.25 Comparison of the lexical categories of transitions in both sub-corpora

Lexical categories	ETs		CTs		Log-likelihood Value*
	RawFrq.	NmlFrq.	RawFrq.	NmlFrq.	
Additions	514	15.64	512	15.43	0.05
Comparisons	231	7.03	101	3.04	53.54****
Consequences	632	19.23	322	9.71	105.57****
Total	1,377	41.90	935	28.18	89.29****

Note: * = significant at $p<0.05$ level; ** = significant at $p<0.01$ level; *** = significant at $p<0.001$ level; **** = significant at $p<0.0001$ level.

With regard to lexical types, teachers in the ET sub-corpus use six types of additions compared with eight types in the CT sub-corpus. Two instances, *at the same* and *besides*, realised by each teacher of the CT sub-corpus, have no occurrence in the ET sub-corpus. However, eleven types of comparisons appear in the ET sub-corpus, while merely three types in the CT sub-corpus. Apart from the shared instances of *but*, *although* and *however*, teachers in the ET sub-corpus also use occasionally *rather than*, *yet*, *even if/though*, *whereas*, *on the other hand*, *thought*, and *while*. As for consequences, both groups of teachers use the same number of six types. Overall, teachers in the ET sub-corpus use 23 types of transitions, as opposed to 17 types in CT sub-corpus. This may again evidence previous research (Friginal et al., 2017) that native English-speaking EAP teachers in the UK have a broader linguistic repertoire than the non-native English-speaking EAP teachers in China do.

In terms of ranges, teachers in both sub-corpora also share considerable similarities in their use of lexical items with relatively wider ranges. In the first place, two lexical items *and* and *also* are used by every teacher in both sub-corpora to act as additive transitional devices, with much higher frequencies compared with other lexical items. Second, each teacher in both sub-corpora employ *but* with comparatively higher frequencies to show comparative relations between two clauses. Third, *so* and *because* are two most frequently and widely used lexical items to indicate consequences by every teacher in both sub-corpora. Overall, both groups of teachers make greater use of transitions markers such as *and*, *but* and *so* respectively to display the additive, comparative and consequential transitions between discourse segments.

In effect, previous research also found that *and* is so prevalent that it is sometimes left out from rhetorical analysis but being regarded as the default option of "marking conjunctive relations" of addition (Hyland & Jiang, 2018, p. 21). The current research may develop this view and demonstrate that *but* and *so* can be the default options of expressing comparative and consequential relations in academic speech contexts. In addition, such considerable similarities in using certain metadiscourse markers across teachers from different cultural and pedagogical backgrounds may be due to the common genre they share. In other words, they all belong to spoken academic discourse, taking place in the classroom instructional contexts. This may evidence once again the argument that the genre constraints of academic spoken discourse may contribute to the common characteristics shared by teachers from different cultural and pedagogical backgrounds (Lee, 2016).

6.4.2 Frame markers

This section seeks to explore the frequency and distribution of frame markers in both ET and CT sub-corpora. Frame markers are generally used to mark text boundaries or elements of schematic text structure. In a similar way to engagement markers and transitions above, the linguistic realisations of transitions are examined in terms of the pragmatic functions in which they are embedded. Based on Hyland (2005), frame markers in the current research can be divided into four pragmatic functions. Specifically, they can be used to sequence parts of a text and act as more explicit additive relations, such as *first*, *then*, and *next*. They can explicitly label text stages, such as *to summarise* and *in sum*. They can announce discourse goals, as in *my purpose is* and *I want to*. Moreover, they can signal topic shifts, for example by using *well*, *right*, and *now*. The pragmatic functions of frame markers, the lexical categories realising these functions, and their corresponding coding examples can be illustrated by Table 6.26 below.

Table 6.26 Linguistic realisations of frame markers

MD markers		Linguistic realisations	Examples with codes*
Interactive MD	Frame markers	Sequencing	First < Fnum >
		Labelling stage	Overall < Fadv >
		Announcing goal	Want < Fverb >
		Shifting topic	So < Fconj >

* Note: metadiscourse markers are coded and annotated based on the initials of metadiscourse subcategory followed by abbreviations of word class and sentence type. For example, *actually* < Badv > means that the metadiscourse marker *actually* belongs booster and it is an adverb in terms of lexical category.

There are some clarifications worth mentioning, in particular with reference to some lexical items that can be explicitly used with multiple metadiscourse functions in the current research. For example, the lexical items *so* can be used as a booster, transition marker, or frame marker. Firstly, it is deemed to be a booster when it emphasises the strong degree of something by mentioning the result or consequence of it. The first instance of *so* in Extract 6.19 below is a booster to modify the degree of effectiveness in explaining the topic the teacher is talking about. Secondly, it is classified as a transition marker when it is used in a sentence to introduce a reason or result for doing the thing mentioned. The second and third instances of *so* in Extract 6.19 below are transition markers to explain the reason why the author adopts a comparison and contrast method. Thirdly, it is regarded as a frame marker when it introduces a new topic, a question or comment about something that has been said. For instance, the occurrence of *so* in Extract 6.20 below, used at the very beginning of a lesson, is a frame marker to introduce a new topic.

Extract 6.19 (CT1)

Teacher: No, yeah, you may give some examples, but still, you may feel it's not *so* effective to explain this topic. *So* the author adopts comparison and contrast. This method, right ↑ *so*, he or she tries to compare the atmosphere of the earth to the window, because the window is something we are very familiar with in our life, right ↑ ?

Extract 6.20 (ET2)

Teacher: Okay, *so*, today, the timetable says we maybe could have a scenario, but I am not going to do that.

The following part reports the overall result of frame markers employed by teachers in the ET and CT sub-corpora. Following the same line of inquiry as the above metadiscourse categories, this section will report the results in terms of two perspectives. The first perspective focuses on the frequency and distribution of frame markers in terms of the overall group of teachers in ET and CT sub-corpora and individual teachers in each of the two sub-corpora respectively. The second perspective deals with the frequency and distribution of frame markers in terms of pragmatic categories of their linguistic realisations. Figure 6.18 below presents an overall landscape of the normalised frequency and distribution of the pragmatic categories used by each teacher in both of the ET and CT sub-corpora.

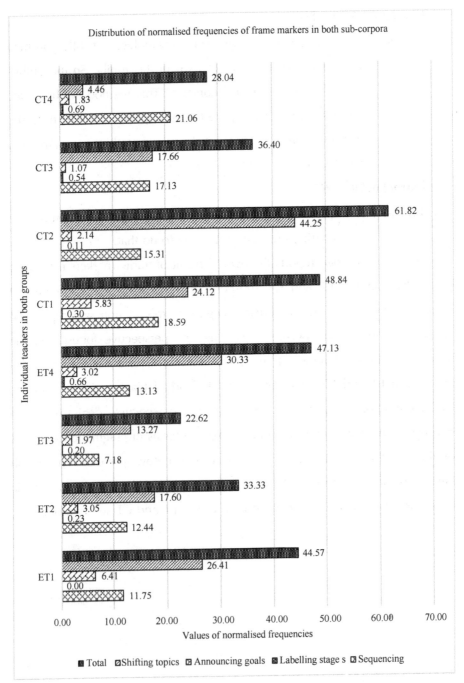

Figure 6.18 Distribution of normalised frequencies of frame markers in both sub-corpora

Figure 6.18 above demonstrates that in terms of individual teachers, two teachers in the CT sub-corpus employ higher frequencies of frame markers than those teachers in the ET sub-corpus do. They are CT2 and CT1, with 61.82 and 48.84 instances per thousand words respectively. However, two other teachers in the CT sub-corpus, CT3 (36.4 ptw) and CT4 (28.04 ptw) use frame markers with lower frequencies than ET4 (47.13 ptw) and ET1 (44.57 ptw). This reveals the complexity of the frequency and distribution of frame markers in the two sub-corpora. Although all teachers in the ET sub-corpus use a higher frequency of frame markers than those in the CT sub-corpus, the results might also vary due to the individual differences of specific teachers. Figure 6.19 below indicates the frequency and distribution of frame markers in terms of all the individual teachers in both sub-corpora. Overall, teachers in the CT sub-corpus employ a higher frequency of frame markers (44.73 ptw) than those in the ET sub-corpus do (35.45 ptw).

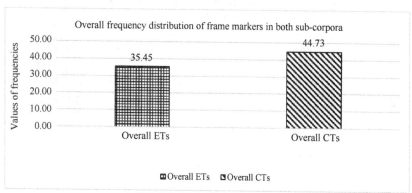

Figure 6.19 Overall frequency distribution of frame markers in both sub-corpora

Figure 6.20 below displays the frequency and distribution of frame markers in terms of their pragmatic categories. It can be seen that the frequency and distribution of the pragmatic categories employed by the two groups of teachers present similar patterns. First, teachers in the ET and CT sub-corpora employ shifting topics with the highest frequencies, followed by sequencing and announcing goals successively. Accordingly, labelling stages is the least frequently used pragmatic function in both sub-corpora. This analysis indicates that both groups of EAP teachers in the UK and China rely heavily on shifting topics in the lesson flow. They use these frame markers to introduce pedagogical tasks for the students. Moreover, they also make use of sequencing devices to outline specific task procedures. In addition, the very low frequencies of labelling stages may suggest that there is not much need for teachers to signpost stages of classroom teaching. This overall distribution pattern is in line with the finding of Yan (2010), who examined the four pragmatic categories of frame markers used in classroom teaching context by non-native English-speaking English teachers in China, and claimed that frame markers for labelling stages might not be a characteristic of spoken language, in particular face-to-face communication. In the following four subsections, the four pragmatic categories realising frame markers will be spelled out.

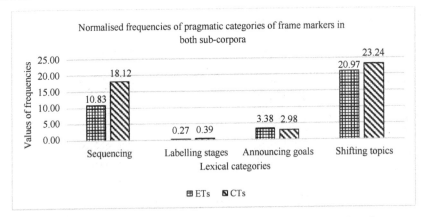

Figure 6.20 Normalised frequencies of pragmatic categories of frame markers in both sub-corpora

To be specific, in terms of frequencies, Table 6.27 below reveals that teachers in the ET sub-corpus employ significantly less frame markers than those in the CT sub-corpus do at a $p < 0.0001$ level. Three of the four pragmatic functional categories, that is, sequencing, labelling stages and shifting topics, also exhibit lower frequencies in the ET sub-corpus than those in the CT sub-corpus. It can be noticed that teachers in the ET sub-corpus use significantly less frequent of sequencing than those in the CT sub-corpus do at $p < 0.0001$ level. Additionally, teachers in the ET sub-corpus use significantly less frequently shifting topics than those in the CT sub-corpus at $p<0.05$ level. However, there are no significant differences across the two groups of teachers in terms of labelling stages and announcing goals. Despite these differences, the frequency and distribution of these four pragmatic categories present a similar pattern across both groups of teachers. Specifically, teachers in both sub-corpora make the most frequent use of shifting topic markers, followed by sequencing, announcing goals and then labelling stages.

Table 6.27 Comparison of the lexical categories of frame markers in both sub-corpora

Lexical categories	ETs		CTs		Log-likelihood Value*
	RawFrq.	NmlFrq.	RawFrq.	NmlFrq.	
Sequencing	356	10.83	601	18.12	-61.11****
Labelling stages	9	0.27	13	0.39	-0.69
Announcing goals	111	3.38	99	2.98	0.81
Shifting topics	689	20.97	771	23.24	-3.86*
Total	1,165	35.45	1,484	44.73	-35.53****

Note: * = significant at $p<0.05$ level; ** = significant at $p<0.01$ level; *** = significant at $p<0.001$ level; **** = significant at $p<0.0001$ level.

In terms of the types of linguistic expressions, both groups of teachers use 36 types in total. Among these various types, 28 types are used by teachers in the ET sub-corpus, whereas 29 types are used by teachers in the CT sub-corpus. Comparatively, teachers in the ET sub-corpus use fewer types of sequencing (ten types by ETs and eleven types by CTs) and labelling stages (four types by ETs and six types by CTs) than those in the CT sub-corpus. On the other hand, teachers in the ET sub-corpus use more types of announcing goals (five types by ETs and four types by CTs) and shifting topics (nine types by ETs and eight types by CTs) than those in the CT sub-corpus. Additionally, one prominent feature was noticed from the shifting topic category is that those two linguistic expressions, *right* and *well*, which are frequently used by teachers in the ET sub-corpus, have very few and even no instances in the CT sub-corpus.

In relation to ranges, teachers in both sub-corpora exhibit considerable similarities. First, every one of the individual teachers in both sub-corpora use *then*, *first*, *second* and *last* as sequencing markers. In each sub-corpus, *then* and *first* are prominently frequent than other lexical items. Second, all of them also employ the linguistic expression *want to* as the most frequent item as announce goal markers. Third, all individual teachers in both sub-corpora use *okay*, *so* and *now* as shifting topic markers, in particular the first two items are extremely more frequent in both sub-corpora. As noted above, these similarities in the use of some frame markers across teachers from different cultural and pedagogical backgrounds may be due to the common genre they share, that is, spoken academic discourse in the classroom instructional contexts. This may further support the argument made in the analyses of hedges and boosters that the genre constraints of academic spoken discourse may contribute to the common features shared by teachers from different cultural and pedagogical backgrounds (Lee 2016).

6.4.3 Endophoric markers

This section sets out to examine the frequency and distribution of endophoric markers in both ET and CT sub-corpora. Endophoric markers are generally linguistic expressions which refer to other places (e.g. *Section X. X*) or time points (e.g. *just now*) of the classroom discourse. First, this metadiscourse category helps to reiterate the addresser's intentions by referring to previous information given to the addressees (e.g. *X earlier*). Second, endophoric markers may also support the addresser's proposition by anticipating something yet to come (e.g. *X later*). Among the four interactive categories, endophoric markers are used with the least frequency by both groups of teachers in the two sub-corpora. A perusal of the data reveals that endophoric markers are realised by three types of lexical category, that is, nouns, adverbs and multiword expressions. However, due to the relatively few instances of endophoric markers, each lexical category will not be examined on its own, as is the case with those of hedges, boosters and attitude markers. Alternatively, endophoric markers in the current research will be investigated with a "lumping" approach (see Ädel, 2010). The overall linguistic realisation and pertinent coding examples are shown in Table 6.28 below.

Table 6.28　Linguistic realisations of endophoric markers

MD markers		Linguistic realisations	Examples with codes*
Interactive MD	Endophoric markers	Nouns	Page < Endnoun >
		Adverbs	X before < Engadv >
		Multi-word expressions	That part < Endmwe >

* The symbol is in the form of initial letter of each category followed by the abbreviation of word class or sentence type. To avoid ambiguity, special forms "Eng" and "End" are used to stand for engagement markers and endophoric markers respectively.

Table 6.29 below illustrates the overall frequency, types and ranges of individual endophoric markers used by teachers in the ET and CT sub-corpora. First of all, the overall frequency of endophoric markers employed by teachers in the ET sub-corpus is less than those teachers in the CT sub-corpus. The log-likelihood value indicates that teachers in the ET sub-corpus use significantly less endophoric markers than their counterparts in the CT sub-corpus at $p<0.05$ level. Both groups of teachers use ten types of endophoric markers. Concerning the ranges of individual lexical items, no instances of endophoric markers are used by all of the individual teachers across the two sub-corpora. Among them, the most commonly used lexical item is *class*, being employed by four teachers in the ET sub-corpus and three teachers in the CT sub-corpus. Another lexical item *X before* is also used fairly common, that is, it is used by four teachers in the ET sub-corpus, however, there is only one instance in the CT sub-corpus. Although *Page X* is not the most widely used lexical item, it is used with the highest frequency in both sub-corpora. Consider the following Extracts 6.21 and 6.22 for an illustration of their usage.

Table 6.29 Summary of endophoric markers in both sub-corpora

No.	Lexical items	ETs RawFrq.	ETs NmlFrq.	ETs Ranges	CTs RawFrq.	CTs NmlFrq.	CTs Ranges	Log-likelihood value*
1	Page X	20	0.61	2	32	0.96	3	-2.38
2	class	6	0.18	4	17	0.51	3	-5.38*
3	just now	2	0.06	1	18	0.54	2	-14.57***
4	X before	15	0.46	4	1	0.03	1	14.83***
5	Example X	4	0.12	1	10	0.30	3	-2.6
6	X later	5	0.15	3	3	0.09	3	0.52
7	that part	0	0.00	0	5	0.15	1	-6.88**
8	X earlier	5	0.15	2	0	0.00	0	6.98**
9	Table X	4	0.12	1	0	0.00	0	5.58*
10	this lesson	2	0.06	1	2	0.06	1	0
11	handout	1	0.03	1	3	0.09	1	-1.03
12	textbook	0	0.00	0	1	0.03	1	-1.38
	Total	64	1.94		92	2.76		-4.79*

Note: * = significant at $p<0.05$ level; ** = significant at $p<0.01$ level; *** = significant at $p<0.001$ level; **** = significant at $p<0.0001$ level.

Extract 6.21   (CT3)

Teacher: Um, okay, and then, let's come to a simple brainstorming. If you have your book with you, let's come to **Page** 326, **Page** 326 ... In brainstorming ... you just write whatever occurs to you, and then you group and classify them. OK. Like here, OK, like here, the author Anna, wrote ...twelve sentences about teenagers and jobs, teenagers and jobs. Okay. And then she reviewed and revised her list of points. She identified three main points to develop in her essay. Okay, let's see, um, the second column on **Page** 327, she writes "No time for real involvement in school and school activities. Students leave right out of school ... blablabla", we have a lot of sentences written by her. Right↑?

Extract 6.22 (CT1)

Teacher: Is that okay for everyone ↑? Tuesday one thirty to three thirty.

Student: Yeah.

Teacher: Is that okay ↑? All right, so, I think we can still get the same room through one thirty to three thirty next weeks. Okay, um so, yeah, what I was suggesting is that for you, your homework. If you can have a look at those writings I gave to you *before*, and see if you can apply any of the normalisation and the cohesion, any of the devices that we've looked at so far, and we'll have a look at that next week. Okay, see you then.

In Extract 6.21 above, the teacher intends to have the students do a brainstorming activity. However, she wants to show the student what brainstorm looks like by referring to an example in the textbook. Therefore, she directs the students explicitly to refer to the exact page number by saying the sentence "let's come to Page 326". Then in the following section, she moves to one specific part of the exemplar passage by the expression "Okay, let's see, um, the second column on Page 327". These uses of endophoric markers help students follow the teacher's instruction and facilitate students' understanding. In a similar way, Extract 6.22 above takes place at the time when the teacher approaches the end of the class. After discussing an appropriate time and location for the next class, she moves to the students' homework. For this, she requires the students to apply the writing devices they have dealt with in that class to previous writings she has handed out to the students. The lexical item *before* in the utterance "If you can have a look at those writings I gave to you before" helps to locate the materials the students can work on.

Overall, there is no obvious difference observed between the types of lexical items being used by the two groups of teachers. Endophoric markers are used with the least frequencies by teachers in both sub-corpora (1.94

ptw by ETs versus 2.76 ptw by CTs). This may be due to the nature of real-time classroom interaction which may turn to other types of linguistic expressions, such as deictic marker *here*, or supplementary teaching materials, for example *the slide*. More importantly, this face-to-face communication may allow for paralinguistic expressions, such as gestures of pointing at the board or slides, to guide students through the lessons. In addition, as proposed by Lee and Subtirelu (2015), teachers may not perceive the necessity to make explicit other parts of the classroom teaching to which the students should refer to in a linear type of classroom instruction within a limited time span.

6.4.4 Code glosses

This section reports the frequency and distribution of code glosses employed by teachers in the ET and CT sub-corpora. Code glosses are mainly used to provide supplementary information, by means of rephrasing, explaining or exemplifying what has been said, to ensure that the addressees are able to understand the addresser's intended meaning. Previous studies on this issue use other alternative terms, such as reformation and exemplifications (e.g. Flowerdew, 1992; Hyland, 2009) and note that these linguistic devices are indispensable to classroom instructions. However, they are not as common as is observed from the current research. Next to endophoric markers, code glosses represent the second least frequently used metadiscourse category among the four interactive devices. This relative lower frequency is in line with the findings of Lee and Subtirelu (2015), who report 4.26 instances per thousand words of code glosses in their EAP teachers' classroom discourse. A careful examination of the dataset for the current research reveals that code glosses are mainly realised by three types of linguistic expressions, that is, verbs, adverbs and multiword expressions. However, as is the case with endophoric markers, this section will not examine code glosses in terms of their individual lexical categories,

Chapter 6 A corpus linguistic analysis of metadiscourse use across native and non-native EAP teachers

but spell out their overall usage with a lumping approach. The linguistic realisations of code glosses and their coding examples can be shown in Table 6.30 below.

Table 6.30 Linguistic realisations of code glosses

MD markers		Linguistic realisations	Examples with codes*
Interactive MD	Code glosses	Verbs	Call < Cverb >
		Adverbs	Namely < Cadv >
		Multi-word expressions	For example < Cmwe >

*Note: metadiscourse markers are coded and annotated based on the initials of metadiscourse subcategory followed by abbreviations of word class and sentence type. For example, *actually* < Badv > means that the metadiscourse marker *actually* belongs booster and it is an adverb in terms of lexical category.

Table 6.31 below illustrates the frequencies, types and ranges of individual code gloss markers used by teachers in the ET and CT sub-corpora. First, code glosses occur 7.59 times per thousand words in the ET sub-corpus, compared to 8.64 times per thousand words in the CT sub-corpus. The log-likelihood value (-2.21) indicates that although teachers in the ET sub-corpus employ code glosses with a higher frequency than those in the CT sub-corpus, there is no significant difference in the use of code gloss markers between the two groups of teachers. The second aspect concerns the types of lexical items. It can be seen that teachers in the ET sub-corpus employ fourteen types of code glosses, one type less than those in the CT sub-corpus. Among the sixteen different types of linguistic expressions, two linguistic expressions, *namely* and *which means*, have no occurrences in the ET sub-corpus. On the other hand, no instances of *specifically* are found in the CT sub-corpus. The third aspect relates to the ranges of individual code glosses. It reveals that compared with other interactive metadiscourse categories, more types of lexical items are used widely by individual teachers of the two sub-corpora. Linguistic expressions such as *like, that is, I mean, or, for example, call(ed)* are used extensively by individual teachers in the two sub-corpora. Consider Extracts 6.23 and

6.24 below for an illustration of the usage of code glosses.

Table 6.31　Summary of code glosses in both sub-corpora

No.	Lexical items	ETs			CTs			Log-likelihood value*
		RawFrq.	NmlFrq.	Ranges	RawFrq.	NmlFrq.	Ranges	
1	like	89	2.71	4	101	3.04	4	-0.65
2	that is	32	0.97	4	75	2.26	4	-17.37****
3	I mean	52	1.58	4	13	0.39	3	25.43****
4	or X	18	0.55	4	44	1.33	4	-11
5	for example	16	0.49	4	20	0.60	3	-0.41
6	called	6	0.18	4	10	0.30	4	-0.97
7	call	10	0.30	4	4	0.12	3	2.71
8	that means	5	0.15	2	5	0.15	3	0.00
9	in fact	7	0.21	2	1	0.03	1	5.12*
10	say/let's say/ that is to say	5	0.15	3	2	0.06	2	1.36
11	such as	2	0.06	2	5	0.15	2	-1.30
12	it means	3	0.09	3	3	0.09	2	0.00
13	in other words	4	0.12	2	1	0.03	1	1.96
14	namely	0	0.00	0	2	0.06	1	-2.75
15	specifically	1	0.03	1	0	0.00	0	1.40
16	which means	0	0.00	0	1	0.03	1	-1.38
	Total	250	7.59		287	8.64		-2.21

Note: * = significant at $p < 0.05$ level; ** = significant at $p < 0.01$ level; *** = significant at $p < 0.001$ level; **** = significant at $p < 0.0001$ level.

Extract 6.23　(ET2)

Teacher: You know in Chinese. What's the name of it ↑? Just find that word in English …

Students: Mao ((Chinese way of saying anchor)), anchor.

Teacher: Yes ↑? Anchor. Anchor. An anchor. The topic sentence is **like** an anchor. Think about your shape as the paragraph. And the topic sentence is the anchor. It's the anchor because it stops the ideas floating away and becoming confused …

Extract 6.24 (CT3)

Teacher: ... In the body part, you have already come up with the three ideas. Now, what you need is sufficient supports, plus transitional words. These connecting words are easy, right ↑? ***Like*** first, second, in addition, something like furthermore, something ***like*** that. You are very good at that. And then, conclusion, for the conclusion part, you may use summary plus final thought, summary plus recommendation, or you can give quest-, you can use a series of questions or predications, suggestions, this kind of things, right ↑? You have already come up with the three ideas. Now, you need the first step ***I mean*** introduction. Now you try to write, um, appealing introduction for the topic you have discussed. Now everyone, please write them down, about five minutes, and then, we'll listen ...

In Extract 6.23 above, the teacher is talking about the topic sentence and its supporting details. She draws a picture of an anchor on the whiteboard, in order to show the similarities of an anchor with the topic sentence, and thus facilitate the students' understanding. At the beginning of the example, she tries to elicit from the students what the picture is. After the students have provided the expected answer, the teacher explains the relationship between a topic sentence and an anchor. By using this metaphor to connect the abstract concept with a concrete one, the teacher makes the function of topic sentence more accessible to the students. In a similar vein, in Extract 6.24 above, the teacher is instructing the students on the general structure of writing a composition. Concerning the main body, the teacher mentions the connecting words. This is a slightly different usage to the one given above, because here the code gloss marker *like* is used to introduce concrete examples of connecting words. Moreover, the teacher also uses *I mean* to make more explicit reference of the specific information "the first step". This may help the students to grasp the meaning of the ideational content the teacher states at certain points in the instructional process.

6.5 Summary

Overall, this chapter has provided a detailed account of metadiscourse use by teachers in the ET and CT sub-corpora. On the one hand, it has revealed the frequency and distribution of metadiscourse markers employed by the two groups of teachers. As the current research is based on a self-compiled small-scale corpus, it allows for a detailed account, not only of the overall frequency and distribution of metadiscourse use between the two teacher groups, but on the other hand also of the metadiscourse use by individual teachers within each sub-corpus. Thus, it offers a more thorough analysis of the dataset compared with previous large-scale corpus analyses of metadiscourse use in written academic discourse.

CHAPTER 7

Conclusion

7.1 Introduction

This chapter concludes the current research with four sections. The first section starts with a brief introduction of the overall content of this chapter. Section Two summarises the major findings as to how they confirm the two assumptions raised at the beginning of the current research. The following section focuses on discussing the main theoretical and pedagogical implications. Section Four points out the limitations of the current research and suggests possible areas for future research.

7.2 Summary of the book

As noted in Section 1.3, the current research was based on two assumptions. First, despite a relative uniformity of teachers' metadiscourse use in EAP classroom teaching imposed by the requirements of the genre, there is significant intercultural variation in the rhetorical preferences of teachers. Second, the use of metadiscourse in the Chinese non-native English-speaking teachers' classroom discourse may be not as diversified as those in the British native English-speaking teachers' classroom discourse. Based on the findings of the current research, three perspectives of these two assumptions are summarised below: 1) uniformity of the two groups of teachers' metadiscourse use in EAP classroom teaching, 2) variations of rhetorical preferences between teachers in the two sub-corpora, and 3) diversifications of lexical types of metadiscourse between teachers in the two sub-corpora.

7.2.1 Uniformity of metadiscourse use

The current research has demonstrated the considerable similarities in metadiscourse use, such as categories and lexical items between teachers in the two sub-corpora. In terms of metadiscourse categories, both groups of teachers make the most frequent use of engagement markers to recognise the presence of their students, guide them through the instruction and involve them in the on-going pedagogical tasks (Hyland, 2005). This is followed by transitions and frame markers, which serve as cohesive or signposting devices at a local and global level respectively, to help relieve the cognitive burden of students in processing the classroom instruction that normally lasts for at least an hour or so (Bu, 2014; Cazden, 2001). They are followed by hedges and boosters, which may fulfil various genre-dependent purposes, such as signposting key points, diminishing authority for solidarity and achieving distinctive pragmatic effects in classroom instruction. Comparatively, the other four types of metadiscourse categories, that is, self-mentions, code glosses, attitude markers and endophoric markers are used with rather lower frequencies in both sub-corpora. This general distributional pattern of metadiscourse markers in both sub-corpora is roughly in line with previous research in teachers' classroom metadiscourse (Lee & Subtirelu, 2015; Yan, 2010).

Teachers in both sub-corpora also share common features in the use of certain lexical items within related metadiscourse categories. First, both groups of teachers employ *just* as the most prevalent hedging marker, which supports Lindemann & Mauranen (2001) in claiming that *just* is the most frequently employed hedging device in spoken academic discourse used to withhold teachers' complete assertion of propositions. Second, teachers from both sub-corpora use the lexical verb *know* with relatively high frequencies, which is used in the phrase *you know* to preface shared knowledge (He & Lindsey, 1998) or mutual experience (Hyland, 2005) that is needed to draw the same conclusion for the addresser and addressees. Third, adjectives such as *important*, *interesting* and *right* are more likely to be used to indicate teachers' "clear stance toward the propositional content" (Hyland, 2009, p.104). The fourth aspect concerns the self-mention marker *I* and several engagement markers. *I* is the most common type of self-mention in both sub-corpora. *You* and inclusive-*we* are two of the central devices for establishing and maintaining high levels of student involvement (Lee, 2009). Moreover, other engagement markers, such as directive marker *let's* co-occurring usually with *see*, *have a look*, *think* or *use* is used to direct students' attention, or provoke their thoughts or actions. In addition, display questions introduced by *what* or *yes/no* questions confirms previous research (e.g. Nunan, 1989) in that teachers normally rely heavily on display questions and questions checking students' comprehension.

The fifth aspect relates to transitions and frame markers. In light of the relatively extensive use of *and*, *but* and *so*, the current research develops Hyland & Jiang (2018) by claiming that in addition to the default form of marking addition by *and*, *but* and *so* can be considered the default options of expressing comparative and consequential relations in academic speech contexts. In addition, the current research echoes Fung & Carter (2007) by observing that discourse markers like *firstly*, *secondly*, and *then* are used frequently in teachers' classroom discourse to signal and segment the logical sequence. Sixth, *okay*, *so* and *now* are used extensively to mark shifting topics at the opening/closing positions of a topic (Carter & McCarthy, 2006). In particular, *okay* is also used to seek students' confirmation as is observed from the current research, which enriched previous studies of the function of *okay* as a discourse marker (e.g. Evison, 2009; Hellermann & Vergun, 2007). Seventh, despite the fact that endophoric markers can refer to other places (e.g. *textbook* or *handout*) or other time points (e.g. *just now* or *later*), it is the reminder of previous knowledge that accounts for a larger proportion. This may be due to the importance of prior knowledge in affecting students' learning achievements (Ausubel et al., 1978). Finally, code glosses such as rephrasing marker *I mean*, explaining marker *that is*, exemplifying marker *like* are used extensively in both sub-corpora to assist students' appreciation of teachers' intended meanings.

7.2.2 Variations of rhetorical preferences

Metadiscourse is considered an important rhetorical resource (Hyland, 2001; Mauranen, 1993b). The current research has identified considerable differences in the rhetorical preferences, or metadiscourse use between teachers in the two cultural backgrounds. Such variations were embodied in two aspects. The first refers to metadiscourse markers with different or even contrastive meanings. The second aspect concerns salient metadiscourse devices within a certain metadiscourse category.

The first aspect includes three pairs of discrepancies, that is, hedges versus boosters, self-mentioning *I* versus inclusive-*we*, and transitions versus frame markers. First, the higher frequency of boosters but lower frequency of hedges employed by teachers in the CT sub-corpus as opposed to their counterparts in the ET sub-corpus, manifested in particular by the extensive use of *have to* and *might* co-occurring with *you* respectively, could be attributed to their different sociocultural constructs. Compared with EAP teachers in the UK, the more authoritative role of EAP teachers in China which could be influenced by Confucianism may lead to their stronger directive tone. Moreover, this may also be due to the impact of cross-linguistic transfer by those teachers' L1 Chinese to their L2, which has been proved in a number of spoken and written contexts (e.g. Kim & Lim, 2013; Mu et al., 2015; Yang et al., 2017). Second, the extensive use of self-mentioning *I* in the CT sub-corpus and engagement marker inclusive-*we* may suggest the effect of individualism and collectivism in these two cultural contexts, as claimed in some written genres (Ohta, 1991; Scollon, 1994; Bloch & Chi, 1995). Third, the more frequent use of the consequential transition marker *so* by ETs and sequencing frame markers *first* and *then* by CTs may suggest that teachers in the two sub-corpora vary in their logical preferences when delivering classroom teachings.

The second aspect entails two types of metadiscourse devices, engagement markers and frame markers. The first type is engagement markers which includes two types of engaging strategies: addressee-oriented mentions and questions. With regard to addressee-oriented mentions, more instances of calling individual students' names may reflect the more interactive teaching approach adopted by teachers in the ET sub-corpus. It may also indicate the impact of class size on teachers' engagement strategies, that is, larger classes in China make it very difficult for teachers to remember every student's name. As for questions, teachers in the ET sub-corpus use a wider variety of tag questions whereas those in the CT sub-corpus rely heavily on *okay*↑ and (*all*) *right*↑, which may echo previous research (e.g. Friginal et al., 2017; Mauranen, 1993b) in suggesting that native English speakers generally have a broader linguistic repertoire than their non-native counterparts. The second type refers to the frame marker *well*, which was used rather frequently in the ET sub-corpus but has no instance in the CT sub-corpus. This may be due to the development order of acquisition, in which discourse markers on the ideational plane such as *but*, *and* and *so* with greater semantic weight are taught and used first, while those more purely pragmatic and interactional ones such as *well* in this case appear later in the subjects' speech.

7.2.3 Diversifications of lexical types of metadiscourse

The current research has also revealed that teachers in the ET sub-corpus employ more lexical items of metadiscourse than those in the CT sub-corpus. It also showed that this discrepancy in the number of lexical types is greater in the interactional category than in the interactive category. On the one hand, 212 types of lexical items are used by teachers in the ET sub-corpus as opposed to 155 types by those in the CT sub-corpus in realising interactional metadiscourse functions. On the other hand, 75 types of lexical items are used by teachers in the ET sub-corpus compared with 71 types by those in the CT sub-corpus in realising interactive metadiscourse functions. Overall, this may further support previous research (e. g. Friginal et al., 2017; Mauranen, 1993b) by showing that native English-speaking EAP teachers probably have a broader linguistic repertoire than their non-native counterparts do.

In addition, this degree of variation in terms of lexical types is consistent with the differences of frequencies between these two broad metadiscourse categories. As noted above, the two teacher groups vary greatly in their interactional metadiscourse use, however, they tend to be relatively convergent in their use of interactive metadiscourse markers. These results may indicate that teachers in the two sub-corpora differ more substantially in their use of interactional metadiscourse strategies. Furthermore, comparison of the current research with metadiscourse use in written academic genres also reveals that contrary to academic written genres, spoken academic discourse generally makes more extensive use of interactional metadiscourse than interactive ones. Such profound analysis has mapped out a clearer landscape of metadiscourse use in spoken academic genres.

Overall, the current research has confirmed the two hypotheses proposed at the beginning of this book. It has presented the uniformity of metadiscourse use constrained by the requirements of the same discourse community, that is, EAP classroom teaching genre. Nevertheless, due to different cultural backgrounds, or variations in discourse communities of these two groups of teachers, they also displayed certain variations in their respective rhetorical preferences and in metadiscourse lexical types. Moreover, as has been highlighted by existing literature in related fields, some other factors that may contribute to these variations were also proposed, such as cross-linguistic transfer, development order of acquisition, and linguistic repertoire resulting from non-native and native discrepancy.

7.3 Implications of the current research

7.3.1 Theoretical implications for the study of metadiscourse markers

The present study fills the gap of cross-cultural analysis of teachers' metadiscourse use in formal instructional contexts. As noted above, existing research into metadiscourse mainly focuses on written academic discourse, very rare studies have been conducted in respect of spoken academic discourse (e.g. Ädel, 2010; Lee & Subtirelu, 2015; Yan, 2010; Zhang, 2017). As pointed out in the literature review section, a bulk of previous research centres on the comparative characteristics of written academic discourse between native and non-native learners of English (e.g. Mauranen, 1993a), and/or between variant groups of native speakers (e.g. Ädel, 2006). Nevertheless, no such cross-cultural investigation has been made in terms of spoken academic contexts, in particular in the classroom instructional context. On the other hand, in EAP instructional contexts, especially in EFL settings, teachers' classroom discourse serves as the primary source of input and means of instruction, and may facilitate or prohibit students' learning (Walsh, 2006b, 2011). Metadiscourse is an important means that teachers can use to organise classroom discourse and to engage students in pedagogical tasks. In light of the above gap in metadiscourse research in spoken academic genres and its significance in classroom teaching process, the current research has drawn its attention to delve into teachers' metadiscourse use across the native and non-native EAP teachers. Consequently, it fills the gap in cross-cultural comparison of metadiscourse use in spoken academic genres, particularly in classroom teaching contexts.

Moreover, the current research develops previous studies of metadiscourse use in spoken academic genres. On the one hand, based on the specific dataset, the current research adapted the widely quoted metadiscourse model proposed by Hyland (2005). As Hyland's (2005) metadiscourse list is based on written discourse, some items specific to written genres are not observed and therefore are deleted in the list of the current research. On the other hand, some items that are specific to spoken academic genres were not listed by Hyland (2005) and therefore were added to the list of the present study. An examination of the very few studies available related to spoken academic discourse reveals that they either do not make explicit the criteria on which their research was based, or merely based their research rigidly on Hyland's (2005) written metadiscourse list. Although a different context may have some newly emerging metadiscourse markers, previous research into spoken metadiscourse has not provided a clear-cut exposition of the identifications or cases for potential similar studies. In response to this phenomenon, the current research provides a detailed metadiscourse list in relation to spoken academic discourse (see Appendix 1), promoting this study in a more accessible way. This may also facilitate replicable research in this field that may enrich the results in the comparative study of metadiscourse use cross teachers or students from different cultural and L1 backgrounds. In turn, the detailed list of metadiscourse items in the current research is available for further research to verify.

7.3.2 Pedagogical implications for language teachers and teacher education

The current research may also have important pedagogical implications for language teachers and teacher education programme. In the first place, the current research into teachers' metadiscourse use intends to raise teachers' classroom language awareness in their classroom teaching. Language awareness is broadly defined as "a person's sensitivity to and conscious awareness of the nature of language and its role in human life" (Donmall, 1985; Cf. Donmall-Hicks, 1997, p. 21). As pointed out by Grundy (2002), "it is not the teacher, or even the learner, who teaches language to learners—rather, it is language that teaches language to learners" (p. 90). Such significance of teacher discourse, in particular in L2 classrooms, appeals to language teachers to raise their awareness of language use. The present study reveals the metadiscourse functions of teachers' classroom discourse and the specific pedagogical functions they can perform. By reflecting on their metadiscourse use, teachers can facilitate effective communication in the classroom teaching and learning process. On the interactive level, appropriate use of metadiscourse markers may contribute to a coherent and logical teacher discourse. On the interactional level, teachers' metadiscourse use may help construct the social relationship between teachers and students.

Secondly, in an EFL educational context, teachers' classroom discourse is particularly important for effective classroom teaching and learning. As mentioned above, it is both the means of lesson organisation and an important resource of language input for students. Furthermore, teachers' classroom discourse may also provide second language learners with "linguistic models of how to interact meaningfully and appropriately in communicative situations, although students at this point in their development may only notice a few at a time" (Friginal et al., 2017, p. 89). In other words, teachers' strategic language use in classrooms may promote students' language acquisition and accordingly language use. Despite such a crucial role for teachers' classroom discourse, most current research into this phenomenon focuses on teacher-students interaction, such as corrective feedback, teachers' questioning strategies, power relationship and identity construction (Lindwall et al., 2015). Whereas how teachers' use of metadiscourse strategies may contribute to the organisation of and interaction in classroom teaching still needs further investigation, in particular the cross-cultural analysis of teachers' metadiscourse use from a comparative perspective. By exploring teachers' metadiscourse use in classrooms in two contexts, the current research may help to raise teachers' language awareness in these pedagogical practices and promote students' language acquisition and practical language use in spoken academic genres.

Thirdly, this cross-cultural research in teachers' metadiscourse use in classrooms may also help to raise teachers' cultural awareness in formal instructions. Arguably, the findings of the current research may help to inform EAP teachers from both contexts of how the sociocultural constructs could affect teachers' metadiscourse use. For example, variations in the use of hedges and boosters may reflect the difference of power distance between the teachers and students in the two cultural contexts (Hofstede, 2001). Moreover, the different preferences in using self-mention marker *I* and inclusive-*we* may reflect the influence of individualism and collectivism valued by respectively by the British and Chinese social contexts (Hyland, 2005; Ohta, 1991; Scollon, 1994; Bloch & Chi, 1995). By making explicit these cultural effects on teachers' classroom metadiscourse use, the present study may better equip teachers with flexible rhetorical strategies in classroom teaching based on their specific student groups.

Fourthly, the current research reveals that non-native English-speaking

EAP teachers in China generally have a limited repertoire of metadiscourse use compared with their native English-speaking counterparts in the UK, lending further support to previous research (e. g. Friginal et al., 2017; Mauranen, 1993b) that native English speakers have a broader linguistic repertoire than non-native learners do. A limited lexical or rhetorical range may in a way affect students' language comprehension or attainment (Kasper & Rose, 1999). However, teachers' strategic use of metadiscourse may make specific linguistic forms and contents stand out and facilitate comprehension (Ellis & Shintani, 2014). In this sense, it is the quality, rather than the quantity of teacher discourse that matters in classroom instruction. Too many instances of metadiscourse may distract students' attention and bury the contents of teacher talk. However, too few uses of metadiscourse may also prohibit fluid and effective classroom communication. The effectiveness of language use needs to be evaluated by linking to specific pedagogical goals in the classroom contexts, which certainly deserves further exploration. Admittedly, the appropriateness of metadiscourse use shall not be judged solely by its quantity. Nevertheless, teachers' rich linguistic repertoire in classroom instruction may be conducive to their students' language input and subsequent output. From this point of view, a comparative study of metadiscourse use between native and non-native EAP teachers may provide insights for the latter to reflect on their own classroom talk and make more diversified and flexible use of metadiscourse makers and rhetoric strategies.

Fifthly, the investigation of metadiscourse use in the present study should be a reciprocal endeavour for both native and non-native EAP teachers. Although teachers' language proficiency is an important prerequisite to be an effective language teacher, it does not necessarily lead to effective language teaching. Nowadays, EAP teachers in the UK face considerable challenges, particularly due to the multi-lingual and multi-cultural backgrounds of their students. In order to achieve the best possible classroom teaching effects, it would be helpful if teachers have a better knowledge of the educational backgrounds of their students who are still in the process of developing the necessary linguistic repertories to allow them to become successful participants in academic life. In an EFL educational context, teachers' classroom discourse is one important sources of students' input. Therefore, knowing non-native EAP teachers' classroom metadiscourse use may be one way of getting to know the partial picture of the students' previous language input. Moreover, as an increasing number of international students in EAP programmes in the UK are from China, such a comparative study can inform native EAP teachers of the instructional backgrounds of their Chinese students, who normally account for a large proportion of their student cohort. Such familiarity with students' educational backgrounds may help teachers to predict students' prior knowledge and anticipate the challenges they might face with their current teacher instructional discourse.

In addition, it may be increasingly desirable to incorporate teachers' classroom language awareness and training into L2 teacher education programmes. It would be crucial for pre-service and in-service teachers to become more "intuitively familiar with the rhetorical acts and recurrent linguistic patterns involved in metadiscourse" (Ädel, 2010, p. 94). Such familiarity would empower EAP teachers to more effectively navigate students through classroom teaching and help students make sense "of the unfolding discourse in the process of developing academic English competence" (Lee & Subtirelu, 2015, p. 61). However, traditional teacher education programme generally incorporates some broader methodological issues concerning teaching pedagogy or curriculum design (Walsh, 2006). The reality is that there is a lack of linguistic reflexivity in the descriptive and pedagogic grammars available to language teachers (Grundy, 2002). In other words, more attention is needed to improve teachers' general English language proficiency, because this is closely related to their classroom

English proficiency (Kamhi-Stein, 2009; Van Canh & Renandya, 2017). In this regard, the current research may serve as the first step towards raising teachers' classroom language awareness and putting general language proficiency on the agenda in teacher training or education programmes.

Furthermore, the current research also attempts to provide a model for language teachers to develop their sensitivity towards the impact that their discourse practices have on students' learning. One way of achieving this is to encourage teachers to reflect on their own teaching practices by examining their classroom teaching discourse (Ellis & Shintani, 2014; Walsh, 2013). Through a recording and transcription of their own classroom teaching, they can then assign predetermined metadiscourse characteristics to their teaching transcripts for a detailed analysis. The current research serves as an example for teachers' reflective practice in this respect.

7.4 Limitations and suggestions for further research

A few limitations of the current research need to be pointed out, four of which are described in this section. In the first place, due to the availability of participants and time constraints, the size of the corpus for the current research, which involves 70,073 words and eight teachers, is relatively small. Therefore, there is inevitably a lack of rigour in the generalisability of the findings in the current research to the broader native and non-native EAP teachers in the UK and China, or in the transferability of those findings to other contexts. In addition, the metadiscourse items identified and listed in the current research are by no means exhaustive, but merely representative of the current research. Those metadiscourse items of the present study were mainly adapted from Hyland's (2005) metadiscourse list in written academic discourse, and they should be reconsidered according to specific contexts being investigated in further research. Bearing this in mind, the current research is not intended to be generalizable or transferrable, but to be explanatory and illustrative of native and non-native English-speaking teachers' classroom discourse in EAP writing courses. Future research may rely on some large-scale corpus to probe into the more generalizable features of teachers' metadiscourse use between teachers in different cultural contexts.

Second, there is some degree of subjectivity in the identification of metadiscourse items. Due to the fuzziness of this concept, there is still a lack of consensus about its definition and taxonomy. Moreover, metadiscourse is context-dependent. Some linguistic units may be metadiscourse in one context, but may be primary discourse in another. In addition, the multi-functionality of certain metadiscourse markers compounds the classification process. Some linguistic expressions may perform different metadiscursive functions in different contexts, whereas other linguistic expressions may perform several functions at the same time. The identification and classification of some metadiscourse markers depends, in a large part, on the researcher's judgement. This will be inevitably affected by some degree of personal subjectivity, despite the fact that inter-rater reliability was checked by a second coder in the current research. However, the clear-cut explanation of the identification and clarification process may help to reduce the effect of subjectivity and provide a reference for future researchers in spoken academic discourse.

Third, more varied sources of data could be used to triangulate the findings of the current research. The current research merely explores the usage and functions of teachers' metadiscourse use based on an examination of the explicit linguistic features, and interprets the similarities and differences between the two groups of teachers' metadiscourse use in light of existing studies in related spoken or written contexts. Future research may use stimulated recall interviews to investigate teachers' perceptions of their classroom metadiscourse use. It may also use semi-structured interviews and questionnaires to explore teachers' perceptions and cognitions of various cultural factors, such as those noted in the current research, and the effect of those cultural factors on teachers' onsite linguistic decisions in classroom teaching processes. Moreover, the current research does not take into account students' uptake of teachers' instructions in relation to their metadiscourse use. Future research may involve questionnaires or interviews with students to obtain their perceptions and viewpoints on teachers' metadiscourse use in classroom teaching and learning contexts.

In addition, the current research mainly investigated the observable linguistic features, but did not involve much of other paralinguistic features such as tones, or non-linguistic features such as gestures. These paralinguistic and non-linguistic features were only referred to when they were observed to have an obvious effect in teachers' metadiscourse use. Previous research has proved that these features also play a vital role in teachers' teaching and students' attainment in classroom contexts (e. g. Royce, 2002; van Leeuwen, 2015). Future research into classroom discourse may benefit from probing into the relationship between these paralinguistic and non-linguistic features, and teachers' metadiscourse use, or exploring the integrative functions of these multimodal features. Further research in these areas would provide us with more insights into the characteristics, reasons and effects of teachers' metadiscourse use in classrooms, and thus empower teachers to better facilitate students' learning and enhance their involvement in pedagogical tasks, and finally improve students' learning outcomes.

References

Abdi, R. (2002). Interpersonal metadiscourse: An indicator of interaction and identity. *Discourse Studies*, 4(2), 139 – 145. https://doi.org/10.1177/14614456020040020101.

Abdollahzadeh, E. (2011). Poring over the findings: Interpersonal authorial engagement in applied linguistics papers. *Journal of Pragmatics*, 43(1), 288 – 297. https://doi.org/10.1016/j.pragma.2010.07.019.

Ädel, A. (2006). *Metadiscourse in L1 and L2 English*. Amsterdam: John Benjamins.

Ädel, A. (2008). Metadiscourse across three varieties of English: American, British, and advanced-learner English. *Contrastive Rhetoric: Reaching to Intercultural Rhetoric*, 169, 45 – 62. https://doi.org/10.1075/pbns.169.06ade.

Ädel, A. (2010). Just to give you kind of a map of where we are going: A taxonomy of metadiscourse in spoken and written academic English. *Nordic Journal of English Studies*, 9(2), 69 – 97. https://doi.org/10.35360/njes.218.

Ädel, A. (2012). "What I want you to remember is …": Audience orientation in monologic academic discourse. *English Text Construction*, 5(1), 101 – 127. https://doi.org/10.1075/etc.5.1.06ade.

Ädel, A. (2017). Remember that your reader cannot read your mind: Problem/solution-oriented metadiscourse in teacher feedback on student writing. *English for Specific Purposes*, 45, 54 – 68. https://doi.org/10.1016/j.esp.2016.09.002.

Ädel, A. & Mauranen, A. (2010). Metadiscourse: Diverse and divided perspectives. *Nordic Journal of English Studies*, 9(2), 1 – 11.

Adolphs, S., et al. (2004). Applying corpus linguistics in a health care context. *Journal of Applied Linguistics*, 1(1), 44 – 49. https://doi.org/10.1558/japl.v1i1.9.

Aijmer, K. (2004). Pragmatic markers in spoken interlanguage. *Nordic Journal of English Studies*, 3(1), 173 – 190.

Allen, J. P. B., Fröhlich, M. & Spada, N. (1984). The communicative orientation of language teaching: An observation scheme. In J. Handscombe, R. A. Orem & B. P. Taylor (Eds.), *On TESOL'83: The Question of Control* (pp. 231 – 252). TESOL.

Allwright, D. & Bailey, K. M. (1991). *Focus on the Language Classroom: An Introduction to Classroom Research for Language Teachers*. Cambridge: Cambridge University Press.

Amiryousefi, M. & Rasekh, A. E. (2010). Metadiscourse: Definitions, issues and its implications for English teachers. *English Language Teaching*, 3(4), 159.

Aull, L. L. & Lancaster, Z. (2014). Linguistic markers of stance in early and advanced academic writing: A corpus-based comparison. *Written Communication*, 31(2), 151 – 183. https://doi.org/10.1177/0741088314527055.

Ausubel, D. P., Novak, J. D. & Hanesian, H. (1978). *Educational Psychology: A Cognitive View* (2nd ed.). New York: Holt, Rinehart and Winston.

BAAL. (2016a). *Recommendations for Good Practice in Applied Linguistics Student Projects*. August 14, 2017, http://www.baal.org.uk/dox/goodpractice-stud.pdf.

BAAL. (2016b). *Recommendations on Good Practice in Applied Linguistics*. August 14, 2017, http://www.baal.org.uk/goodpractice-full-2016.pdf.

Babbie, E. R. (1992). *The Practice of Social Research*. London: Macmillan.

Baker, P. (2010). *Sociolinguistics and Corpus Linguistics*. Edinburgh: Edinburgh University Press.

Bal-Gezegin, B. (2016). A corpus-based investigation of metadiscourse in academic book reviews. *Procedia-Social and Behavioral Sciences*, 232, 713 – 718. https://doi.org/10.1016/j.sbspro.2016.10.097.

Basturkmen, H. (2010). *Developing Courses for English for Specific Purposes*. London: Palgrave Macmillan.

Bateson, G. (1972/1999). *Steps to an Ecology of Mind: Collected Essays in Anthropology, Psychiatry, Evolution, and Epistemology*. Chicago: The University of Chicago Press.

Bayer, J., Häussler, J. & Bader, M. (2016). A new diagnostic for cyclic wh-movement: Discourse particles in German questions. *Linguistic Inquiry*, 47(4), 591 – 629. httos://doi.org/10.1162/LING_a_co224.

Beauvais, P. J. (1989). A speech act theory of metadiscourse. *Written Communication*, 6(1), 11 – 30.

Bellack, A., et al. (1966). *The Language of the Classroom*. New York: Teachers College Press.

Biber, D. (2006). *University Language: A Corpus-Based Study of Spoken and Written Registers*. Amsterdam: John Benjamins.

Biber, D., Conrad, S. & Reppen, R. (1994). Corpus-based approaches to issues in applied linguistics. *Applied Linguistics*, 15(2), 169 – 189. https://doi.org/10.1093/applin/15.2.169.

Bidaoui, A. (2016). Discourse markers of causality in maghrebi and egyptian dialects: A socio-pragmatic perspective. *Open Linguistics*, 2(1), 5292 – 5609. https://doi.org/10.1515/opli-2016-0032.

Blakemore, D. (1988). "So" as a constraint on relevance. In M. K. Ruth (Ed.), *Mental Representations: The Interface Between Language and Reality* (pp. 183 – 195). Cambridge: Cambridge University Press.

Bloch, J. & Chi, L. (1995). A comparison of the Citations in Chinese and English academic discourse. In D. Belcher & G. Braine (Eds.), *Academic Writing in a Second Language: Essays on Research and Pedagogy* (pp. 231 – 276). Ablex.

Bloome, D., et al. (2004). *Discourse Analysis and the Study of Classroom Language and Literacy Events: A Microethnographic Perspective*. London: Routledge.

Bondi, M. (2010). Metadiscursive practices in introductions: Phraseology and semantic sequences across genres. *Nordic Journal of English Studies*, 9(2), 99 – 123.

Brown, J. D. & Rodgers, T. S. (2002). *Doing Second Language Research: An Introduction to the Theory and Practice of Second Language Research for Graduate/Master's Students in TESOL and Applied Linguistics, and Others*. Oxford: Oxford University Press.

Bu, J. (2014). Towards a pragmatic analysis of metadiscourse in academic lectures: From relevance to adaptation. *Discourse Studies*, 16(4), 449 – 472. https://doi.org/10.1177/1461445613519019.

Buysse, L. (2011). The business of pragmatics. The case of discourse markers in the speech of students of business English and English linguistics. *ITL: International Journal of Applied Linguistics*, 161, 10 – 30. https://doi.org/10.1075/itl.161.02buy.

Buysse, L. (2012). So as a multifunctional discourse marker in native and learner speech. *Journal of Pragmatics*, 44(13), 1764 – 1782. https://doi.org/10.1016/j.pragma.2012.08.012.

Bychkovska, T. & Lee, J. (2017). At the same time: Lexical bundles in L1 and L2 university student argumentative writing. *Journal of English for Academic Purposes*, 30, 38 – 52. https://doi.org/10.1016/j.jeap.2017.10.008.

Cameron, D. (2000). *Good to Talk? Living and Working in a Communication Culture*. Thousand Oaks, CA: Sage.

Campbell, P. N. (1975). The personae of scientific discourse. *Quarterly Journal of Speech*, 61

(4), 391-405. https://doi.org/10.1080/00335637509383302.

Cancino, M. (2015). Assessing learning opportunities in EFL classroom interaction: What can conversation analysis tell us? *RELC Journal*, 46(2), 115-129. https://doi.org/10.1177/0033688214568109.

Çandarli, D., Bayyurt, Y. & Marti, L. (2015). Authorial presence in L1 and L2 novice academic writing: Cross-linguistic and cross-cultural perspectives. *Journal of English for Academic Purposes*, 20, 192-202. https://doi.org/10.1016/j.jeap.2015.10.001.

Carter, R. & McCarthy, M. (2006). *Cambridge Grammar of English: A Comprehensive Guide: Spoken and Written English Grammar and Usage*. Cambridge: Cambridge University Press.

Cazden, C. B. (2001). *Classroom Discourse: The Language of Teaching and Learning*. Portsmouth, NH: Heinemann.

Cazden, C. B. (1986). Language in the classroom. *Annual Review of Applied Linguistics*, 7, 18-33.

Celce-Murcia, M. & Olshtain, E. (2000). *Discourse and Context in Language Teaching*. Cambridge: Cambridge University Press.

Chaudron, C. (1988). *Second Language Classrooms: Research on Teaching and Learning*. Cambridge: Cambridge University Press.

Chaudron, C. & Richards, J. (1986). The effect of discourse markers on the comprehension of lectures. *Applied Linguistics*, 7(2), 113-127. https://doi.org/10.1093/applin/7.2.113.

Cheng, S. W. (2012). "That's it for today": Academic lecture closings and the impact of class size. *English for Specific Purposes*, 31(4), 234-248. https://doi.org/10.1016/j.esp.2012.05.004.

Cohen, L., Manion, L. & Morrison, K. (2013). *Research Methods in Education*. London: Routledge.

Coxhead, A. (2000). A new academic word list. *TESOL Quarterly*, 34(2), 213-238. https://doi.org/10.2307/3587951.

Craig, R. T. (1999). Metadiscourse, theory, and practice. *Research on Language & Social Interaction*, 32(1-2), 21-29.

Craig, R. T. (2005). How we talk about how we talk: Communication theory in the public interest. *Journal of Communication*, 55(4), 659-667.

Craig, R. T. (2016). Metacommunication. In K. B. Jensen, E. W. Rothenbuhler & J. D.

Pooley and R. T. Craig (Eds.), *The International Encyclopaedia of Communication Theory and Philosophy* (pp. 1 – 8). New York: John Wiley & Sons, Inc. https://doi.org/10.1002/9781118766804.wbiect232.

Crawford, C. B. (2005). Adjusting a business lecture for an international audience: A case study. *English for Specific Purposes*, 24(2), 183 – 199. https://doi.org/10.1016/j.esp.2004.05.002.

Creese, A. (2008). Linguistic ethnography. In K. A. King & N. H. Hornberger (Eds.), *Encyclopedia of Language and Education* (2nd ed., pp. 229 – 241). Boston, MA: Springer.

Creswell, J. W. & Poth, C. N. (2018). *Qualitative Inquiry & Research Design: Choosing Among Five Approaches* (4th ed.). Thousand Oaks, CA: Sage Publications.

Crismore, A. (1983). *Metadiscourse: What It Is and How It Is Used in School and Non-School Social Science Texts.* (No. 237). Center for the Study of Reading, University of Illinois, Urbana-Champaign.

Crismore, A. (1984). The rhetoric of textbooks: Metadiscourse. *Journal of Curriculum Studies*, 16(3), 279 – 296. https://doi.org/10.1080/0022027840160306.

Crismore, A. (1989). *Talking with Readers: Metadiscourse as Rhetorical Act*. New York: Peter Lang.

Crismore, A. (1990). Metadiscourse and Discourse processes: Interactions and issues. *Discourse Processes*, 13(2), 191 – 205. https://doi.org/10.1080/01638539009544753.

Crismore, A. & Farnsworth, J. (1990). Metadiscourse in popular and professional science discourse. In W. Nash (Ed.), *The Writing Scholar: Studies in Academic Discourse* (pp. 118 – 136). Thousand Oaks, CA: Sage Publications.

Crismore, A. & Farnsworth, R. (1989). Mr. Darwin and his readers: Exploring interpersonal metadiscourse as a dimension of ethos. *Rhetoric Review*, 8(1), 91 – 112. https://doi.org/10.1080/07350198909388880.

Crismore, A., Markkanen, R. & Steffensen, M. S. (1993). Metadiscourse in persuasive writing: A study of texts written by American and Finnish university students. *Written Communication*, 10(1), 39 – 71. https://doi.org/10.1177/0741088393010001002.

Cuenca, M. & Marín, M. (2009). Co-occurrence of discourse markers in Catalan and Spanish oral narrative. *Journal of Pragmatics*, 41(5), 899 – 914. https://doi.org/10.1016/j.pragma.2008.08.010.

Dahl, T. (2004). Textual metadiscourse in research articles: A marker of national culture or of academic discipline? *Journal of Pragmatics*, 36(10), 1807 – 1825. https://doi.org/10.

1016/j. pragma. 2004. 05. 004.

Deroey, K. L. B. (2012). What they highlight is …: The discourse functions of basic wh-clefts in lectures. *Journal of English for Academic Purposes*, 11(2), 112 – 124. https://doi.org/10.1016/j.jeap.2011.10.002.

Dobbs, C. L. (2014). Signalling organization and stance: Academic language use in middle grade persuasive writing. *Reading and Writing*, 27(8), 1327 – 1352. https://doi.org/10.1007/s11145 – 013 – 9489 – 5.

Donmall, B. G. (1985). *Language Awareness (NCLE Papers and Reports, Vol. 6)*. Centre for Information on Language Teaching and Research.

Donmall-Hicks, B. G. (1997). The history of language awareness in the United Kingdom. In L. van Lier & D. Corson (Eds.), *Encyclopedia of Language and Language Education: Knowledge About Language*, Vol. 6 (pp. 21 – 30). Kluwer. https://doi.org/10.1007/978-94-011-4533-6_3.

Dörnyei, Z. (2007). *Research Methods in Applied Linguistics: Quantitative, Qualitative and Mixed Methodologies*. Oxford: Oxford University Press.

Dunkel, P. A. & Davis, J. N. (1994). The effects of rhetorical signaling cues on the recall of English lecture information by speakers of English as a native or second language. In J. Flowerdew (Ed.), *Academic Listening: Research Perspectives* (pp. 55 – 74). Cambridge: Cambridge University Press.

Dunning, T. (1993). Accurate methods for the statistics of surprise and coincidence. *Computational Linguistics*, 19(1), 61 – 74.

Ellis, R. & Shintani, N. (2014). *Exploring Language Pedagogy through Second Language Acquisition Research*. Oxford: Routledge.

Enkvist, N. E. (1978). *Tekstilingvistiikan Peruskiisitteitii*. Jyvaskyla, Finland: Gaudeamnus.

Estaji, M. & Vafaeimehr, R. (2015). A comparative analysis of interactional metadiscourse markers in the introduction and conclusion sections of mechanical and electrical engineering research papers. *Iranian Journal of Language Teaching Research*, 3(1), 37 – 56.

Evison, J. M. (2009). Academic discourse. In L. Cummings (Ed.), *The Pragmatics Encyclopaedia* (pp. 27 – 29). Oxford: Routledge.

Fischer, K. (2006). *Approaches to Discourse Particles*. Amsterdam: Elsevier.

Flanders, N. A. (1960). *Interaction Analysis in the Classroom: A Manual for Observers*. Ann Arbor: University of Michigan Press.

Flowerdew, J. (1992). Definitions in science lectures. *Applied Linguistics*, 13(2), 202–221. https://doi.org/10.1093/applin/13.2.202.

Flowerdew, J. & Tauroza, S. (1995). The effect of discourse markers on second language lecture comprehension. *Studies in Second Language Acquisition*, 17(4), 435–458. https://doi.org/10.1017/S0272263100014406.

Fortanet, I. (2004). The use of "we" in university lectures: Reference and function. *English for Specific Purposes*, 23(1), 45–66. https://doi.org/10.1016/S0889-4906(03)00018-8.

Fraser, B. (1988). Types of English discourse markers. *Acta Linguistica Hungarica*, 38(1–4), 19–33. https://www.jstor.org/stable/44362602.

Fraser, B. (1990). An approach to discourse markers. *Journal of Pragmatics*, 14(3), 383–398. https://doi.org/10.1016/0378-2166(90)90096-V.

Fraser, B. (1999). What are discourse markers? *Journal of Pragmatics*, 31(7), 931–952. https://doi.org/10.1016/S0378-2166(98)00101-5.

Friginal, E., et al. (2017). *Exploring Spoken English Learner Language Using Corpora: Learner Talk*. Cham, Switzerland: Palgrave Macmillan.

Fu, X. (2012). The use of interactional metadiscourse in job postings. *Discourse Studies*, 14(4), 399–417. https://doi.org/10.1177/1461445612450373.

Fu, X. & Hyland, K. (2014). Interaction in two journalistic genres: A study of interactional metadiscourse. *English Text Construction*, 7(1), 122–144. https://doi.org/10.1075/etc.7.1.05fu.

Fuertes-Olivera, P. A., et al. (2001). Persuasion and advertising English: Metadiscourse in slogans and headlines. *Journal of Pragmatics*, 33(8), 1291–1307. https://doi.org/10.1016/S0378-2166(01)80026-6.

Fuller, J. M. (2003). Discourse marker use across speech contexts: A comparison of native and non-native speaker performance. *Multilingua*, 22(2), 185–208. https://doi.org/10.1515/mult.2003.010.

Fung, L. & Carter, R. (2007). Discourse markers and spoken English: Native and learner use in pedagogic settings. *Applied Linguistics*, 28(3), 410–439. https://doi.org/10.1093/applin/amm030.

Galton, M., et al. (1999). *Inside the Primary Classroom: 20 Years On*. London: Routledge.

Gee, J. P. (1996). *Social Linguistics and Literacies: Ideology in Discourses* (2nd ed.). London: Taylor & Francis.

Gee, J. P. & Green, J. L. (1998). Discourse analysis, learning, and social practice: A methodological study. *Review of Research in Education*, 23(1), 119-169. https://doi.org/doi:10.2307/1167289.

Gholami, J. & Ilghami, R. (2016). Metadiscourse markers in biological research articles and journal impact factor: Non-native writers vs. native writers. *Biochemistry and Molecular Biology Education*, 44(4), 349-360. https://doi.org/10.1002/bmb.20961.

Gil, G. (2002). Two complementary modes of foreign language classroom interaction. *ELT Journal*, 56(3), 273-279. https://doi.org/10.1093/elt/56.3.273.

Gilmore, A. (2015). Research into practice: The influence of discourse studies on language descriptions and task design in published ELT materials. *Language Teaching*, 48(4), 506-530. https://doi.org/10.1017/S3261444815000269.

Givón, T. (1995). Coherence in text vs. coherence in mind. In M. A. Gernsbacher & T. Givón (Eds.), *Coherence in Spontaneous Text* (pp. 59-115). Amsterdam: John Benjamins.

Godó, ÁM. (2012). Are you with me? A metadiscursive analysis of interactive strategies in college students' course presentations. *International Journal of English Studies*, 12(1), 55-78. https://doi.org/10.6018/ijes.12.1.118281.

Goffman, E. (1974). *Frame Analysis: An Essay on the Organization of Experience*. Cambridge, MA: Harvard University Press.

Golmohammadi, S., et al. (2014). Socio-cognitive perspective to the analysis of the strategic features of the discussion section of research articles in applied linguistics: Native vs. non-native researchers. *Procedia-Social and Behavioral Sciences*, 98, 604-613. https://doi.org/10.1016/j.sbspro.2014.03.457.

González, R. A. (2005). Textual metadiscourse in commercial websites. *Ibérica*, 9, 33-52.

Granger, S. (2009). The contribution of learner corpora to second language acquisition and foreign language teaching. *Corpora and Language Teaching*, 33, 13-32. https://doi.org/10.1075/scl.33.04gra.

Green, J. L., Franquiz, M. & Dixon, C. (1997). The myth of the objective transcript: Transcribing as a situated act. *TESOL Quarterly*, 31(1), 172-176. https://doi.org/10.2307/3587984.

Green, J. L. & Joo, J. (2017). Classroom interaction, situated learning. In S. Wortham, D. Kim & S. May (Eds.), *Discourse and Education* (3rd ed., pp. 55-70). Boston, MA: Springer.

Grundy, P. (2002). Reflexive language in language teacher education. In H. R. Trappes-Lomax & G. Ferguson (Eds.), *Language in Language Teacher Education* (pp. 83 – 94). Amsterdam: John Benjamins.

Halliday, M. A. K. (1973). In L. R. Waugh & M. Monville-Burston (Eds.), *Explorations in the Functions of Language*. New York: Elsevier North-Holland, Inc.

Halliday, M. A. K. (1977). Text as semantic choice in social contexts. In T. A. van Dijk & J. S. Petöfi (Eds.), *Grammars and Descriptions: Studies in Text Theory and Text Analysis* (pp. 176 – 225). Berlin: Mouton de Gruyter.

Halliday, M. A. K. (1985). *An Introduction to Functional Grammar*. London: Edward Arnold.

Halliday, M. A. K. (1994). *An Introduction to Functional Grammar*. London: Edward Arnold.

Halliday, M. A. K. & Hasan, R. (1976). *Cohesion in English*. London: Longman.

Hansen, M. M. (1998). *The Function of Discourse Particles: A Study with Special Reference to Spoken Standard French*. Amsterdam: John Benjamins.

Harris, Z. (1959). The transformational model of language structure. *Anthropological Linguistics*, 1(1), 27 – 29.

Harris, Z. (1970). Linguistic transformations for information retrieval. *Papers in Structural and Transformational Linguistics* (pp. 458 – 471). Boston, MA: Springer. https://doi.org/10.1007/978-94-017-6059-1_24.

Hasebe, Y. (2015). Design and implementation of an online corpus of presentation transcripts of TED talks. *Procedia-Social and Behavioral Sciences*, 198, 174 – 182. https://doi.org/10.1016/j.sbspro.2015.07.434.

Hasselgård, H. (2016). Discourse-organizing metadiscourse in novice academic English. In B. M. J. López-Couso, et al. (Eds.), *Corpus Linguistics on the Move: Exploring and Understanding English through Corpora* (pp. 106 – 131). Leiden: Brill Academic Publishers. https://doi.org/10.1163/9789004321342_007.

He, A. W. & Lindsey, B. (1998). "You know" as an information status enhancing device: Arguments from grammar and interaction. *Functions of Language*, 5(2), 133 – 155. https://doi.org/10.1075/fol.5.2.02he.

Hellermann, J. & Vergun, A. (2007). Language which is not taught: The discourse marker use of beginning adult learners of English. *Journal of Pragmatics*, 39(1), 157 – 179. https://doi.org/10.1016/j.pragma.2006.04.008.

Heritage, J. (1985). Analysing news interviews: Aspects of the production of talk for an overhearing audience. In T. A. van Dijk (Ed.), *Handbook of Discourse Analysis* (pp. 95 –

117). London: Academic Press.

Heshemi, R., et al. (2012). The effect of metadiscourse on EFL learners' listening comprehension. *Journal of Language Teaching and Research*, 3(3), 452–457. https://doi.org/10.4304/jltr.3.3.452-457.

Hinkel, E. (1995). The use of modal verbs as a reflection of cultural values. *TESOL Quarterly*, 29(2), 325–343. https://doi.org/10.1002/tesq.409.

Ho, D. (2006). *Classroom Talk: Exploring the Sociocultural Structure of Formal ESL Learning*. Oxford: Peter Lang.

Ho, V. (2016). Discourse of persuasion: A preliminary study of the use of metadiscourse in policy documents. *Text & Talk*, 36(1), 1–21. https://doi.org/10.1515/text-2016-0001.

Hofstede, G. (2001). *Culture's Consequences: Comparing Values, Behaviours, Institutions and Organizations Across Nations* (2nd ed.). Thousand Oaks, CA: Sage Publications.

Holsti, O. R. (1969). *Content Analysis for the Social Sciences and Humanities*. Reading, MA: Addison-Wesley.

Hong, H. & Cao, F. (2014). Interactional metadiscourse in young EFL learner writing: A corpus-based study. *International Journal of Corpus Linguistics*, 19(2), 201–224. https://doi.org/10.1075/ijcl.19.2.03hon.

Hsieh, H. & Shannon, S. E. (2005). Three approaches to qualitative content analysis. *Qualitative Health Research*, 15(9), 1277–1288. https://doi.org/10.1177/1049732305276687.

Hu, G. & Cao, F. (2015). Disciplinary and paradigmatic influences on interactional metadiscourse in research articles. *English for Specific Purposes*, 39, 12–25. https://doi.org/10.1016/j.esp.2015.03.002.

Huang, Y. (2009). *Pragmatics*. Beijing: Foreign Language Teaching and Research Press.

Hunston, S. (2002). *Corpora in Applied Linguistics*. Cambridge: Cambridge University Press.

Huth, T. (2011). Conversation analysis and language classroom discourse. *Language and Linguistics Compass*, 5(5), 297–309. https://doi.org/10.1111/j.1749-818X.2011.00277.x.

Hyland, K. (1994). Hedging in academic writing and EAF textbooks. *English for Specific Purposes*, 13(3), 239–256. https://doi.org/10.1016/0889-4906(94)90004-3.

Hyland, K. (1998a). Exploring corporate rhetoric: Metadiscourse in the CEO's letter. *The Journal of Business Communication*, 35(2), 224–244. https://doi.org/10.

1177/002194369803500203

Hyland, K. (1998b). Persuasion and context: The pragmatics of academic metadiscourse. *Journal of Pragmatics*, 30(4), 437-455. https://doi.org/10.1016/S0378-2166(98)00009-5.

Hyland, K. (2000). *Disciplinary Discourses: Social Interactions in Academic Writing*. London: Longman.

Hyland, K. (2001). Humble servants of the discipline? Self-mention in research articles. *English for Specific Purposes*, 20(3), 207-226. https://doi.org/10.1016/S0889-4906(00)00012-0.

Hyland, K. (2004). Disciplinary interactions: Metadiscourse in L2 postgraduate writing. *Journal of Second Language Writing*, 13(2), 133-151. https://doi.org/10.1016/j.jslw.2004.02.001.

Hyland, K. (2005). *Metadiscourse: Exploring Interaction in Writing*. London: Continuum.

Hyland, K. (2006). *English for Academic Purposes*. London: Routledge.

Hyland, K. (2009). *Academic Discourse: English in a Global Context*. London: Continuum.

Hyland, K. (2010). Metadiscourse: Mapping interactions in academic writing. *Nordic Journal of English Studies*, 9(2), 125-143.

Hyland, K. (2017). Metadiscourse: What is it and where is it going? *Journal of Pragmatics*, 113, 16-29. https://doi.org/10.1016/j.pragma.2017.03.007.

Hyland, K. & Jiang, F. (2016). Change of attitude? A diachronic study of stance. *Written Communication*, 33(3), 251-274. https://doi.org/10.1177/0741088316650399.

Hyland, K. & Jiang, F. (2018). "In this paper we suggest": Changing patterns of disciplinary metadiscourse. *English for Specific Purposes*, 51, 18-30. https://doi.org/10.1016/j.esp.2018.02.001.

Hyland, K. & Tse, P. (2004). Metadiscourse in academic writing: A reappraisal. *Applied Linguistics*, 25(2), 156-177. https://doi.org/10.1093/applin/25.2.156.

Intaraprawat, P. & Steffensen, M. S. (1995). The use of metadiscourse in good and poor ESL essays. *Journal of Second Language Writing*, 4(3), 253-272. https://doi.org/10.1016/1060-3743(95)90012-8.

Ivanic, R. (1998). *Writing and Identity: The Discoursal Construction of Identity in Academic Writing*. Amsterdam: John Benjamins.

Jakobson, R. (1980). Metalanguage as a linguistic problem. In R. Jakobson (Ed.), *The Framework of Language* (pp. 81-92). Ann Arbor: Michigan Studies in the Humanities.

Jakobson, R. (1998). *On Language: Roman Jakobson*. Cambridge, MA and London: Harvard University Press.

Jalilifar, A. & Alipour, M. (2007). How explicit instruction makes a difference: Metadiscourse markers and EFL learners' reading comprehension skill. *Journal of College Reading and Learning*, 38(1), 35–52. https://doi.org/10.1080/10790195.2007.10850203.

Jaworski, A. & Coupland, N. (2004). Metalanguage: Why now? In A. Jaworski, N. Coupland & D. Galasiński (Eds.), *Metalanguage: Social and Ideological Perspectives* (pp. 105–106). Berlin: Mouton de Gruyter.

Jefferson, G. (2004). Glossary of transcript symbols with an introduction. In G. H. Lerner (Ed.), *Conversation Analysis: Studies from the First Generation* (pp. 13–31). Amsterdam: John Benjamins.

Jiang, F. & Hyland, K. (2015). "The fact that": Stance nouns in disciplinary writing. *Discourse Studies*, 17(5), 529–550. https://doi.org/10.1177/1461445615590719.

Jiang, F. & Hyland, K. (2016). Nouns and academic interactions: A neglected feature of metadiscourse. *Applied Linguistics*, 39(4), 508–531. https://doi.org/10.1093/applin/amw023.

Jung, E. H. S. (2006). Misunderstanding of academic monologues by nonnative speakers of English. *Journal of Pragmatics*, 38(11), 1928–1942. https://doi.org/10.1016/j.pragma.2005.05.001.

Jung, S. (2003). The effects of organization markers on ESL learners' text understanding. *TESOL Quarterly*, 37(4), 749–759. https://doi.org/10.2307/3588223.

Kamhi-Stein, L. (2009). Teacher preparation and nonnative English-speaking educators. In A. Burns & J. Richards (Eds.), *The Cambridge Guide to Second Language Teacher Education* (pp. 91–101). Cambridge: Cambridge University Press.

Kan, M. O. (2016). The use of interactional metadiscourse: A comparison of articles on Turkish education and literature. *Educational Sciences: Theory & Practice*, 16, 1639–1648. https://doi.org/10.12738/estp.2016.5.0196.

Kasper, G. & Rose, K. (1999). Pragmatics and SLA. *Annual Review of Applied Linguistics*, 19, 81–104. https://doi.org/10.1017/S0267190599190056.

Keller, E. (1979). Gambits: Conversational strategy signals. *Journal of Pragmatics*, 3(3–4), 219–238. https://doi.org/10.1016/0378-2166(79)90032-8.

Kennedy, G. (2014). *An Introduction to Corpus Linguistics*. London: Routledge.

Khabbazi-Oskouei, L. (2013). Propositional or non-propositional, that is the question: A new approach to analysing "interpersonal metadiscourse" in editorials. *Journal of Pragmatics*, 47(1), 93–107. https://doi.org/10.1016/j.pragma.2012.12.003.

Khabbazi-Oskouei, L. (2016). Orality in Persian argumentative discourse: A case study of editorials. *Iranian Studies*, 49(4), 677–691. https://doi.org/10.1080/00210862.2015.1026250.

Khedri, M., Heng, C. S. & Ebrahimi, S. F. (2013). An exploration of interactive metadiscourse markers in academic research article abstracts in two disciplines. *Discourse Studies*, 15(3), 319–331. https://doi.org/10.1177/1461445613480588.

Kim, L. C. & Lim, J. M. (2013). Metadiscourse in English and Chinese research article introductions. *Discourse Studies*, 15(2), 129–146. https://doi.org/10.1177/1461445612471476.

Kintsch, W. & Yarbrough, J. C. (1982). Role of rhetorical structure in text comprehension. *Journal of Educational Psychology*, 74(6), 828–834. https://doi.org/10.1037/0022-0663.74.6.828.

Kuhi, D., Asadollahfam, H. & Anbarian, K. D. (2014). The effect of metadiscourse use on Iranian EFL learners' lecture comprehension. *Procedia-Social and Behavioral Sciences*, 98, 1026–1035. https://doi.org/10.1016/j.sbspro.2014.03.513.

Kuhi, D. & Mojood, M. (2014). Metadiscourse in newspaper genre: A cross-linguistic study of English and Persian editorials. *Procedia-Social and Behavioral Sciences*, 98, 1046–1055. https://doi.org/10.1016/j.sbspro.2014.03.515.

Kumaravadivelu, B. (1999). Critical classroom discourse analysis. *TESOL Quarterly*, 33(3), 453–484. https://doi.org/10.2307/3587674.

Labov, W. & Fanshel, D. (1977). *Therapeutic Discourse: Psychotherapy as Conversation*. London: Academic Press.

Lakoff, G. (1973). Hedges: A study in meaning criteria and the logic of fuzzy concepts. *Journal of Philosophical Logic*, 2(4), 458–508. https://doi.org/10.1007/BF00262952.

Lamb, S. M. (1998). *Pathway of the Brain: The Neurocognitive Basis of Language*. Amsterdam: John Benjamins.

Lautamatti, L. (1978). Observations on the development of the topic in simplified discourse. In V. Kohonen & N. E. Enkvist (Eds.), *Textlinguistics, Cognitive Learning and Language Teaching* (pp. 71–104). Turbu: University of Turku.

Lautamatti, L. (1987). Observations on the development of the topic in simplified discourse. In

U. Connor & R. B. Kaplan (Eds.), *Writing Across Languages: Analysis of L2 Text* (pp. 87–114). Reading, MA: Addison-Wesley.

Lee, J. (2009). Size matters: An exploratory comparison of small- and large-class university lecture introductions. *English for Specific Purposes*, 28(1), 42–57. https://doi.org/10.1016/j.esp.2008.11.001.

Lee, J. (2011). *A Genre Analysis of Second Language Classroom Discourse: Exploring the Rhetorical, Linguistic, and Contextual Dimensions of Language Lessons* (PhD thesis). Available from: Applied Linguistics and English as a Second Language Dissertations. http://digitalarchive.gsu.edu/alesl_diss/20. (date of access: 12 June 2017).

Lee, J. (2016). "There's intentionality behind it ...": A genre analysis of EAP classroom lessons. *Journal of English for Academic Purposes*, 23, 99–112. https://doi.org/10.1016/j.jeap.2015.12.007.

Lee, J. & Casal, J. (2014). Metadiscourse in results and discussion chapters: A cross-linguistic analysis of English and Spanish thesis writers in engineering. *System*, 46, 39–54. https://doi.org/10.1016/j.system.2014.07.009.

Lee, J. & Deakin, L. (2016). Interactions in L1 and L2 undergraduate student writing: Interactional metadiscourse in successful and less-successful argumentative essays. *Journal of Second Language Writing*, 33, 21–34. https://doi.org/10.1016/j.jslw.2016.06.004.

Lee, J. & Subtirelu, N. (2015). Metadiscourse in the classroom: A comparative analysis of EAP lessons and university lectures. *English for Specific Purposes*, 37, 52–62. https://doi.org/10.1016/j.esp.2014.06.005.

Lee, M. (2004). Structure and cohesion of English narratives by Nordic and Chinese students. *Nordlyd*, 31(2), 290–302. https://doi.org/10.7557/12.4.

Leech, G. (2004). Recent grammatical change in English: Data, description, theory. Paper presented at the *Advances in Corpus Linguistics: Papers from the 23rd International Conference on English Language Research on Computerized Corpora* (ICAME 23). Göteborg, Sweden.

Leibbrand, M. P. (2015). The language of executive financial discourse. *Studies in Communication Sciences*, 15(1), 45–52. https://doi.org/10.1016/j.scoms.2015.03.006.

Levinson, S. C. (1983). *Pragmatics*. Cambridge: Cambridge University Press.

Li, T. & Wharton, S. (2012). Metadiscourse repertoire of L1 mandarin undergraduates writing in English: A cross-contextual, cross-disciplinary study. *Journal of English for Academic Purposes*, 11(4), 345 – 356. https://doi.org/10.1016/j.jeap.2012.07.004.

Liddicoat, A. J. (2011). *An Introduction to Conversation Analysis* (2nd ed.). London: Bloomsbury Publishing.

Liddicoat, A. J. (2007). *An Introduction to Conversation Analysis*. London: Continuum.

Lin, C. (2010). " … That's actually sort of you know trying to get consultants in … ": Functions and multifunctionality of modifiers in academic lectures. *Journal of Pragmatics*, 42(5), 1173 – 1183. https://doi.org/10.1016/j.pragma.2009.10.001.

Lin, C. (2012). Modifiers in BASE and MICASE: A matter of academic cultures or lecturing styles? *English for Specific Purposes*, 31(2), 117 – 126. https://doi.org/10.1016/j.esp.2011.08.003.

Lin, C. (2017). "I see absolutely nothing wrong with that in fact I think …": Functions of modifiers in shaping dynamic relationships in dissertation defenses. *Journal of English for Academic Purposes*, 28, 14 – 24. https://doi.org/10.1016/j.jeap.2017.05.001.

Lincoln, Y. S. & Guba, E. G. (1985). *Naturalistic Inquiry*. Newburg Park, CA: Sage.

Lindemann, S. & Mauranen, A. (2001). "It's just real messy": The occurrence and function of *just* in a corpus of academic speech. *English for Specific Purposes*, 20, 459 – 475. https://doi.org/10.1016/S0889-4906(01)00026-6.

Lindwall, O., Lymer, G. & Greiffenhagen, C. (2015). The sequential analysis of instruction. In N. Markee (Ed.), *The Handbook of Classroom Discourse and Interaction* (pp. 142 – 158). New York: John Wiley & Sons, Inc.

López-Ferrero, C. & Bach, C. (2016). Discourse analysis of statements of purpose: Connecting academic and professional genres. *Discourse Studies*, 18(3), 286 – 310. https://doi.org/10.1177/1461445616634553.

Lyons, J. (1977). *Semantics*. Cambridge: Cambridge University Press.

Makkonen-Craig, H. (2011). Connecting with the reader: Participant-oriented metadiscourse in newspaper texts. *Text & Talk*, 31(6), 683 – 704. https://doi.org/10.1515/text.2011.033.

Malmström, H. (2014). Engaging the congregation: The place of metadiscourse in contemporary preaching. *Applied Linguistics*, 37(4), 561 – 582. https://doi.org/10.1093/applin/amu052.

Mao, L. R. (1993). I conclude not: Toward a pragmatic account of metadiscourse. *Rhetoric Review*, 11(2), 265 – 289. https://doi.org/10.1080/07350199309389006.

Markkanen, R., Steffensen, M. S. & Crismore, A. (1993). Quantitative contrastive study of metadiscourse problems in design and analysis of data. *Papers and Studies in Contrastive Linguistics*, 28, 137 – 151.

Marmorstein, M. (2016). Getting to the point: The discourse marker yaʕni (lit. "it means") in unplanned discourse in Cairene Arabic. *Journal of Pragmatics*, 96, 60 – 79. https://doi.org/10.1016/j.pragma.2016.03.004.

Martin, J. & Rose, D. (2003). *Working with Discourse: Meaning Beyond the Clause*. London: Continuum.

Martín-Laguna, S. & Alcón, E. (2015). Do learners rely on metadiscourse markers? An exploratory study in English, Catalan and Spanish. *Procedia-Social and Behavioral Sciences*, 173, 85 – 92. https://doi.org/10.1016/j.sbspro.2015.02.035.

Marton, F. & Tsui, A. B. (Eds.). (2004). *Classroom Discourse and the Space of Learning*. Mahwah, NJ: Lawrence Erlbaum.

Mauranen, A. (1993a). Contrastive ESP rhetoric: Metatext in Finnish-English economics texts. *English for Specific Purposes*, 12(1), 3 – 22. https://doi.org/10.1016/0889-4906(93)90024-I.

Mauranen, A. (1993b). *Cultural Differences in Academic Rhetoric: A Textlinguistic Study*. Frankfurt: Peter Lang.

Mauranen, A. (2001). Reflexive academic talk: Observations from MICASE. In R. Simpson & J. M. Swales (Eds.), *Corpus Linguistics in North America* (pp. 165 – 178). Ann Arbor: University of Michigan Press.

Mauranen, A. (2010). Discourse reflexivity—a discourse universal? The case of ELF. *Nordic Journal of English Studies*, 9(2), 13 – 40.

McCarthy, M. (1991). *Discourse Analysis for Language Teachers*. Cambridge: Cambridge University Press.

McEnery, T. & Hardie, A. (2012). *Corpus Linguistics: Method, Theory and Practice*. Cambridge: Cambridge University Press.

McEnery, T. & Wilson, A. (2001). *Corpus Linguistics: An Introduction* (2nd ed.). Edinburgh: Edinburgh University Press.

McKay, S. L. (2006). *Researching Second Language Classrooms*. London: Routledge.

Medgyes, P. (2017). *The Non-Native Teacher*. Callander: Swan Communication.

Mehan, H. (1979). *Learning Lessons: Social Organization in the Classroom*. Cambridge, MA: Harvard University Press.

Mercer, N. (2004). Sociocultural discourse analysis: Analysing classroom talk as a social mode of thinking. *Journal of Applied Linguistics*, 1(2), 137–168. https://doi.org/10.1558/japl.v1.i2.137.

Mercer, N. (2010). The analysis of classroom talk: Methods and methodologies. *British Journal of Educational Psychology*, 80(1), 1–14. https://doi.org/10.1348/000709909X479853.

Mercer, N. & Dawes, L. (2014). The study of talk between teachers and students, from the 1970s until the 2010s. *Oxford Review of Education*, 40(4), 430–445. https://doi.org/10.1080/03054985.2014.934087.

Meyer, B. J. F. (1975). *The Organisation of Prose and Its Effects on Memory*. Amsterdam: North-Holland.

Meyer, B. J. F., Brandt, D. M. & Bluth, G. J. (1980). Use of top-level structure in text: Key for reading comprehension of ninth-grade students. *Reading Research Quarterly*, 72–103.

Mollin, S. (2007). The hansard hazard: Gauging the accuracy of British Parliamentary transcripts. *Corpora*, 2(2), 187–210. https://doi.org/10.3366/cor.2007.2.2.187.

Mondada, L. (2013). The conversation analytic approach to data collection. In J. Sidnell & T. Stivers (Eds.), *The Handbook of Conversation Analysis* (pp. 32–56). New York: John Wiley & Sons, Ltd. https://doi.org/10.1002/9781118325001.ch3.

Morell, T. (2004). Interactive lecture discourse for university EFL students. *English for Specific Purposes*, 23(3), 325–338. https://doi.org/10.1016/S0889-4906(03)00029-2.

Morell, T. (2007). What enhances EFL students' participation in lecture discourse? Student, lecturer and discourse perspectives. *Journal of English for Academic Purposes*, 6(3), 222–237. https://doi.org/10.1016/j.jeap.2007.07.002.

Moreno, A. I. (1997). Genre constraints across languages: Causal metatext in Spanish and English RAs. *English for Specific Purposes*, 16(3), 161–179. https://doi.org/10.1016/S0889-4906(96)00023-3.

Mori, J. & Zuengler, J. (2008). Conversation analysis and talk-in-interaction in classrooms. *Encyclopedia of Language and Education* (pp. 773–785). New York: Springer.

Morse, J. (2003). Principles of mixed methods and multimethod research design. In A. Tashakkori & C. Teddlie (Eds.), *Handbook of Mixed Methods in Social and Behavioral Research* (pp. 189–208). Thousand Oaks, CA: Sage Publications.

Mu, C., et al. (2015). The use of metadiscourse for knowledge construction in Chinese and English research articles. *Journal of English for Academic Purposes*, 20, 135 – 148. https://doi.org/10.1016/j.jeap.2015.09.003.

Mukherjee, J. (2009). The grammar of conversation in advanced spoken learner English. *Corpora and Language Teaching*, 33, 203.

Nash, W. (1992). *An Uncommon Tongue*. London: Routledge.

Nassaji, H. & Wells, G. (2000). What's the use of "triadic dialogue"?: An investigation of teacher-student interaction. *Applied Linguistics*, 21(3), 376 – 406. https://doi.org/10.1093/applin/21.3.376.

Noble, W. (2010). Understanding metadiscoursal use: Lessons from a "local" corpus of learner academic writing. *Nordic Journal of English Studies*, 9(2), 145 – 169.

Nunan, D. (1989). *Understanding Language Classroom*. Cambridge: Prentice Hall.

Nystrand, M. (1997). *Opening Dialogue: Understanding the Dynamics of Language and Learning in the English Classroom. Language and Literacy Series*. New York: Teachers College Press.

Ohta, A. (1991). Evidentiality and politeness in Japanese. *Issues in Applied Linguistics*, 2(2), 183 – 210.

Oxford English Dictionary. (2018). *Adverb*. April 16, 2018. https://dictionary.cambridge.org/dictionary/english/adverb.

Ozdemir, N. O. & Longo, B. (2014). Metadiscourse use in thesis abstracts: A cross-cultural study. *Procedia-Social and Behavioral Sciences*, 141, 59 – 63. https://doi.org/10.1016/j.sbspro.2014.05.011.

Peplow, D., et al. (2015). *The Discourse of Reading Groups: Integrating Cognitive and Sociocultural Perspectives*. London: Routledge.

Pérez, M. A. & Macià, E. A. (2002). Metadiscourse in lecture comprehension: Does it really help foreign language learners? *Atlantis*, 24(1), 7 – 22.

Pérez-Llantada, C. (2006). Signaling speaker's intentions: Towards a phraseology of textual metadiscourse in academic lecturing. In C. Pérez-Llantada & G. R. Ferguson (Eds.), *English as a Globalization Phenomenon: Observations from a Linguistic Microcosm* (pp. 59 – 86). Asociación Europea de Lenguas para Fines Específicos.

Pérez-Llantada, C. (2010). The discourse functions of metadiscourse in published academic writing: Issues of culture and language. *Nordic Journal of English Studies*, 9(2), 41 – 68.

Peterlin, A. P. (2005). Text-organising metatext in research articles: An English-Slovene contrastive analysis. *English for Specific Purposes*, 24(3), 307 – 319. https://doi.org/10.1016/j.esp.2004.11.001.

Peterlin, A. P. (2008). Translating metadiscourse in research articles. *Across Languages and Cultures*, 9(2), 205 – 218. https://doi.org/10.1556/Acr.9.2008.2.3.

Peterlin, A. P. (2010). Hedging devices in Slovene-English translation: A corpus-based study. *Nordic Journal of English Studies*, 9(2), 171 – 193.

Peterlin, A. P. & Moe, M. Z. (2016). Translating hedging devices in news discourse. *Journal of Pragmatics*, 102, 1 – 12. https://doi.org/10.1016/j.pragma.2016.06.009.

Polat, B. (2011). Investigating acquisition of discourse markers through a developmental learner corpus. *Journal of Pragmatics*, 43(15), 3745 – 3756. https://doi.org/10.1016/j.pragma.2011.09.009.

Poos, D. & Simpson, R. (2002). Cross-disciplinary comparisons of hedging: Some findings from the michigan corpus of academic spoken English. In R. Reppen, S. M. Fitzmaurice & D. Biber (Eds.), *Using Corpora to Explore Language Variation* (pp. 3 – 23). Amsterdam: John Benjamins.

Potter, W. J. & Levine-Donnerstein, D. (1999). Rethinking validity and reliability in content analysis. *Journal of Applied Communication Research*, 27(3), 258 – 284. https://doi.org/10.1080/00909889909365539.

Preston, D. (2004). Folk metalanguage. In A. Jaworski, N. Coupland & D. Galasiński (Eds.), *Metalanguage: Social and Ideological Perspectives* (pp. 75 – 101). Berlin: Mouton de Gruyter.

Redeker, G. (1990). Ideational and pragmatic markers of discourse structure. *Journal of Pragmatics*, 14(3), 367 – 381. https://doi.org/10.1016/0378-2166(90)90095-U.

Redeker, G. (1991). Linguistic markers of discourse structure. *Linguistics*, 29(6), 1139 – 1172. https://doi.org/https://doi.org/10.1515/ling.1991.29.6.1139.

Rex, L. & Green, J. L. (2008). Classroom discourse and interaction: Reading across the traditions. In B. Spolsky & F. Hult (Eds.), *The Handbook of Educational Linguistics* (pp. 571 – 584). Malden, MA: Blackwell Publishing.

Rex, L., Steadman, S. & Graciano, M. (2006). Researching the complexity of classroom interaction. In J. Green, G. Camilli & P. Elmore (Eds.), *Handbook of Complementary Methods in Education Research* (pp. 727 – 771). London: Routledge.

Rich, M. H. & Craig, R. T. (2012). Habermas and bateson in a world gone MAD: Metacommunication, paradox, and the inverted speech situation. *Communication Theory*,

22(4), 383-402.

Rogers, L. E. & Escudero, V. (2014). *Relational Communication: An Interactional Perspective to the Study of Process and Form*. London: Psychology Press.

Rossiter, J. C. M. (1974). Instruction in metacommunication. *Communication Studies*, 25(1), 36-42.

Royce, T. (2002). Multimodality in the TESOL classroom: Exploring visual-verbal synergy. *TESOL Quarterly*, 36(2), 191-205. https://doi.org/10.2307/3588330.

Ruesch, J. & Bateson, G. (1951/1968). *Communication: The Social Matrix of Psychiatry*. New York: Norton.

Sacks, H., Schegloff, E. A. & Jefferson, G. (1974). A simplest systematics for the organization of turn-taking for conversation. *Language*, 50(4), 696-735. https://doi.org/10.2307/412243.

Salas, M. D. (2015). Reflexive metadiscourse in research articles in Spanish: Variation across three disciplines (linguistics, economics and medicine). *Journal of Pragmatics*, 77, 20-40. https://doi.org/10.1016/j.pragma.2014.12.006.

Schiffrin, D. (1980). Meta-talk: Organizational and evaluative brackets in discourse. *Sociological Inquiry*, 50(3-4), 199-236. https://doi.org/10.1111/j.1475-682X.1980.tb00021.x.

Schiffrin, D. (1987). *Discourse Markers*. Cambridge: Cambridge University Press.

Schourup, L. (1985). *Common Discourse Particles in English Conversation*. New York: Garland.

Schourup, L. (1999). Discourse markers. *Lingua*, 107(3-4), 227-265.

Schreier, M. (2012). *Qualitative Content Analysis in Practice*. Thousand Oaks, CA: Sage Publications.

Scollon, R. (1994). As a matter of fact: The changing ideology of authorship and responsibility in discourse. *World Englishes*, 13(1), 33-46. https://doi.org/10.1111/j.1467-971X.1994.tb00281.x.

Seedhouse, P. (2004). *The Interactional Architecture of the Language Classroom: A Conversation Analysis Perspective*. Malden, MA: Blackwell.

Seedhouse, P. (2012). Conversational analysis and classroom interaction. In C. Chappele (Ed.), *Encyclopaedia of Applied Linguistics* (pp. 1-5). Oxford: Wiley-Blackwell.

Seedhouse, P. (2015). L2 classroom interaction as a complex adaptive system. In N. Markee (Ed.), *The Handbook of Classroom Discourse and Interaction* (pp. 373-389). New

York: John Wiley & Sons, Inc.

Sert, O. (2015). *Social Interaction and L2 Classroom Discourse*. Edinburgh: Edinburgh University Press.

Shi, R. (2015). The relationship between metadiscourse and discourse marker. *Journal of Ningbo University*, 28(4), 13–18.

Shokouhi, H., Norwood, C. & Soltani, S. (2015). *Evidential in Persian Editorials*. Thousand Oaks, CA: Sage Publications.

Simons, H. W. (1994). "Going meta": Definition and political applications. *Quarterly Journal of Speech*, 80(4), 468–481.

Simpson, R. C., et al. (1999). *The Michigan Corpus of Academic Spoken English*. Ann Arbor: The Regents of the University of Michigan.

Simpson-Vlach, R. (2006). Academic speech across disciplines: Lexical and phraseological distinctions. In K. Hyland & M. Bondi (Eds.), *Academic Discourse Across Disciplines* (pp. 295–316). Frankfurt: Peter Lang.

Simpson-Vlach, R. (2013). Corpus analysis of spoken English for academic purposes. In C. A. Chapelle (Ed.), *The Encyclopaedia of Applied Linguistics* (pp. 1–8). Malden, MA: Blackwell Publishing.

Simpson-Vlach, R. & Ellis, C. (2010). An academic formulas list: New methods in phraseology research. *Applied Linguistics*, 31(4), 487–512. https://doi.org/10.1093/applin/amp058.

Sinclair, J. & Coulthard, M. (1975). *Towards an Analysis of Discourse: The English Used by Teachers and Pupils*. London: Oxford University Press.

Sinclair, J. (1981). Planes of discourse. In S. N. K. Rizvi (Ed.), *The Two-Fold Voice: Essays in Honour of Ramesh Mohan* (pp. 70–89). Salzburg: Salzburg Universtiy Press.

Sinclair, J. (1991). *Corpus, Concordance, Collocation*. Oxford: Oxford University Press.

Skukauskaite, A., et al. (2015). Understanding classroom discourse and interaction. In N. Markee (Ed.), *The Handbook of Classroom Discourse and Interaction* (pp. 44–59). New York: John Wiley & Sons, Inc.

Spada, N. & Fröhlich, M. (1995). *COLT Observation Scheme*. Sydney: National Centre for English Language Teaching and Research.

Speed, J. G. (1893). Do newspapers now give the news? Paper presented at the *Forum*, 15, 705–711.

Strobelberger, K. (2012). *Classroom Discourse in EFL Teaching: A Cross-Cultural Perspective*.

Hamburg: Diplomica Verlag.

Strodt-Lopez, B. (1991). Tying it all in: Asides in university lectures. *Applied Linguistics*, 12(2), 117 – 140. https://doi.org/10.1093/applin/12.2.117.

Stubbs, M. (1983). *Language, Schools and Classrooms*. London: Methuen.

Stukker, N. & Sanders, T. (2012). Subjectivity and prototype structure in causal connectives: A cross-linguistic perspective. *Journal of Pragmatics*, 44(2), 169 – 190. https://doi.org/10.1016/j.pragma.2011.06.011.

Swales, J. (2001). Metatalk in American academic talk: The cases of point and thing. *Journal of English Linguistics*, 29(1), 34 – 54. https://doi.org/10.1177/00754240122005189.

Swales, J. & Malczewski, B. (2001). Discourse management and new-episode flags in MICASE. In R. Simpson & J. Swales (Eds.), *Corpus Linguistics in North America* (pp. 145 – 164). Ann Arbor: University of Michigan Press.

Tang, K. (2017). Analysing teachers' use of metadiscourse: The missing element in classroom discourse analysis. *Science Education*, 101(4), 548 – 583. https://doi.org/10.1002/sce.21275.

Tanghe, S. (2016). Position and polyfunctionality of discourse markers: The case of Spanish markers derived from motion verbs. *Journal of Pragmatics*, 93, 16 – 31. https://doi.org/10.1016/j.pragma.2015.12.002.

Tannen, D. (1993). *Framing in Discourse*. Oxford: Oxford University Press.

Taylor, T. J. (1997). *Theorizing Language: Analysis, Normativity, Rhetoric, History*. Amsterdam: Pergamon.

Ten Have, P. (2007). *Doing Conversation Analysis*. Thousand Oaks, CA: Sage Publications.

Thompson, G. (2001). Interaction in academic writing: Learning to argue with the reader. *Applied Linguistics*, 22(1), 58 – 78. https://doi.org/10.1093/applin/22.1.58.

Thompson, P. A. (2006). A corpus perspective on the lexis of lectures with a focus on economics lectures. In K. Hyland & M. Bondi (Eds.), *Academic Discourse Across Disciplines* (pp. 253 – 270). Frankfurt: Peter Lang.

Thompson, S. (2003). Text-structuring metadiscourse, intonation and the signalling of organisation in academic lectures. *Journal of English for Academic Purposes*, 2(1), 5 – 20. https://doi.org/10.1016/S1475-1585(02)00036-X.

Thoms, J. J. (2012). Classroom discourse in foreign language classrooms: A review of the literature. *Foreign Language Annals*, 45(s1), s8 – s27. https://doi.org/doi.org/10.1111/j.1944 – 9720.2012.01177.x.

Tsui, A. B. (2008). Classroom discourse: Approaches and perspectives. In J. Cenoz & N. H. Hornberger (Eds.), *Encyclopaedia of Language and Education* (Vol. 6: *Knowledge About Language*) (pp. 261 – 272). New York: Springer.

Tsui, A. B. (2015). Classroom discourse: Theoretical orientations and research approaches. In J. Cenoz, D. Gorter & S. May (Eds.), *Language Awareness and Multilingualism. Encyclopedia of Language and Education.* New York: Springer. https://doi.org/10.1007/978-3-319-02240-6_15.

Tsui, A. B. (2017). Classroom discourse: Theoretical orientations and research approaches. In J. Cenoz, D. Gorter & S. May (Eds.), *Language Awareness and Multilingualism* (pp. 187 – 203). New York: Springer.

University of Aberdeen. (2016). *College of Arts and Social Sciences Policy and Procedure for the Ethical Review of Research.* August 14, 2017, https://www.abdn.ac.uk/cass/documents/CASS_Research_Ethics_Policy_2016.pdf.

Valero-Garcés, C. (1996). Contrastive ESP rhetoric: Metatext in Spanish-English economics texts. *English for Specific Purposes*, 15(4), 279 – 294. https://doi.org/10.1016/S0889-4906(96)00013-0.

van Canh, L. & Renandya, W. A. (2017). Teachers' English proficiency and classroom language use: A conversation analysis study. *RELC Journal*, 48(1), 67 – 81. https://doi.org/10.1177/0033688217690935.

van Dijk, T. A. (2008). *Discourse and Context: A Sociocognitive Approach.* Cambridge: Cambridge University Press.

van Leeuwen, T. (2004). Metalanguage in social life. In A. Jaworski, N. Coupland & D. Galasiński (Eds.), *Metalanguage: Social and Ideological Perspectives* (pp. 107 – 130). New York: Mouton de Gruyter.

van Leeuwen, T. (2015). Multimodality in education: Some directions and some questions. *TESOL Quarterly*, 49(3), 582 – 589. https://doi.org/10.1002/tesq.242.

Vande Kopple, W. J. (1980). *Experimental Evidence for Functional Sentence Perspective.* (Unpublished doctoral dissertation). Chicago: The University of Chicago.

Vande Kopple, W. J. (1985). Some exploratory discourse on metadiscourse. *College Composition and Communication*, 36(1), 82 – 93. https://doi.org/10.2307/357609.

Vande Kopple, W. J. (2002). Metadiscourse, discourse, and issues in composition and rhetoric. In F. Barton & C. Stygall (Eds.), *Discourse Studies in Composition* (pp. 91 – 113). Cresskill, NJ: Hampton Press.

Vásquez, C. (2015). "Don't even get me started ...": Interactive metadiscourse in online consumer reviews. In E. Darics (Ed.), *Digital Business Discourse* (pp. 19–39). New York: Palgrave.

Wallace, M. (1998). *Action Research for Language Teachers*. Cambridge: Cambridge University Press.

Wallace, M. J. (1991). *Training Foreign Language Teachers: A Reflective Approach*. Cambridge: Cambridge University Press.

Walsh, S. (2006a). *Investigating Classroom Discourse*. London: Routledge.

Walsh, S. (2006b). *Analysing Classroom Discourse: A Variable Approach*. Oxon: Routledge.

Walsh, S. (2011). *Exploring Classroom Discourse: Language in Action*. London: Taylor & Francis.

Walsh, S. (2013). *Classroom Discourse and Teacher Development*. Edinburgh: Edinburgh University Press.

Walsh, S., Morton, T. & O'Keeffe, A. (2011). Analysing university spoken interaction: A corpus linguistics/conversation analysis approach. *International Journal of Corpus Linguistics*, 16(3), 325–345. https://doi.org/10.1075/ijcl.16.3.03wal.

Weber, R. P. (1990). *Basic Content Analysis*. Thousand Oaks, CA: Sage Publications.

Wells, G. (1993). Reevaluating the IRF sequence: A proposal for the articulation of theories of activity and discourse for the analysis of teaching and learning in the classroom. *Linguistics and Education*, 5(1), 1–37. https://doi.org/10.1016/S0898-5898(05)80001-4.

Williams, J. (1981). *Style: Ten Lessons in Clarity and Grace*. Chicago: Scott Foresman.

Williams, J. (1985). *Style: Ten Lessons in Clarity and Grace* (2nd ed.). Chicago: Scott Foresman.

Willoughby, L., Starks, D. & Taylor-Leech, K. (2015). *What Their Friends Say About the Way They Talk: The Metalanguage of Pre-Adolescent and Adolescent Australians*. London: Taylor & Francis.

Wouk, F. (1999). Gender and the use of pragmatic particles in Indonesian. *Journal of Sociolinguistics*, 3(2), 194–219.

Yan, Y. (2010). *A Corpus-Based Study of EFL Teachers' Metadiscourse in Classroom Teaching*. (Unpublished PhD thesis). Shanghai: Shanghai International Studies University.

Yang, M., Cooc, N. & Sheng, L. (2017). An investigation of cross-linguistic transfer between Chinese and English: A meta-analysis. *Asian-Pacific Journal of Second and Foreign Language Education*, 2(15), 28 October 2018. https://doi.org/10.1186/s40862-017-

0036-9.

Yang, Y. (2013). Exploring linguistic and cultural variations in the use of hedges in English and Chinese scientific discourse. *Journal of Pragmatics*, 50(1), 23 – 36. https://doi.org/10.1016/j.pragma.2013.01.008.

Yeh, K. & Huang, C. (2016). Mandarin-speaking children's use of the discourse markers *hao* "okay" and *dui* "right" in peer interaction. *Language Sciences*, 57, 1 – 20. https://doi.org/10.1016/j.langsci.2016.04.004.

Zare, J. & Tavakoli, M. (2017). The use of personal metadiscourse over monologic and dialogic modes of academic speech. *Discourse Processes*, 54(2), 163 – 175. https://doi.org/10.1080/0163853X.2015.1116342.

Zhang, L. (2017). *Classroom Discourse in Content-Based Instruction in Higher Education: A Focus on Teachers' Use of Metadiscourse*. (Unpublished PhD thesis). Hong Kong: University of Hong Kong.

Appendix 1 List of metadiscourse items

Interactional metadiscourse markers

Hedges

a bit
a little
a little bit
a quick bit
about
almost
appears
argue
assume
assumes
claim
could
couldn't
fairly
feel
feels
felt
frequently
generally
guess
in general
in most cases
in my opinion
indicate
just
kind of
likely
mainly
may
maybe
might
more or less
mostly
often
perhaps
possible
possibly
practically
presumably
pretty
probable
probably
quite
rather
seem
seems
should
slightly

sometimes
sort of
suggest
suggested
suggesting
suggests
suppose
supposed
technically
tend to
tended to
tends to
think
thought
unlikely
usually
would
wouldn't

Boosters
a lot
actually
always
apparently
believe
certain
certainly
clear(er/est)
clearly
definite

definitely
demonstrate
found
have to
in fact
indeed
know
known
knows
lots of
must (possibility)
need to
never
obvious
obviously
of course
realised
really
show
showed
showing
shown
shows
so
sure
too
totally
very

Attitude markers

agree
appropriate
appropriately
correct
correctly
difficult
easy
essential
essentially
even X
expected
fantastic
hopefully
important
importantly
interesting
meaningful
natural
necessary
practical
prefer
preferably
right
significant
straightforward
unexpected
unfortunately
unusual
usual
usually

wrong

Engagement markers
Directives
add
agree
analyse
apply/applying
archive
arrange
ask
brainstorm
build
call
choose
classify
code
comb
come
come on
comment
compare
connect
consider
continue
contrast
convey
cross out
decide
deliver

develop	label
disagree	learn
discuss	let you
do	let's
do not / don't	like
draw	look through
evaluate	make
explain	make sure
express	mark
figure it out	match
fill	move on
follow	narrow
get	need
give	notice
go	number
go ahead	open up
go on	organise
go through	pair up with
group	paraphrase
hang on	pass
have	pay attention (to)
have a look	persuade
(have a) look at	pick
have a think	prepare
help	present
highlight	press
identify	probe into
illustrate	provide
improve	put
keep	read

regard
remember
remind
review
say
see
select
send
set
show
spend
stand
state
strengthen
summarise
suppose
take
talk
think
try
try to
turn
underline
understand
use
work
worry
write

Addressee-oriented mentions

anybody
anyone
our (inclusive)
ourselves
some (of you)
some students
student name
us (inclusive)
we (inclusive)
you
your
yours
yourself
yourselves

Questions

Wh-question

how
how many
how much
what
where
which
who
whose
why

Tag-question

(all) right ↑
aren't they ↑

aren't you ↑
didn't you ↑
does it ↑
doesn't it ↑
don't we ↑
don't you ↑
is it ↑
isn't it ↑
okay ↑/OK ↑
shall we ↑
was it ↑
wasn't it ↑
yeah ↑
yes ↑

Yes-no-question
auxiliary verbs
statement with interrogative tone

Self-mentions
I
me
mine
my
we

Interactive metadiscourse markers
Transition markers
Additive
again

also
and
at the same time
besides
equally
further
still

Comparative
although
but
even if
even though
however
on the other hand
rather than
though
whereas
while
yet

Consequential
as a result
because
since
so
so that
therefore
thus

Frame markers
Sequencing
begin
first
first of all
firstly
last
next
second
secondly
start(s/ing)
then
third

Labelling stages
all in all
at this point
conclude
for the moment
repeat
restate
so far
sum up
summarise

Announcing goals
aim
focus
purpose(s)
want to
would like to
would like you to

Shifting topics
alright / all right
back to
move
move on
now
OK/okay
right
so
well

Endophoric markers
Example X
handout
just now
Page X
Table X
textbook
that part
this class / today's class
this lesson
X before
X earlier
X later

Code glosses
call

called	namely
for example	or X
I mean	say / let's say / that is to say
in fact	specifically
in other words	such as
it means	that is
like	that means
(used when introducing examples)	which means

Appendix 2   Participant information sheet

Research topic: Metadiscourse in the classroom: A comparative analysis of non-native and native EAP teachers

Researcher: Xinxin Wu

Supervisors: Prof. Robert Millar, Dr. Agni Connor

I am a PhD student in Linguistics at the University of Aberdeen, UK. Currently, I am researching classroom discourse in China and the UK. This study endeavours to compare the use of discourse in non-native and native EFL classrooms. The purpose of this study is to provide some insights into the EFL teaching and learning in China, and contribute to the EFL teacher training and development both in China and other EFL countries.

Do you have to take part?

The whole participation process is voluntary, and you are free to make the decision to take part in the investigation or not. Refusing to participate or withdrawing participation will not affect any other aspects of the way you are treated.

What will you do in the project?

The researcher will collect the data through video-recording of the classroom of the participants. I will carry out research at mutually convenient times; we will negotiate ways that will minimise disruption to your schedule. It will not be a burden to you. Where possible, you have the right to review the transcripts of the recording for clarification and correction, and be provided with a summary of research findings and an opportunity for debriefing after taking part in the research.

What are the potential risks to you in taking part?

This research will not pose any threat or burden to you. The research in the classroom will only be used for research purposes. You will not be judged on your teaching.

What happens to the information in the project?

Your dignity and interests will be respected at all times, and steps will be taken to ensure that no harm will result from participating in the research. All necessary steps will be taken to protect the privacy and ensure the anonymity and non-traceability of participants—for example, by the use of pseudonyms or codes, for both individual and institutional participants, in any written reports or other forms of dissemination derived from the research. Data generated by the research (e. g. transcripts of research interviews) will be kept on a password-protected computer system. No information will be released to a third party; it will be used purely for the purposes of the research project (including the dissemination of findings). No one except research colleagues, supervisors or examiners will have access to any of the data collected.

Who has ethically reviewed the project?

The University of Aberdeen is registered with the Information Commissioner's Office, which implements the UK Research Integrity Office Code of Practice for Research (2009). All personal data on participants will be processed in accordance with the provisions of the UK Research Integrity Office Code of Practice for Research 2009 and the University of Aberdeen's Advisory Group on Research Ethics and Governance (AGREG) 2014.

What happens next?

If you are happy to be involved in the project, please sign the attached consent form to confirm this. Where possible, you will be provided with a summary of research findings and an opportunity for debriefing after taking part in the research.

Researcher contact details

Thank you for reading this information. Please ask any questions if you are unsure about what is written here. If you have any other questions about this study, you may contact me by email (r01xw15@ abdn). ac.uk.

Chinese version of Participant Information Sheet

研究参与者须知

研究课题：中英高校教师课堂元话语研究

研究人员：仵欣欣

指导教师：Prof. Robert Millar, Dr. Agni Connor

尊敬的老师：

您好！

我是英国阿伯丁大学语言学专业的一名博士研究生，目前正在做一项关于中英教师课堂话语的研究。该研究旨在通过比较两国教师的课堂话语，优化教师课堂话语质量，并为中国及其他英语作为外语国家的教师发展和培训提供有益借鉴。您的参与将会对我的研究带来极大帮助，并对该研究项目做出重大贡献。

整个参与过程遵循自愿原则，您有权决定是否参与接受研究，并有权随时退出，拒绝和退出研究不会对您的工作和生活造成任何影响。

该研究需要对您的课堂进行录像。关于时间安排，我会尊重您的日程安排，选择您方便的时间进行，尽量减少对您的打扰。根据需要，您有权对录像的转写材料进行检查和修改，我也可以向您汇报研究进展情况和研究结果。

该研究搜集的数据仅作为科学研究使用，不会对您的课堂教学进行评价，不会对您造成任何形式的威胁和挑战，所以请您不要有任何心理负担。

整个研究过程中，我会严格保障和尊重您的权益，确保不会因为您的参与对您造成任何形式的危害。该研究参与者均采用匿名形式进行编码，研究数据将被加密，并保存在有密码保护的电子数据库中。该研究的任何信息不会透漏给除研究者、导师或者论文审阅专家之外的任何人员。

英国阿伯丁大学设有专门的学术伦理审查部门，对每名研究者的研究伦理进行评估，确保所有研究数据的处理严格遵守英国学术研究伦理规范（2009）和阿伯丁大学学术伦理委员会章程（2014）。

感谢您阅读该须知，若您任何时候有任何疑问，欢迎您随时提出。

如果您同意参与该研究，请在下面的同意书中签字。

联系人：
仵欣欣　　　　　　Email：r01xw15@abdn.ac.uk
导师姓名：
Prof. Robert Millar　　Email：r.millar@abdn.ac.uk
Dr. Agni Connor　　　Email：agni.conner@abdn.ac.uk

Appendix 3 Consent form for teachers

Consent form for participation in metadiscourse in the classroom: A comparative analysis of native and non-native EAP teachers

I, the undersigned, confirm that (please tick below as appropriate):

Item	Description	Yes	No
1.	I have read and understood the information about the project, as provided in the Information Sheet.		
2.	I have been given the opportunity to ask questions about the project and my participation.		
3.	I voluntarily agree to participate in the project.		
4.	I understand I can withdraw at any time without giving reasons and that I will not be penalised for withdrawing nor will I be questioned on why I have withdrawn.		
5.	The procedures regarding confidentiality have been clearly explained (e.g. use of names, pseudonyms, anonymization of data, etc.) to me.		
6.	Terms of consent for the forms of data collection such as interviews and video have been explained and provided to me.		
7.	The use of the data in research, publications, sharing and archiving has been explained to me.		
8.	I understand that other researchers will have access to this data only if they agree to preserve the confidentiality of the data and if they agree to the terms I have specified in this form.		
9.	I, along with the researcher, agree to sign and date this informed consent form.		

Participant:

_____   _____   _____
Name of Participant   Signature   Date

Researcher:

_____   _____   _____
Name of Researcher   Signature   Date

Chinese Version of Consent Form for Teachers

参与研究同意书

课题名称：中英高校教师课堂元话语研究

我同意在下面签字（请根据需要打对号）：

项目	内容	是	否
1.	我已经阅读并同意该研究相关信息。		
2.	我有权就该研究和我的参与提出问题。		
3.	我自愿参与该研究项目。		
4.	我明白我可以任何时候无条件地退出研究，并不会为此受到任何惩罚或质问。		
5.	我清楚了解该研究中关于对参与者进行保密的信息。		
6.	研究者为我解释了访谈、录像等形式的数据收集方式。		
7.	研究者为我解释了研究数据的使用、出版及存档的相关事项。		
8.	我了解其他研究者可能会接触这些数据，但他们应严格遵照本表格中所述保密条款。		
9.	我同意与研究者共同就该研究在下方签字。		

参与者：

姓名_____   签字_____   日期_____

研究者：

姓名_____   签字_____   日期_____

Appendix 4　Consent form for students

Consent form for participation in metadiscourse in the classroom: A comparative analysis of native and non-native EAP teachers

I, the undersigned, confirm that (please tick below as appropriate):

Item	Description	Yes	No
1.	I have read and understood the information about the project, as provided in the Information Sheet.		
2.	I have been given the opportunity to ask questions about the project and my participation.		
3.	I voluntarily agree to participate in the project.		
4.	I understand I can withdraw at any time without giving reasons and that I will not be penalised for withdrawing nor will I be questioned on why I have withdrawn.		
5.	The procedures regarding confidentiality have been clearly explained (e.g. use of names, pseudonyms, anonymization of data, etc.) to me.		
6.	Terms of consent for the forms of data collection such as interviews and video have been explained and provided to me.		
7.	The use of the data in research, publications, sharing and archiving has been explained to me.		
8.	I understand that other researchers will have access to this data only if they agree to preserve the confidentiality of the data and if they agree to the terms I have specified in this form.		
9.	I, along with the researcher, agree to sign and date this informed consent form.		

Date:　　　　　　　　　　Date:

Participant:　　　　　　　Researcher:

Chinese Version of Consent Form for Students

参与研究同意书

课题名称：中英高校教师课堂元话语研究

我同意在下面签字（请根据需要打对号）：

项目	内容	是	否
1.	我已经阅读并同意该研究相关信息。		
2.	我有权就该研究和我的参与提出问题。		
3.	我自愿参与该研究项目。		
4.	我明白我可以任何时候无条件地退出研究，并不会为此受到任何惩罚或质问。		
5.	我清楚了解该研究中关于对参与者进行保密的信息。		
6.	研究者为我解释了采访和录像等形式的数据收集方式。		
7.	研究者为我解释了研究数据的使用、出版及存档的相关事项。		
8.	我了解其他研究者可能会接触这些数据，但他们应严格遵照本表格中所述保密条款。		
9.	我同意与研究者共同就该研究在下方签字。		

日期：　　　　　　　　　　日期：

参与者：　　　　　　　　　研究者：

Appendix 5 Transcription conventions

The transcription conventions employed in this research are mainly adapted from Gail Jefferson (2004) and Sert (2015).

(6)	Numbers enclosed in parentheses indicate a pause in seconds. The number represents the duration of the pause, to one decimal place. In this case, it represents a pause of six seconds.
(( ))	Doubled parentheses shows transcriber's additional descriptions or comments, for instance, about the features of the contextual information.
[ ]	Square brackets around portions of utterances show that these portions overlap with a portion of another speaker's utterance. The left bracket indicates the point of overlap onset, while the right bracket indicates the point at which the two overlapping utterances end.
> <	"Greater than" and "less than" signs bracketing an utterance or utterance-part indicate that the bracketed material is noticeably faster than the surrounding talk.
< >	"Less than" and "greater than" signs bracketing an utterance or utterance-part indicate that the bracketed material is noticeably slower than the surrounding talk.
=	Equal signs indicate no break or gap. A single equal sign indicates no break in an ongoing piece of talk, where one might otherwise expect it, e.g. after a completed sentence. A pair of equal signs, one at the end of one line and one at the beginning of the next, indicate no break between the two lines of talk.
Italics	English translation
CAPITAL	Capital letters show that the speaker spoke the capitalised portion of the utterance at a higher volume than the speaker's normal volume.
°word°	Degree signs bracketing an utterance or utterance-part indicates that the sounds are softer than the surrounding talk.
-	A hyphen indicates an abrupt cut-off, where the speaker stops speaking suddenly.

↓ ↑	Upward or downward arrows used preceding a syllable to indicate there is a rising or falling of intonation in it.
.	A period indicates slightly falling intonation.
,	A comma indicates a continuation of tone.
:	A colon after a vowel or a word is used to signal that the sound is extended. The number of colons shows the length of the extension.
(utterance)	An utterance appear in parentheses indicates that the transcriber has guessed as to what was said, because it was indecipherable on the tape.
(inaudible)	Audible appear in parentheses indicates that the transcriber was unable to guess what was said, nothing appears within the parentheses.
£word£	Sterling signs are used to indicate a smiley or jokey voice.
(hh)	This is onomatopoeic representation of the audible exhalation of air or plosiveness associated with laughter. The more "h"s, the longer the exhalation or plosiveness.
.hh	A dot-prefixed row of "h"s indicates an audible inhalation of air. The more "h"s, the longer the in-breath.